LAURENCE BC

LOVE at 24FPS

or

Gillian's 100 Films + 1

SIXTH AVENUE PRESS

AVANT-PROPOS

In May, 2014, I was enjoying a simple lunch with an old and dear friend of mine at his North London home, when his wife quite suddenly popped up with a question – could I make her a list of 100 films to see? Her husband murmured the gentlest of reproofs, suggesting that, surely, maybe, wouldn't perhaps a dozen or so be enough, but, no, she wanted a hundred….I saw her point – why not? In for a penny, in for a pound…? The idea quietly sunk in …

It was only some months later, however, on the other side of the world in faraway Manila, installed in the sanctuary of a modest but charming little Apartelle in Makati, surrounded by the clatter and struggle of daily Filipino life, that I got down to the business of trying to do something about meeting her request…

49 days later, and this is what emerged… Not a 100, but 101…Funny, isn't it, what a simple lunch can lead to..?

LB., Makati Apartelle, Manila, 2015

© Laurence Boulting, 2016

Published by Sixth Avenue Press

All rights reserved. No part of this book may be reproduced, adapted, stored in a retrieval system or transmitted by any means, electronic, mechanical, photocopying, or otherwise without the prior written permission of the author.

The rights of Laurence Boulting to be identified as the author of this work have been asserted in accordance with the Copyright, Designs and Patents Act 1988.

A CIP catalogue record for this book is available from the British Library.

ISBN 978-0-9955687-0-9

Book layout by Clare Brayshaw

Prepared and printed by:

York Publishing Services Ltd
64 Hallfield Road
Layerthorpe
York YO31 7ZQ

Tel: 01904 431213

Website: www.yps-publishing.co.uk

For Gill and Mark,
who lit the blue touch paper to make this book
and my beloved daughter, Teresa, who has lit up everything else

INTRODUCTION

24 frames per second is the speed at which film runs through the camera, the speed which most closely corresponds to our perceived sense of real-life time – its what (I read somewhere) is called our *'akinesis'*. Run the film faster at, let's say, 72fps and everything, when projected back at 24fps, will go into slow motion. And vice versa, at 8fps, everything faster. Were we, for instance, a common house fly (and should we be a Jain or a Buddhist, perhaps we think once we were or one day will be), rudely disturbed by a human hand approaching with intent to swat us, we would still have plenty of time to finish our breakfast, wipe our mouths and complete the last clue in the Times Crossword (if that's your fancy) before stepping smartly out of harm's way – because, as flies, our *akinesis* is around 4fps and the human hand would appear to us as ridiculously, even risibly, slow. Ditto a trout evading the fingers endeavouring to tickle it out of the water and into the frying pan to become someone's tasty *Truite Meunière*…

For me, though, 24fps is also something more than a measurement of how we perceive the motion of real time. And for me, whenever I watch film celluloid clattering through a projector – and being able to see even there, like a Muybridge photo, as they pass whirring through the gate, one by one, the actual motion of the events those frames are presenting – 24fps also becomes the portal leading me through into another world in which reality and meaning themselves are being gauged. 24fps becomes the window into this strange 'other world', which exists in a very different time and space relationship to us – the world of Art, so mysterious and hard to capture in a definition, and which has its own exclusive *akinesis*. And because Film is a medium that has been my constant, if capricious and frequently bloody-minded, even cruel companion throughout my life, it is also, for me, Love at 24fps…

This is a simple anthology of films. Not necessarily of the greatest films ever made, but of 100 + 1 of those which, for diverse reasons, have shaped and influenced my own personal life through the years. Quite possibly, therefore, what I see as 'Me' can also be glimpsed reflected in them. It is not a "Top 101", they are not numbered in rank – for they are all equals in sharing a common quality: a special and creatively original grasp of craft coupled to a real curiosity and concern about the differing aspects of our common humanity …

They are all, in their own different ways, thinking films and they have the great virtue of making the enormously complex elements of this craft appear to be both inevitable and also simple.

As far as possible, I have relied on my memory to re-evoke them here, but memories are fickle and elusive beasts and the pathway through all those billions of chattering electro-chemical brain cells to retrieve them is famously unreliable at times. They are there, however, they haven't gone away and can be conjured up and experienced in many different ways other than the word. Nevertheless, I admit without any shame that I have had to recourse, at times, to knocking on the door of The Mighty Search Engine they call Google for a dose of its own brand of Electro Convulsive Therapy to jolt those memories back into the foreground. Where there are errors and inaccuracies, however, the blame can be safely assumed to be mine and mine alone… I am not, nor wish to be a Film historian, but "to err is human, forgive divine" etc, so I am depending on the generosity of the reader to indulge me whenever I slip on the lurking banana skin nor to laugh too much at the spectacle of my falling on it .

The lights go down, the curtains swish back, the beam of the projector hits the screen, the searchlights sweep the sky and 20th Century's rolling drums and fanfare (God, I love it – must have it at my funeral!) herald the start of the film,…And I still feel that same shiver of excitement as I did 60 years ago…Film!

Love at 24fps – here we go…

1. "ANDREI RUBLEV"

(1966. Director: Andrei Tarkovsky)

Tarkovsky was a very great film director – but I have chosen this film as my opening shot because it deals with a fundamental challenge faced by any creative artist: belief. Belief in what you are doing and the faith and courage to continue doing it. In some respects, the film fulfills the poet René Char's dictum:" *Il faut marcher avec le front contre la nuit"*

Andrei Rublev was a great 15th century Russian icon artist – a humanist who, in the face of the barbaric cruelty, greed, ignorance and oppression he saw all around him, lost faith, took a vow of silence and abandoned painting altogether for a number of years. His gifts were restored to him when he witnessed an act of pure faith performed by somebody else and flowered into the glorious icons for which he is known to this day. Divided into chapters, Tarkovsky's magnificent film is as much a portrait of the medieval Russia in which Rublev lived, as it is of the artist himself. Religion, freedom, the role of the artist, political repression, the nature of humanity itself are all threads running through this epic piece of film craftsmanship.

Rublev and two companions have left their monastery and make a living as itinerant monks through commissions to paint churches with their icons. It is a time in which paganism still exists, when power rivalry and intrigue divide families, a time of instability and deprivation. Disillusion and cynicism, a world weariness threaten the tenets of faith and challenge Rublev's humanist belief in the essential goodness to be found in mankind. It is a dark time..

To be perfectly honest, at the distance of some 45 years or so, much of this film is now beyond my conscious recall. Yet some parts were so vividly expressed that they can never be forgotten. The marauding Tartars and the carnage they brought with them as they sack a city, raping and pillaging, contains such brutal imagery that they have lingered in me forever. A sequence in which they set fire to and destroy a church in which the citizens have taken refuge and which Rublev has just painted is equally unforgettable. They are scenes of terrible power and horror to which we, like Rublev, become unwilling witnesses.

Above all, however, I remember so well a fantastic chapter in which, at the command of its Prince, a new bell is cast for a city. When messengers are sent to summon the Master Bell-maker, they arrive to find that he is dead. His young adolescent son, however, swears that the secret of bell-making had been passed onto him by his father before he died. So this boy, not much more than a child, is given the charge to make the bell and command a large workforce to construct the outdoor foundry and mould in which it will be cast. He knows, too, that if he fails in his mission his life will be instantly forfeit. Tarkovsky shows us the mechanics of this complex process(fascinating) and builds the tension up through the uncertainty of the outcome. Throughout the casting, Rublev stands by as a silent observer. When the bell is finally removed from its mould, hoisted up to the city and then up to the tower of the church, everyone – Prince, the nobility, the church and people – waits in anticipation, for agonizing minutes, to see if the bell will ring true. The clapper swings slowly back and forth – and finally it rings, pure and perfect... Seeking out the boy, Rublev finds him collapsed on the ground and sobbing his heart out – confessing that his father, in fact, had never ever told him the secret of bell-making and what he had achieved was an act of pure faith alone. It makes Rublev break his years of silence and he vows to return to painting his icons. At this moment, the film, which is in black and white, bursts into colour to show us the glorious fruits of Rublev's labours. It is wonderful.

Tarkovsky seems as much at home in handling large crowds as he is with more intimate scenes. Indeed, there is a real epic feel to the film – not simply because of its 3 hours plus duration – but springing from its scope, its grand compositions and action, the structure of its passage through time and history. I was blown quite a few feet sideways when I saw it, moved and impressed not only by its craft but by its compassionate enquiry into the nature of belief and faith – its spiritual depths. The Soviet authorities were less impressed – as good atheists they didn't take to the religious tone to the film. It was banned, heavily cut and only re-emerged intact some years later. The director of the next picture didn't fare much better either…

2. "TO LIVE"

(1994. Director: ZHANG YIMOU)

This is a kind of 'Rake's Progress' in reverse – a dissolute who is redeemed by the exigencies of the history taking place around him. The massive historical background of China in revolution – followed by the ghastly follies of 'The Great Leap Forward' and then 'The Cultural Revolution' unfold in the hands of a director whose technical mastery of the craft is truly amazing and whose visual imagery is never less than sumptuously beautiful.

The film, not unlike Tarkovsky's, is set in different periods and its hero, if one can call him such, is a foolish member of a rich family who is gambling everything away. One evening this includes the family home as well. His wife(the beautiful actress, Gong Li) leaves him taking their two children with her. Although re-united with his family, this idle product of the nobility is now reduced to scraping a living by mounting shadow puppet shows. It is the time of the Civil War and the Kuomintang forcibly conscript him into their army to fight the revolutionaries who, in turn, capture him and put him to work entertaining the Red Army with his shows. Fearful of his noble background being discovered and condemning him, a life he had taken so much for granted through the privilege of his birth must be re-evaluated if he has any chance of survival. As he is beginning to learn, he is at the mercy, beyond his vanity and ego, of the vagaries of history and fate intertwining, and the misfortune and pain they so often can bring on their wake. This is real Life and he must learn to accept it. Yes, he must learn "to live".

During the revolution, lack of proper medical care leaves his only daughter with her hearing and speech badly impaired – and this brands her as something of a social misfit. While the 'Great Leap

Forward' is under way, with everyone compelled to provide the required quotas of any metals that could be melted down for that disastrous "leap" into the modern industrial age, his only son is crushed to death. Later, during the Cultural Revolution, his daughter now married to a gentle man, himself semi-crippled by an industrial accident, dies from loss of blood while giving birth, simply because the only doctor around has been banned from practising for being 'over-educated' and the so-called nurses, vanguard standard-bearers of the Little Red Book, simply haven't a clue what to do. At the end, left only with his wife, grandchild and son-in-law, a chastened and humbled man, living in very reduced circumstances, can now sit down quietly for an evening meal and still gently profess his belief that things will get better and that life is good to live…It is very moving.

As you would expect with Zhang Yimou, there are some spectacular images in this complex, ambiguous film – our hero, cowering with fear, as thundering over the brow of a hill, what appears to be the entire Red Army charge past him with more important things to pursue than him; the wretched home-made furnaces glowing during the Great Leap; the hysterical panic of the Nurses tending his daughter's labour and the ghastly irony of the old doctor, dragged back to the hospital by the lure of sweet buns, lying almost comatose and incapable of saving the life bleeding out of her, so bloated by drinking water with them the buns have swollen to seven times their size. Awful!

The film was immediately banned in China and the few copies which got out soon disappeared. Zhang Yimou was forbidden to make a film for 2 years….and thereafter has become a great artist whose tongue has been cut….Brilliant, but without the passion of his scream. He produced the opening ceremony of the Beijing Olympics – dazzling, but without the impassioned soul of his earlier works….But this is a film which understands how humility is an essential tool for human happiness – and that's just one of the reasons why, for me, this is an important film…Its terribly wonderful.

* * *

From big canvasses to a small one…but a very rich one for all that, packing a punch far above it's apparent weight. It needs no encouragement to spring immediately into focus in the foreground of my mind, as it is a work which has influenced and shaped my understanding of film – in particular my sense of the inherent drama possible in so-called 'documentary film' – and left an indelible impression. It is not an exaggeration to say that, like the two previous films, it's effect upon me has been gently seismic…

3. "LISTEN TO BRITAIN"

(1942. Director: Humphrey Jennings)

There are very few true poets in English cinema, but Jennings was most certainly one of them. This 15 minute jewel is quite simply a masterpiece of film language. Despite the absolutely absurd prefix the Crown Film Unit and the COI insisted on attaching for fear the public wouldn't understand it, Jennings paints a picture of wartime Britain through an elision of images and their sounds which, logically, should defy juxtaposition. There is no Narrator – just sounds and images of wartime Britain…the hiss of a steam engine, the sound of an unseen plane passing overhead, the factories, the homes – the rich and the poor. Flanagan and Allen sing to the workers in their canteen, the Queen Mother listens to Myra Hess playing the piano in a National Gallery stripped of its paintings…the images and sounds glide effortlessly twined into the current Jennings has created. He also understood that the British don't like their propaganda stuffed down their throats – and this portrait of a nation unified by 'wartime socialism' is very affecting precisely because it allows the images and sounds to become the message and do the job for themselves. It's a knock-out and incredibly moving beyond its simplicity. It taught me, too, how sound can act as kind of punctuation, pointing up and sharpening the inner sense of any image. It's a film every student should study again and again – pure cinema, transcending all the limits of any "genre"(documentary, drama, etc) just to be a work of art in itself.

4. "OTTO E MEZZO" (8 1/2)

(1963. Director: Federico Fellini)

In many ways, this next film is a courageous one – it takes guts to look at your daemons straight in the eye and wrestle with a creative paralysis which perhaps seizes all artists at different times in their lives...

A famous director (Marcello Mastroianni) confronts the complicated web of reasons preventing him from making the film he wants to make but cannot find. He is stuck, lost – and so is his life. He has a sophisticated and understanding wife (Anouk Aimée), a tarty but endearing mistress (Sandra Milo), but remains dissatisfied and still searching for the 'ideal woman'. He embodies his idea of what she should be in an actress (Claudia Cardinale). In his fantasy day-dreams, he wishes they could all be harmoniously in his life together. Yes, he is stuck...!

Wrestling with both the daily production demands being made on him as well as the daemons in his head, he delves into his memories, back to childhood...the adoring mother and women surrounding him in his innocent days, the fierce giantess of a prostitute performing her magnificent rumba on the seashore, his dead father rising to counsel him from the grave...He visits a spa to consult with a Cardinal so old and frail he is more stick insect than living human...He listens to the advice of an intellectual 'dramaturge', who goes on and on, but secretly wishes (and imagines) he would go out and hang himself ... He imagines his wife and mistress taking coffee together in a cafe, delighted in each other's company...He sees his actress, dressed all in white, tiptoeing to his bedside to administer soothing comfort and adoring understanding...Flashbacks and reality weave in and out of one another with dolphin-like ease and grace, often blurring the line between the two states.

At the end of the film, in front of a gigantic set of some kind of spacecraft, the director leads all the different elements of his life in a dance around the edge of a circus ring....There is some kind of resolution...The vision fades and marching into the centre of the ring, a little boy in uniform stands in the spotlight with his fife playing the theme, before turning smartly to his right and marching us all away. The show is over...

This is the world of Fellini – so it is deliciously extravagant in its fantasies; touchingly vulnerable in its regret of lost innocence; witty in its compassion and, at the last count, surely a splendid hymn to our muddled understanding of love and life. Photographed in black and white by the great Gianni di Venanzo (heavens, how those Italians are so gifted as cinematographers), it is beautiful to look at, and superbly played by an extraordinary cast of characters (and hats!).

Nino Rota's score is, as always, really fine and, altogether, this is Fellini at his best – magnificent, but thankfully a little flawed as well – after all, as the Arab proverb goes: "God abhors a straight line"... or – as Joe E. Brown famously says at the end of Billy Wilder's "Some Like it Hot" – "Nobody's perfect!"... He was a national treasure, and when Federico Fellini died, they gave him a State funeral...now how many film directors ever get that?!

5. "AMARCORD"

(1973. Director; Federico Fellini)

Ten years later, Fellini made this glorious film, returning to his childhood and coming of age in a small seaside town in the 1930's. Between them, the Fascists and the Church controlled pretty well everything – and Fellini, of course, has a lot of irreverent fun at the expense of both those institutions. But although the film is very much a human comedy, there is a darker undercurrent running through it about this period of Italian (and indeed European) history when the country seemed in danger of losing sight of its moral bearings. Not that the band of adolescents, through whom Fellini guides us through the film, could be conscious of this undertow as they grow up and celebrate the joys, follies, absurdities and desires of the life around them.

And what a collection of characters Fellini parades before us! The blind accordionist, constantly taunted by the boys; the village idiot; the town beauty, romantic and soft-hearted; the nymphomaniac; the working class father of the central boy in the film and his apoplectic rages; his narcissistic brother-in-law, forever in a hair net cultivating his moustache and sponging off the family; and the academic who steps before camera, from time to time, to give us the town history; the priests, the teachers, the fascist dignitaries – the list goes on and on...and, of course, plenty of girls with big busts whom the boys lust over in their masturbatory fantasies, to the despair of their priest... Its glorious...and gloriously funny.

Some scenes stick especially vividly in the memory – the father, with his socialist leanings, subjected to a treatment much favoured by the Fascists, namely a bottle of castor oil down his throat. Fellini manages to make his humiliating indignity, as he returns to his family having shat himself senseless, both funny but touching… A marriage performed before a portrait of Mussolini which is hilariously absurd, but also a little alarming… The town beauty sent to make the noble and romantic sacrifice of 'entertaining' a visiting Prince, an almost effetely delicate creature who looks as if he has just stepped out of a Modigliani painting…. The townsfolk going out in their boats at night to watch a majestic ocean liner sailing by through the fog…Then, in a wonderful sequence, the boy's uncle they take on an outing from his asylum who forgets to open his trousers before taking a pee, before shooting up into a tree, shouting "I want a woman", refusing to come down until a midget Nun arrives from the hospital to chide him and whom he meekly obeys….A glorious wedding lunch held in the dunes to celebrate the town beauty's marriage to a balding, paunchy *carabinieri* who makes a toast, not to his lovely new bride, but to "Viva Italia" in a squeaky falsetto tenor reducing her to understandable tears of regret, while the blind accordionist plays on…Delicious.

The film starts with balm of trees floating like snowflakes through the town square announcing the return of Spring…and it ends the same way. Indeed, this is a springtime film, so full is it with the promise of life, of warm, affectionate and tender scenes and a laughter which never mocks but rather celebrates human absurdities. Nino Rota wrote yet another unforgettable score, and Guiseppe di Rotunno (God, another Italian genius with light) photographed it memorably.

Earthy, romantic, wistful, compassionate, the film is mature Fellini and quite simply a life-affirming joy! I want it again…

* * *

There are delightfully cheeky scenes in "Amarcord" taking a poke at all the boys' different school-teachers – and how very amusing they are – which quite suddenly prod my memory about my own prep-school days…and how I sort of came of age with Film. This prompts me to pause here, take a breather and indulge in a not altogether irrelevant anecdotal digression…

Every fortnight, a screen went up, the blinds came down on the long windows and we prep-school boys were treated to a film show in the main hall. Apart from Popeye, whom I loved and who is undoubtedly responsible for my continuing appreciation of spinach to this day, I really didn't think too much of the films they screened for us – at a certain age you begin to tire of Hopalong Cassidy and his ruddy "Heigh-ho, Silver and away!" and begin to crave more serious fare. So I had the temerity with one C.Wales (we only had surnames and initials at school) to make a kind of broadsheet, hand written in green ink and laid out in the format of a newspaper, in which we criticized the quality of the films we were being shown. This had come to the attention of the Master in charge of booking them, a certain Mr Odell, nicknamed 'The Turkey'. He challenged me on what we had written with the words, "So, Boulting Minor, do you think you could do any better?". There and then, I vowed to myself that one day I would ... through a glass darkly, I perceived what I most wanted to do was to make films...

What I looked forward to at these film shows, however, were not the films so much as to be beside the projectionist and his son while they set up their equipment and loaded the 16mm Bell and Howell projector on the balcony above the hall. I loved seeing them set the spools on their spindles, how they looped the film through a series of sprockets to clatter smoothly through the gate – but above all I loved the smell and touch of the film itself. It was intoxicatingly special and grown-up. My parents had divorced when I was an infant, and I had only a shadowy sense of my very absent father but dimly knew he might have had something to do with films also. This may have explained my longing to be at this projectionist's side, be part of his team, to touch and carry the film and be useful to him and his son – yes, I was a little boy looking for his Daddy and the nearest I could get to him, it seemed, was by standing close to a projectionist in a chocolate brown jacket with graying hair and a pronounced Dorsetshire accent.

One day all that changed forever. I don't remember precisely how or when it happened, but I do remember vividly the moment I saw the projectionist suddenly crashing down the wide staircase from the balcony and falling at my feet. He lay there, his head writhing, his face puce, gasping frantically for breath. I had sunk to my knees beside him, too shocked to know what to do except to stare back into his imploring, desperate eyes. Then he stopped and was still. And I knew he was dead. Dead – and, irrationally, I felt somehow it was all my fault for writing that childish broadsheet...for, strangely enough, he died on the very same spot where 'Turkey' Odell had thrown down his gauntlet at me... I carried this uneasy sense of guilt with me until, some days later, I was called out of class to the Headmaster's study to be interviewed by the police – who very gently explained to me that I had done nothing wrong, was in no way responsible but, as I was the only eye-witness, perhaps I could describe to them what I had seen. And, thankfully, the very act of re-living that terrible moment and blurting it out in words to the kindly policeman was, in itself, cathartic and comforting .Not surprisingly, however, these events have stayed with me forever – and you could say they opened my eyes to the fact that Life, as well as Film, could be a pretty serious business..."Well, Boulting Minor, do you think you can do any better...?"

Not long after, my father came into my life and came into it pretty damn seriously too. It was 1956, I was 11 years old and he took me and my elder brother to the cinema (it was the Swiss Cottage Odeon). I was mildly surprised and curious why we didn't have to buy tickets and why the Cinema Manager personally led us to seats at the front of what in those days was still called the 'Royal' Circle, but I was even more surprised when the curtains parted and up on the screen came the words "The Boulting Brothers present..." Boulting?! – my name...my father...film...It was like coming home, arriving at the place I most naturally belonged...Love at 24fps had suddenly woken up and begun to make sense – (Incidentally, I didn't remember a thing about the film, their very successful satirical comedy "Private's Progress") – and life thereafter was never ever going to be the same again...

But shoot forward in time and back to Italy ...back to the list!

6. "LA GRANDE BELLEZZA"

(2013. Director: Paolo Sorrentino)

In some ways, Sorrentino is the natural heir to Fellini – and this delightful film has no shame in paying direct homage to him. 'The Great Beauty' of the title is, of course, Rome itself, and this film meanders slowly, even lazily, as the Tiber through it. Eschewing a conventional narrative line and so-called realism, Sorrentino constructs a bewitching mosaic of the different facets of Roman life and spirit, both internal and external, contemporary and historic. Like Fellini in "La Dolce Vita" with his character Marcello, a single individual is Sorrentino's vehicle to take us on the journey. He's a charming but slightly decadent gentleman socialite who has just turned 65 years of age. Celebrated for his one and only novel, written years before, he is an indispensable asset at high-society parties. Dry of wit, impeccable in manner, both sartorial and social, 65 years suddenly find him disappointed with himself and the life he has been living. A nocturnal stroll through Rome re-awakens questions and brings him into contact with a series of little incidents through which he can re-appraise his life, his loves and Rome itself. Warm, affectionate, discursive, the apparent ease with which he moves us from one situation to another is deceptive: this is a very carefully constructed piece of film executed with all the skill of a juggler. Heir as he might be to Fellini, Sorrentino nevertheless has his own distinctive voice which he puts to work with great elegance and fluidity of style. Beautifully photographed by Luca Bigazzi (God, those Italians!), exceptionally well performed, this is another joy to behold!

7. "I ALBERO DEGLI ZOCCOLI"
("The Tree of the Wooden Clogs")

(1978. Director: Ermanno Olmi)

I'm staying in Italy and am likely to do so awhile longer – so bear with me. Ermanno Olmi is one of the finest directors – and this, for me, his finest film. Made against the odds on 16mm then blown up to 35mm, it emerges out of the very best in the neo-realist tradition (non-professional actors, natural settings, social realism) which has been so influential in the history of cinema. I think it was Fellini who said that you don't need professional actors in Italy because all Italians are natural-born actors anyway – and in this film, depicting the oppressed lives of farm labourers tied to their landowners, Olmi has assembled a cast whose authenticity is sometimes exquisitely moving.

Set at the end of the 19th century in Lombardy, the film looks at the lives of a group of families all tied to the same farmhouse and landlord. They labour on the land, take in the crops, slaughter the animals, subsist on very little as they struggle with hunger and the problems of feeding yet more children. Meanwhile in the 'big house' the rich show off their own pampered child playing classical music, oblivious to the lives of the people who are providing them with their wealth. The wooden clogs of the title are those made from a tree one of the peasants cuts down illegally in order to give shoes to his child. His offence is discovered and he and his family expelled from the farmhouse. Such is the fragility of all their existences. During the story, a young couple are wed and, in a beautiful scene, are entertained on their wedding night in a convent – the groom the only shy and bewildered man present amongst the nuns celebrating their nuptials in plain chant. In another scene, an old grandfather teaches his grandson the secret of cultivating the best tomatoes...

Such is the film, gentle, sad and caring, as it depicts the cycle of life lived by these people.

Olmi is a kind of spiritual socialist –(don't forget he also made a wonderful film about Pope John XXIII – "the people's Pope") – and his humanity and care for social justice glows in every frame. See it and be moved. It won a lot of prizes, including the Palme D'Or at Cannes, and deserves its place as a classic piece of film-making. There is an innate modesty in Olmi's work which I admire enormously – from "Il Posto" through "I Fidanzati" and "Un Cierto Giorno" to his late "Legend of the Holy Drinker", his films have a loving regard for humanity which I think sets him up there amongst the greats.

8. "THE BICYCLE THIEVES"

(1948. Director: Vittorio de Sica)

Olmi leads us back to where it all began – de Sica's masterpiece was in the vanguard of the neo-realist school – and has been a classic ever since it was made. The story of the poor worker, dependent on his bicycle to keep him just about in work, and his relationship to his young son is also about social injustice, the squalor and degradation of poverty, the bonds of humanity played by a cast of non-professional unknowns with complete conviction and sincerity.

Amidst the economic ruins of post-war Rome, an unemployed man is offered the chance of work pasting billboards if he has a bicycle. His wife promptly sells the family linen to redeem his bike from the pawnshop and now he can stand tall in front of his adoring young son. But not for long – his bicycle is stolen. In vain, he tries to track down and catch the thief, but to no avail. Father and son sit on the kerbside together, utterly defeated in all their attempts to retrieve the instrument of earning the family livelihood. Then, in his desperation, he is tempted when he sees an unattended bicycle and, after agonizing hesitation, he, in turn, becomes the bicycle thief. Except, in his case, he doesn't get away with it. Shamed in front of his son, he is denounced by the jeering, buffeting crowd and handed over to the police. It seems he just cannot win…At the very end, however, the owner of the bike he has stolen takes pity on him and he is released. Tearful father and tearful son walk home, hand in hand. It is heart-breaking.

The celebrated Cesare Zavattini wrote the script with de Sica and it is a superb portrait of the struggle to survive in Rome in the aftermath of war. By centering on the relationship between father and son, de Sica enhances the sense of just how bloody unfair life can seem to the innocent eyes of a child and how painful it is for a father to disappoint and be so publicly humiliated in front of him. De Sica has a natural tendency towards sentimentality, but somehow manages to get away with it. The film immediately had every superlative heaped upon it outside Italy – but was received with a degree of hostility by many Italians. *Plus ça change...*

Warning: best viewed with a decent supply of tissues at hand – blubbing is unavoidable with this one!

9. "THE GOSPEL ACCORDING TO ST MATTHEW"

(1964. Director: Piero Paolo Pasolini)

I can't quite leave Italy without mentioning another director whose work has had a lasting impact on me.

Pasolini takes the neo-realist school a step forward – using the actual text of the Gospel as his script, side-stepping any big 'dramatics', he just gets on with it: angels appear, deliver their messages, go; the Three Kings arrive, pay their homage without any fuss, depart; miracles are performed; the sermons are given – all as if they were ordinary bland day-to-day events. The effect is compelling and curiously all the more believable by being so 'commonplace'. Following neo-realist tradition, his cast are non-professionals and his locations rugged and gritty. There are none of the usual idealizations, these are common people of flesh and blood. I was reminded a little of the medieval Mystery Plays in which the local butcher might well have played Christ and the baker the apostle Peter – and recognizably so for their audience. Like the Mystery Plays, this simplicity and the straightforward use of the gospel text itself has the effect of making the words step into our own time and belong to us today. For me, it is far and away the best 'bible' film ever made – and Hollywood's pious attempts, however sincere their intentions, pale by comparison. Pasolini also takes the bold step of using the blues singer Odetta and her song 'Sometimes I feel like a motherless child' over some of the sequences: it works! And, despite coming from an intellectual left-wing atheist such as Pasolini was, it is nevertheless curiously devout....

10. "TEOREMA"

("Theorem") (1968. Director: Piero Paolo Pasolini)

Nor can I depart Italy without finally including this altogether more abstract and intellectual work in which Pasolini steps beyond neo-realism into a measured formalism – employing professional actors, a non-naturalist structure and a style more cerebral than emotional.

An anonymous stranger (played by Terence Stamp) steps into the lives of a wealthy and conventional bourgeois family. One by one, he proceeds to seduce them – the maid, (Laura Betti), the repressed mother (Silvana Mangano), the withdrawn daughter, (Anne Wiazemsky) the son and finally the disillusioned and weary father of the family(Massimo Girotti). The effect upon them – just through his mere presence – is a catalyst disrupting the veneer of their "order" and unleashing their repressions and desires...But he also offers them each comfort, counsel and even vision. And then he goes on his way, leaving them to get on with their lives. Who is he? Was this the intervention of a divine spirit?

The maid quits the household and returns to her village where, levitating over the roof of her farmhouse, she starts to perform miracles, before immolating herself in a state of ecstasy ((Laura Betti was fantastic in this role). The mother starts taking up with young men to satisfy her sexual desires (the beautiful Silvana Mangano humiliating herself in a roadside ditch is unforgettable). The son leaves home as well to fulfill his repressed creative desires to become a painter, whilst his sister falls into a kind of catatonic trance. As for the father, he gives away his factory to his workers, strips off his clothes and wanders naked into the wilderness...

I found it a disturbing and challenging film when I saw it – but utterly arresting. I knew at the time that the language Pasolini was employing to craft his film was in some way setting us free from the cinematic conventions preceding it. Abstruse and enigmatic as it is, Pasolini handles his material with an assured and direct simplicity. It has an interestingly 'modernist' score by the versatile Enrico Morricone and is handsomely photographed by Giusseppe Ruzzolini…..It haunts like a lingering dream…

* * *

By the time Pasolini was making "Teorema" I had already set out on the treacherous road of making films myself – with a short film called "Margins" made in 1965. Co-written with my university friend Mark Fisher, who later went on wisely to leave the film business and enter politics where he sat in Parliament and government with some distinction, God only knows what "Margins" was all about – but it did have the one virtue of having a music score written for it by the then unknown Harrison Birtwhistle. I doubt much else can be said in its favour… But I still mark the beginning of this journey back to 1956, when 'Turkey' Odell challenged to me to do "any better"; a projectionist in a brown jacket came crashing down those stairs to die at my feet; and my father took me to sit in The Royal Circle of the Swiss Cottage Odeon and see my own surname appearing in the title "The Boulting Brothers present". In the following 3 years, this embryonic awakening took on more shape, as prep became public school and tormented puberty the anguished awakenings of adolescence.

It was also around about this time that "those bloody twins", Roy and John, joined the board of British Lion, the 'independent distributor' and alternative 'voice' of British Cinema. It was (and was intended to be) a direct challenge to the creatively asphyxiating duopoly wielded by the two major distributors/exhibitors/producers, Rank and ABPC who, between them, controlled the two major theatre circuits, Odeon and ABC, and thus could pretty well ordain what did or did not get made and released. Rank, in particular, in the shape of its managing director, John Davis, came in for the contempt and loathing of the Boulting Bros and I vividly remember a

21

framed photograph of Davis hanging in their office. They had doctored it so as to clamp Davis' pudgy smiling face and head into a steel contraption not unlike the early electric chairs or those machines dreamt up by mad boffins in 'B' movies to zap some life-giving voltage into the monsters they were trying to create. The twins had titled the picture, "John Davis in the Boulting Brothers Patent Head Shrinking Machine" – typical of their relish in debunking anything or anybody which had a vague whiff of the phoney or corrupt hiding behind a veneer of respectability. Nor was there any shortage of such insalubrious characters to be found within the film fraternity and, indeed, Wardour Street, then the hub of the film industry, had been dubbed "the only street in London which is shady on both sides". As far as I know, John Davis wasn't necessarily shady, but the Boulting Bros were not the only ones to find him a rather odious character, whose head might well benefit from some shrinking. Of course, there were also those who felt that the Boulting Twins themselves could do with a dose of head-shrinking: "those bloody twins" could be obstreperous, bloody-minded, opinionated, arrogant in their self-belief, yet simultaneously possessed of considerable charismatic charm and wit which few could resist. Their double-act of identical twins, telepathically tuned into one another and working together in a pincer movement could prove to be formidable if you crossed their path. Another distinguished director, Sidney Gilliat, a fellow on the British Lion board, once lamented with wry affection that "when they came into a meeting, the entire boardroom suddenly seemed full of fucking Boultings!". However, few denied their creative talent either, nor the fact they really were champions of independent film-making and generous in their support and encouragement of emerging talent, as many film-makers, actors and technicians could testify to. Following in the wake of the flamboyant producer, Alexander Korda, who had first built up and then brought British Lion to its knees, I think they believed (as Korda had)that, in order to be a healthy and dynamic part of the cultural fabric of society, the making of films should be left in the hands of and guided by real professional film-makers, not by accountants and business people often more interested in the sales of ice-creams in their theatres than the quality of the films themselves. Although they recognized (as my father, Roy, often repeated to me) that Film was "Art conducted on an industrial scale" and commercial considerations could not be ignored and were an inevitable, if thorny, part of the equation, nor could the aesthetic and creative ambitions of film-makers be ignored either. The balancing act between the two would always be precarious but, unless you were prepared at times to take the risk on a project you believed in and go out on a limb, back it, get it made and into the theatres, then you would be short-changing not only Film as a medium which can also enlarge our understanding of life and humanity, but also the sensibilities and intelligence of the very audiences to whom the films were being directed. It would be an act of impoverishment all round. And John Davis (as well as those of his ilk then and since), with or without a rigorous session in the Patent Head-Shrinking Machine, was for the Boulting Brothers representative of a coarse mediocrity more usually associated with the Vandals – and we all know how dangerous they can be. Put more simply, for all their short-comings, the Boultings were truly passionate about Film – indeed, they loved it ... probably more than they loved anything else, apart from each other, indissolubly glued together as they were by their twinship.

In his last years, it amused my father, Roy, to hang a framed cartoon (I think by Vicky)on the wall above his bed in the modest one-bedroomed flat in the village of Eynsham, where he lived in what are euphemistically referred to as 'greatly reduced circumstances' until his death on Guy Fawke's Day, 2001. It was captioned 'The End' and, while he awaited his own, he slept beneath this cartoon which depicted a dejected lion trussed upside down on a pole being carried off through the jungle by two smug hunters, complete with khaki shorts and solar topees. The lion, of course, was British Lion and the hunters the duopoly of Rank/ABPC. The demise came in 1976 when British Lion, despite a valiant struggle to survive, was finally taken over by EMI. Nevertheless, for almost 20 years, British Lion made an important and significant contribution to the health of independent British Cinema – and, without the stewardship of the Boulting Brothers and Launder and Gilliat, I wonder what the fate would have been for independent and even ground-breaking films such as Karel Reisz' "Saturday Night, Sunday Morning", Tony Richardson's "The

Entertainer" and "A Taste of Honey", or John Schlesinger's first feature, "A Kind of Loving", had they not known that British Lion was there to ensure they got a decent theatrical release? Or Joseph Strick's controversial "Ulysses", and later on Nic Roeg's terrific "Don't Look Now"? As another director, Christopher Miles, once commented to me, "It was very simple – if you had a project which was in any way out of the ordinary, original, 'difficult', then you went to the Boultings – because nobody else was going listen to you!". On more than one occasion, quite apart from listening and encouraging, they also dug into their own pockets to put their money where their collective mouth was – "those bloody twins" could be more generous than is generally known, although it is also true to say that their own budgets were kept pretty tight to a point of questionable frugality – or, rather, they saw no reason to over-price their films with exorbitant salaries just because the Americans, taking advantage of both our lower costs and also undoubtedly high technical skills, were bringing their productions over here and doing so by jacking up costs and salaries, left, right and centre. This sometimes unfairly gave the Boultings a reputation for being stingy – others might say, however, their relative thriftiness was just being realistic – it was hard enough to recoup your investment and make a profit on any film, so why make life even more difficult for yourself by inflating your budget by awarding yourself with what the Boultings frequently saw as excessive upfront fees driven by nothing less than greed? And there was plenty of that, too, going in and out of the doorways of shady Wardour Street: the film business was a magnet for 'quick buck' merchants...and perhaps it still is.

The flagship for British Lion production was Shepperton Studios, back in 1959 a mighty enterprise with a huge permanent work-force – not the 4-waller it has become today – servicing every aspect of film-making from start to finish. To keep it afloat required keeping the 8 stages (including the massive Stage 'H', the biggest in Europe and called the 'Silent Stage' because it wasn't baffled for sound) busy with productions for as much of the year as possible. This was in the face of the competition from the other major studios, principally Pinewood and Boreham Wood at Elstree, trying to do exactly the same thing. But just how many productions, from home or abroad, were there going to be at any given moment...? British Lion – the big studios generally – were facing an uphill task and, some would say, were doomed to bat on a losing wicket. Of course, as a 14 year-old adolescent, I was unaware of all this – I was too caught up in the excitement of visiting the different sets, watching how they were painstakingly lit, seeing the huge baffled Mitchell cameras panning and tilting on the amazingly geared Moy heads in the skilled hands of the Operator, or gliding silently across the floor on a dolly to bring this actor or that actress into Close-up during those special, highly concentrated and focused moments which envelop any set during a take. If I wasn't on one of the stages, then perhaps I was hearing 35mm clattering noisily through the old upright Movieolas in the Editing Block and watching an Editor mark a frame with his Chinagraph pencil, a cut being made and joined(still by cement glue in those days)surrounded by streams of film hanging in their bins and giving off that compelling scent of the emulsion which all too frequently brought on flashbacks of that awful day at prep-school when a man with graying hair and brown jacket came crashing down the staircase to die...."Well, Boulting Minor ... do you think you could do any better?" ... How much, I was was beginning to understand, there was to learn.

My father, realizing I had caught the film 'bug', encouraged me to learn about all the different facets of film-making – and so took me down to Shepperton as often as possible during the school holidays for an altogether different kind of education. And what a good one it was. By 1959 I had been allowed to put in the clapper-board(respectfully wearing suit and tie)to mark the scene and take, had learnt how to help the Grips push a dolly silently across the boards (as a result, I have a special affection and affinity to Grips to this day), and I had begun to feel a sense of belonging to the strange world of film. However, I wasn't around to see my Uncle John directing "I'm Alright Jack", with Peter Sellers giving one of his finest and most memorable performances as Fred Kite, the union shop steward, nor to see my father directing Terry Thomas as "Carlton-Browne of the F.O." in the same year. Both of these films are what you would call 'conventional' studio pictures in style – but just across the Channel, on the *streets of Paris, something far more radical was taking place in Cinema – a young Frenchman was making a film which also dealt with the trials and tribulations of adolescence – and, dear God, what a film it was!*

11. "LES QUATRE CENTS COUPS"
("The 400 Blows")

(1959. Director: François Truffaut)

This was a heady time in French cinema and *La Nouvelle Vague* was like an unexpected dousing in cold water: a stimulating and refreshing shock to the system! Truffaut's highly autobiographical film about his childhood is raw, gritty, bursting with vitality and cinematically unfettered by tradition.

This was the film that introduced us to the character of Antoine Doinel, played by Jean-Pierre Léaud, himself a disturbed young man for whom Truffaut became a mentor and father figure. There were to be 4 more 'Antoine Doinel' films, all of them semi-autobiographical, but it is "Les Quatre Cent Coups" which is far and away the most memorable. Antoine is a troubled boy moving into adolescence, neglected at home and picked upon at school by his teacher. Whenever possible, he runs away from both – he's a 'problem' kid. The only inspiration in his life is Balzac for whom he has constructed a makeshift shrine in the box-room which serves as his bedroom. Sometimes showered with sudden affection by his neglectful mother and her husband (one night Antoine even catches her in the arms of another man), for the most part he is viewed by all as a trouble-maker and a liar (there's a wonderful scene in which he gets himself out of trouble at school by saying his mother's dead, earning a moment of sympathy from his cantankerous teacher until he discovers its yet another lie). With plans of running away from home again, Antoine steals a typewriter to sell it, is caught, spends the night in a jail with prostitutes and common thieves, before ending up in a harsh reform school, close to the sea. One day he manages to escape and starts running. He runs and runs and runs and then, suddenly, there it is – the ocean he has always dreamt of seeing. Standing at the edge of the shore, he turns into Camera and stares. His vulnerable, wounded face becomes a Freeze Frame and the film ends.

Antoine's Paris is the one of Montmartre, Pigalle, sleazy and run-down and far from being romantic. The fine cinematographer, Henri Decae, films it so that you can almost feel the grime on the walls, the dust of chalk in the schoolroom, the malodorous damp of his dingy home. Apart from J-P Léaud, there are uniformly good performances all round, and the entire film has the voice of an authentic and original talent. Tender, funny, compassionate, this was La Nouvelle Vague showing its teeth – and they all came out to lend a helping hand. There's Jeanne Moreau playing a little cameo, Jean-Claude Brialy … and see if you can spot Truffaut himself at the funfair Antoine's mother takes him to in a moment of guilty remorse. Or Jacques Démy as a policeman. I believe Godard and Belmondo are somewhere there as voices too. It's a truly wonderful film. I loved it then – and I love it now.

* * *

In fact, when I was asked what I would like for my 21st birthday, I asked for a screening of it – and got it, plus a rather good lunch to liven me up beforehand! Truffaut made so many fine films – the captivating "Jules et Jim", "Le Dernier Métro", "L'Enfant Sauvage", the strange "La Chambre Verte" and his work was never less than interesting. But, although I saw "Jules et Jim" more times than I can care to remember, I have chosen another Truffaut film for this list – because it is so much a film-maker's film.

12. "LA NUIT AMERICAINE"
("Day for Night")

(1973. Director: François Truffaut)

Of all the films made about film-making itself, this surely is one of the very best. 'Day for Night' is, of course, the term used to describe a night-time scene shot during the day. The French, rather more poetically, call it 'La Nuit Americaine'. With Truffaut himself playing the role of a director, faced with having to answer a thousand questions every day, the film explores all the artifices, trick, devices – the lies which become the 'truth' – which film-making involves. Plus the stresses, endless adaptations that have to be made alongside the emotional vagaries of both cast and crew alike.

The magnificent Valentina Cortese plays an ageing diva opposite an equally ageing male star, the dapper Jean-Pierre Aumont. They are making something of a soap opera melodrama of a movie in which the younger love element is provided by Jacqueline Bisset and Jean-Pierre Léaud who, off-screen, is having an affair with a singer(I think) played by Dani. Miss Bisset, too, is arousing curiosity about her marriage to a much older man whom no-one can identify. Jean-PIerre Aumont also raises eyebrows a little when introducing the good-looking young man he refers to as his 'godson'. As for Ms. Cortese, her problem is her liking for a tipple or two too many – drunk on set she cannot remember her lines or which door she is meant to exit through, ending up in the kitchen cupboard or the broom closet in take after take. Even with her lines written out and pasted up in strategic parts of the set, she's still having to struggle. Its delicious. On the side, between set-ups, the Prop Man has a quick bout of sex with the Script Girl, an actress due to play a swimming pool scene reveals she is heavily pregnant, a cat takes an interminable age to do what its meant to do, and Jean-Pierre Léaud throws a major wobbly when Dani ups sticks and leaves him. He can only be coaxed back on the set when Ms. Bisset allows him to fall into her arms for the night…And so it goes on, wittily, delightfully and shrewdly observed. Towards the end, The Completion Guarantors have to be brought in and deny more funds, necessitating a quick re-write and a compromised re-shoot. "Can we do it with snow?", pleads the Script Girl……and out come the foam machines…For anyone involved in film-making, they will recognize the accuracy of Truffaut's film; for everyone who isn't, they will be enlightened about the challenges faced and the tricks employed to meet them. Put together it is a celebration of film and a declaration of Truffaut's love for his art. The distinguished Georges Delerue, who worked on so many of Truffaut's films, wrote the score(and appears in it as himself) and the entire film was shot at the old Victorine Studios above Nice where Carné had made "Les Enfants du Paradis" so many years before in 1945 (and before it came right into the flight path of the nearby Nice airport!). Look carefully and you might also just catch a glimpse of Graham Greene, up the road from his home in Antibes, making his one and only (uncredited) appearance as a Completion Bond official. Truffaut has made a heart-warming but intelligent film which, quite deservedly, went on to win the Palme D'Or down the road at nearby Cannes. A film-maker's film for everyone.

* * *

In "Les Quatre Cents Coups", Antoine Doinel reveres the writer, Balzac. In Cinema, Truffaut had a special reverence for another master …and maybe the master of us all…certainly a surrogate father figure…Jean Renoir.

13. "LA RÈGLE DU JEU"
("The Rules of the Game")

(1939. Director: Jean Renoir)

Renoir, of course, is one of the giants of cinema; but when this film came out in 1939 it was an instant flop. Not for the first time, Renoir found himself taking another of his father's paintings down from the wall to get himself out of a scrape. It was to be some years before it was re-issued and become recognized as a masterpiece.... the rest is history: and now "La Règle du Jeu" is rightly esteemed as one the finest films ever made. But why…? Superficially, this is not much more than the story of a weekend party in a grand chateau with the predictable class divisions above and below stairs. Love and jealousy lurk in both spheres and lead to a tragic accident. *Eh voilà* – end of story… But this is no Downton Abbey soap: and Renoir has no polemic, no judgement, no moral pronouncement to make – rather, with again a technically beguiling simplicity, he is driven by a compassionate humanity for all and everyone, be they high or low, to observe the human condition and love it warts and all.

A famous aviator (Roland Toutain) is in love with Christine (Nora Gregor) who is married to the suave Marquis, Robert (Marcel Dalio – and watch out for him later after he fled to America to escape the Nazis – and see him pop up in "Casablanca"). All of them have a friend in Octave (chubby Renoir himself). Christine also has a devoted maid, Lisette, (Paulette Dubost) who cares more for her mistress than for her jealous husband, Schumacher (Gaston Modot) who is gamekeeper on the Marquis' estate. Throw in a leery poacher, Marceau (Julien Carette) whom the Marquis fancies to employ and who has more than a passing eye for Lisette, plus a mistress for the Marquis himself and you have more than enough ingredients to foresee trouble in store. But the rules of the game, the social etiquette both above and below stairs can mask the simmering passions and contain them from openly boiling over. Yet they remain there, and they will have their day. The gentlemen shoot, the servants cook and buttle, there is a masquerade and the Marquis amuses his guests with a fabulous musical machine while below stairs Marceau beguiles Lisette with a little music box. Love is secretly declared, plans to elope forged, and disaster is no further away than a jealous finger on the trigger of a shotgun. And that finger is the finger of the gamekeeper – in the darkness of the night, what he assumes to be his wife, Lisette, about to run off with no less than Octave, he shoots and kills the aviator who intends to elope with Christine. "Chers amis….sad", declares the Marquis, with the politest shrug of regret "sad…but an accident…" The party is over…and so is a certain world order…

The film radiates goodwill, even in its sorrows. Sure, there are hints of the inevitable changes to this social system in the air; there is regret and frustration observed and watched through a dispassionate (and innovative deep focus) lens. Nor does he condone the social system that brings such misfortune, yet he never falls into the trap of condemning. Rather he tries to make us understand and rejoice in our common humanity and thus sorrow in our common failings and the pitfalls it can lead us into. And this is why, for me, it makes it such a very BIG film, big of heart, big with life, and why one understands the very considerable influence it has exercised on film-makers following on from it.

14. "LA GRANDE ILLUSION"

(1937. Director: Jean Renoir)

There are many of Renoir's films which could be included in this list – in particular the wonderful "Boudu Sauvé des Eaux" ("Boudu saved from Drowning") with Michel Simon as the anarchic tramp who creates havoc in the liberal bourgeois household who take him in, but "La Grande Illusion", made in 1937 and 2 years before "La Règle du Jeu", is somehow seminal Renoir and anticipates themes in his work to which he would return again, in different ways, in later years. Set during the Great War, Pierre Fresnay plays the aristocratic airman who, with his working-class co-pilot, Jean Gabin is shot down over enemy lines. Their captor, the equally aristocratic and gentlemanly Erich von Stroheim, entertains them for lunch before apologetically packing them off to a POW camp. Eventually, their paths cross again when Fresnay and Gabin are transferred to another camp – a mighty escape-proof castle now under von Stroheim's command. He has been incapacitated by wounds and is now strapped into a monstrous neck brace, but remains the perfect old-fashioned gentleman – indeed, the film is as much about the etiquette and duties of honour as it is about war breaking down the class barriers which precede it. Because of their shared social backgrounds, von Stroheim and Fresnay are mutually respectful and friendly, yet inevitably obliged, by their different positions as captive and captor, to be in conflict. Also amongst the prisoners is a wealthy *nouveau riche* Jew (Marcel Dalio again), recipient of generous food parcels which he willingly shares with everyone. There is also a large cast of minor but important characters; and, being Renoir, they are treated to his signature compassion and gently ironic humour – an excited batch of Russian prisoners, for instance, receiving a gift from the Tsarina, only to discover it is not the food and clothing they so badly need, but a crate full of bibles, is painfully funny and speaks volumes (if you'll forgive the pun).

Gabin and Dalio plot to escape – and when the hour arrives for them to make their bid for freedom, Fresnay gallantly provides distraction by appearing on the roof of the castle. Von Stroheim's pleas to him, as one gentleman to another, to come down are to no avail and reluctantly von Stroheim draws his pistol intending to wing him – missing and shooting Fresnay in the stomach. As he lies dying, the apologetic von Stroheim at his side, Fresnay regrets the passing of the values they both adhere to which will disappear after the war. Gabin and Dalio, in the meanwhile, make their way towards Switzerland, taking refuge with a German woman who has lost all her family in the war. She and Gabin fall in love and he promises to come back for her after the war…At the end, he and Dalio are seen tramping through the snow and over the border. A German patrol watching them decide they will not shoot…

The underlying theme accompanying the narrative is of how the common bond of humanity, in certain situations, can transcend the divisions of class, social background, nationality and beliefs. It is a motif to which Renoir would return in 1962 with "Le Caporal Epinglé"("The Vanishing Corporal"), a lovely film, too, but without the same impact of its earlier predecessor. "La Grande Illusion" remains one of my favourites – Fresnay, Gabin and Dalio are a joy to watch …and von Stroheim, in that extraordinary neck-brace, absolutely impeccable!

* * *

If the amiable chubby figure of Jean Renoir casts a hugely influential shadow over La Nouvelle Vague, and Truffaut in particular, nevertheless we have to go a few years further back than him, however, to find, in the works of another director, the flowering of French radical cinema, and whose few films – only 4 – doubtless cast a shadow over Renoir as well as it did over everyone else – then and since …

15. "ZÉRO DE CONDUITE"
("Zero for Conduct")

(1933.Director: Jean Vigo)

… And here it is in one of the most anarchic, iconoclastic and anti-institutional films of all time, echoes of which can be found in French cinema for the rest of the century…No more than 44 minutes long,"Zéro de Conduite" is a riot of irreverence, Gallic "Je suis Moi" individualism and sheer "Je m'en fou-tism", made with poetic relish by one of Cinema's lost masters. Drawing from his own experiences, it tells the story of the uprising and revolution of the boys incarcerated in a boarding school, gleefully sticking two fingers in the air at all and every notion of Authority. As radical in its techniques as it is in its thinking, Vigo's brilliant film is, at times, almost surreally beautiful (think of the pillow-fight scene with all the feathers floating like snow). The phrase 'poetic realism', often used to describe Vigo's work, doesn't do it justice: it is a little god of a film – (Lindsay Anderson's much later "If"(1968), surely heavily influenced by it, comes nowhere near reaching its sublime heights) – assured of a place in the pantheon of the greats forever. It was considered so subversive (and its worth noting Vigo was the son of a militant Catalan anarchist, who spent much of his life on the run) that it was banned by the French government until after the war. The only feature film Vigo made, "L'Atalante" didn't have much luck either and was pretty well hacked to death by the distributors. All his films lost money and Vigo, tubercular and always frail, died at the very early age of 29, leaving behind a wife and little daughter. What a loss to Cinema! Everything about him is extraordinary: "Zero de Conduite" has the beauty of true freedom and Vigo himself the marks and scars of a true hero.

* * *

The French take their Cinema seriously – or rather, they actually and actively LIKE it, incorporating it quite naturally into their culture as one of the Arts in a way we, the Brits, have never quite managed or are vaguely reluctant to do. It is part of their life, as much as their cuisine, and, although that is maybe changing now (as is the standard of that celebrated cuisine), back in the '60's, 70's and into the '80's their appreciation of Film seemed almost genetically hard-wired into their sensibility. Paris alone could boast over 270 cinema and all doing business -, as compared to what in London? 50 maybe? France and French Cinema has exerted its charm and influence over me ever since my adolescence, and I am an unabashed Francophone (irrespective of the absurdly rude posturings of some Parisiens)so I don't want to leave French Cinema quite just yet without including 4 other directors whose work I admire...The first of these is hardly known to the general public but is considered by many of his peers to be head and shoulders above them all. His name is Maurice Pialat ...

16. "VAN GOGH"

(1991. Director: Maurice Pialat)

The French singer, Jacques DuTronc plays the artist in this quite extraordinary cinematic *tour de force*. Forget about Kirk Douglas, dimpled chin and all, rampaging around the Provençal countryside, in Minelli's perfectly respectable but banal biog "Lust for Life" – this is a very different animal indeed, centering more on Van Gogh, the man, during his last 2 months in Auvers under the care of Dr Gachet. It is also about his relationship with his brother Theo, his wife and her younger sister, more than it is about the paintings themselves. And about the 'love life' of a moody, irascible man given to headaches and moping about with whores – not about paint being slapped on canvas or ears being cut off or going blind on absinthe. Long, sustained shots, stripped bare of any dramatic ornamentation, rigorously compressed into almost minimalist frames, build up a really powerful portrait of the artist's struggle with his life as much as the creative process itself. In one sequence, set in a brothel, Van Gogh participates in a dance, a kind of folk dance quadrille, I suppose, in which the dancers, dressed in lines facing one another, repeat the same clunking steps again and again and again, joining the partner opposite and advancing towards a fixed camera, peeling off and coming back again, with Dutronc's expression devoid of any emotion throughout. Where most directors would have cut out of the action long before or, at the very least, varied the camera angles, Pialat is relentless and holds the scene in one shot until it is almost unbearable. Knock out – burning itself into my memory forever. The film, as a whole, seized me, froze me almost, with the 'purity' of its film language and its unflinching discipline in keeping away from any cheap sentiment or easy effect. A humbling film experience.

17. "CÉLINE ET JULIE VONT EN BATEAUX"
("Céline and Julie go boating")

(1974. Director: Jacques Rivette)

Truffaut wrote that *La Nouvelle Vague* really began because of Rivette, (with his film "Paris Nous Appartient" in 1961) which I find a bit odd, since Truffaut himself had already made "Les Quatre Cents Coups" 2 years earlier. But its true Rivette has never received the public attention he really merits. I was once taken to meet him by the actress Bulle Ogier (who also plays in this film) and found him living in a room covered floor to ceiling in newspaper to keep out the drafts and cold …and not much else. That's sometimes the price…. just think of poor Jean Vigo, or Renoir having to sell off another of his father's paintings. Highly prized by his peers, Rivette is a special and original talent – but not immediately accessible.

This film, with Juliet Berto and Dominique Labourier as Céline and Julie, is a strange dream-like drama in which the lives of two friends (are they friends?) is continually interrupted by a bizarre, possibly surreal boudoir story which keeps on intruding. It was thought to have been improvised – in the sense of being ad-libbed. It wasn't… it was carefully developed by Rivette (a pre-cursor of Mike Leigh and his working methods?) who shaped the story/stories provided by his cast. When I saw it, I could not honestly say I understood it very well – except to know that I was watching an authentic and very special piece of film and that my conventional sense of film was being challenged. " Go boating" is also slang for " go crazy"…and this is certainly a crazy film. So Rivette has to be on this list – and the next one too….

18. "LE GENOU DE CLAIRE" ("Claire's Knee")

(1970. Director: Eric Rohmer)

Rohmer was one of the last of the directors to get going in *La Nouvelle Vague* and the one who is perhaps its most 'intellectual' or certainly most *verbal*. He has won more attention over the years than either Pialat or Rivette with a raft of films banded together under the general title of " 6 Moral Tales". Each of them deals, in different ways and in different situations, with the moral dilemmas and uncertainties of love, fidelity, attraction, responsibility – digging wittily and shrewdly into the psychology of human relationships. Dialogue and dialectic debate predominate in his very simply crafted films – so restrained and 'ordinary' at times that one begs the question as to whether they are really cinema at all…Yet, somehow, so judiciously constructed are they, that one cannot deny them their place as real film. Moreover, as much if not more than his *nouvelle vague* contemporaries his films found a willing and appreciative public within a more commercial spectrum. (Gosh – 'art films' can actually make money????)

Shot on and around Lake Annecy, the dilemma facing Jean-Claude Brialy is whether he can, should, should not, will not touch the knee of the young and precocious Claire (played with great aplomb by the unknown Béatrice Romand). In the best French tradition there is endless *discours* about the nature of attraction, sexual boundaries, love etc. Far from being a bore, it is all delightfully witty and as deliciously chaste as snow. And, yes, he does get to touch that knee! Highly enjoyable – and ferociously clever!

* * *

In the same year Truffaut was metaphorically re-writing the rule book with "Les Quatre Cents Coups", (as was, incidentally, John Cassavetes, a kindred spirit over in New York with "Shadows" – also released in the UK by British Lion), another great French talent emerged into public Close Up and I cannot possibly leave France behind(or return later) without including a director of the stature of Alain Resnais...

19. "HIROSHIMA, MON AMOUR"

(1959. Director: Alain Resnais)

I was deeply moved and affected by this film when I saw it at the age of 16. Scripted by Marguerite Duras, the film is structured as a long conversation about memory, forgetfulness … but it is also dealing with the wounds man inflicts upon his fellow man in war. The film is set in both Nevers during World War 2 and Hiroshima of today. The wounds of the girl in Nevers, played by Emmanuelle Riva, are those of the brutal punishment meted out on her for collaborating by taking a German lover…hair shorn, ostracized and spat upon, that is the trauma she must suffer for the mistake of her love. The wounds of Hiroshima are those of the 'keloids' or radiation scars, together with the trauma of the Bomb itself, suffered by a Japanese architect (Eiji Okada) she takes as a passing lover years later while, as an actress, she is making an anti-war film. He was present in Hiroshima when the Bomb fell – and how both remember their traumas is told in quick flashbacks, with both of them questioning the accuracy of each other's memories. Indeed, memory and our individual perceptions of the reality of memory run through Resnais' work, from "L'Année Dernière à Marienbad", and on through "Muriel" and "Providence", but perhaps never so tellingly as in this earlier film. It is a haunting piece, stately in form and style, imbued with a sadness and melancholy, marked by restless and fluid camerawork, and established Resnais as the very great talent he had already shown he promised to be with his previous "Nuit et Brouillard" ('Night and Fog') his short and chilling documentary film about the Nazi concentration camps. Resnais's formalism has sometimes been criticized as 'cold' and his films lacking in 'human feeling', but, for all its cool detachment and stylized discipline, "Hiroshima, mon Amour" is anything but 'cold'. It not only influenced the Nouvelle Vague, but has continued to influence directors from all over the world ever since: Resnais quite deservedly hangs in the gallery with the gods.

* * *

Another little digression...À propos the so-called 'épuration' of French collaborators at the end of the war, I particularly like the story of the great actress and national icon, Arletty ("Les Enfants du Paradis", "Hotel du Nord" etc) who was arraigned and brought to court for having had an affair with a German Luftwaffe Officer. When quizzed on the substance of the charge against her, she rose to her feet in the dock and regally declared to the court at large: " Mon Coeur appartient à La France – mais mon Cul au Monde!" (I'm sure you can translate!). So pleased was the judge with this reply and its witty play on the 2 'c' words that he dismissed the charges there and then. Apocryphal or not, the story has always struck me as being so deliciously French! (In reality, however, like so many versions of their wartime history, the truth was rather different – and I believe Arletty did indeed have to serve a few months in a French jail, but at least they didn't dare shave her head!...)

* * *

I want to take a breather from French Cinema for awhile – and cross the pond to the other side...

In so doing, I am no more than following in the footsteps of so many fine film-makers who fled persecution in their native Germany or Austria to find refuge and an expression for their talents in Hollywood. It is easy to forget that so many of these great film-makers were of Austro-German blood and most, if not all of them Jewish...Billy Wilder, Ernst Lubitsch, Fritz Lang, Joseph von Sternberg, Fred Zinneman(whose parents both died in The Holocaust)...all refugees from the Nazis who, along with so many other talents in writing, music, art direction, editing, etc, could be said to have been instrumental in forging the idea of what we call American Cinema today...What they brought with them, of course, were the traditions of European culture and sensibility which inevitably they began to graft onto the American vision, refining and developing it to high standards of craft and creative technique – and, in some instances, into Art...However, my first of these 'giants', although Polish Jewish and an émigré, did not come to America to flee the Nazis, but much earlier – in search of a better life than being the son of a hat-maker. He was nicknamed 'The Man you Love to Hate' – but, for me, Erich von Stroheim is a film-maker I love to love...

20. "GREED"

(1924: Director: Erich von Stroheim)

This is a whopper of a film! Huge! And, at some eight hours plus long (I think) when originally completed by von Stroheim, quite a journey! Greed – and the lengths to which man will go, abandoning all his conventional human decencies and values, in order to acquire and covet little more than a pot of gold – is depicted for all its futility and baseness with majestic authority by von Stroheim. In so doing, he hardly endeared himself to the studio bosses – because, after all, gold and not art was what they really wanted for themselves too.

It has been a very long time indeed since I saw "Greed", and, like the two protagonists in "Hiroshima, Mon Amour", I question my memory... A woman (Zasu Pitts) wins a lottery ticket, but refuses to spend it. Her husband, (Gibson Gowland) reduced to poverty by her miserliness, longs to lay his hands on it. And his friend (Jean Hersholt) covets the money, too, believing it rightfully should have come to him. Husband is set against wife, friend against friend – money and greed, a toxic mix! Sharp flashes of memory: in despair to get hold of the money, in a fit of rage the husband bites his wife's hand – the wound goes septic and her fingers are amputated. But she still won't part with the money – she wants to touch it, hold it, smell it – she lays it out on her bed and lies on it. Husband and wife confront each other once again – this time he beats her to death, steals the money and goes on the run. He is pursued by his erstwhile friend, still hellbent on grabbing the cash himself. In the unforgettable final sequence, they confront each other in the dry, pitiless heat of Death Valley. Their horse gets shot, their only water bottle punctured....the friend is overcome but somehow has managed to handcuff himself to the husband before he dies. Alone in this remorseless landscape, unable to move, shackled to a dead body, starved of water, without a horse, the husband pays for his greed ... with the bag of money forever just beyond his reach.

Although the film was not recognized as a masterpiece at the time – in subsequent years it has always been voted into the Top Ten of the 'best films ever'. Quite apart from the moral complexities of the plot, it is stamped with von Stroheim's legendary (and time-consuming) obsession with detail and shows a sense of realism far ahead of its time. It was savagely cut by Irving Thalberg ... and to compound the wound, more's the shame, von Stroheim himself was deemed too 'difficult' a director to be trusted, being successively fired from subsequent pictures and then effectively side-lined altogether. Hollywood was to do the same thing to Orson Welles later on... as it had already done to D.W.Griffith... The conflict between the chink of silver and the chink of light has always characterized the essential dilemma facing film-makers...Erich von Stroheim was one of the early victims...But his film lives on where so many thousands of other lie buried forever in the dust of Death Valley too...

Consolation of sorts...Von Stroheim, himself, left the States and returned to Europe and France where, as he pointed out, your artistry was honoured and you were not considered 'only as good as your last film', or appreciation of your creativity overshadowed by any ensuing failures(principally at the box-office) which may have also accompanied your career ... And it was there in France that he died – in my book, as good a place as any in which to pop your clogs – fulsomely admired by the emerging talents of *La Nouvelle Vague*, and at least graced with a *Legion D'Honneur* with which the French like to acknowledge and honour a true artist when they see one, and preferably while they're still alive to enjoy it.

* * *

Back in 1967, I witnessed an example of this fickle Hollywood loyalty at first hand, while I was fortunate enough to be a house guest of the actor Richard Widmark and his family in Los Angeles. They introduced me to that strange, sometimes unreal world of Hollywood and, through him, I got to meet some of the 'legends' – including one evening, in a Japanese restaurant, the director Fred Zinnemann. His superbly crafted "A Man for All Seasons" had recently scooped 6 Oscars (and would gather a total of 27 prizes in all) and, not for the first time, he was currently something of the talk of the town. I was struck by both his impeccable manners and also by his completely uncontrived modesty – he was a natural gentleman. At some point in the evening, a couple approached the table to greet Zinnemann, like a long-lost friend. Hurt reproach combined with an effusively affectionate outpouring of questionable sincerity, as they reproached him with "Fred! FRED! Long time! Where have you BEEN!? We've missed you, for Crissake! Its been so LONG!" etc, etc. In response Zinnemann was the model of civility, and betrayed no sign of anything other than quiet friendliness. It was only afterwards that Richard Widmark explained to me that, prior to the success of "A Man for All Seasons", Zinneman had flopped badly (in particular with "Behold, a Pale Horse") and Hollywood society – such as this couple – had had no hesitation in turning its back on him. Now, of course, they all wanted to know him again. Zinnemann was far too intelligent and sensitive to be fooled by such 'fair weather friends', but that's not to say that he didn't feel the hurt. Born a Polish Jew but brought up in Austria, he had seen enough in his life to understand the value of loyalty and distinguish between true friendship and its shallow counterfeit – all too often apparent, I'm afraid to say, in the film world wherever you find it...Like von Stroheim, Zinnemann returned to Europe for his last years and last films, dying in London in 1997 at the age of 89. A consummate craftsman, I am grateful to have spent those few hours in his company...

21. "SUNSET BOULEVARD"

(1950 – Director: Billy Wilder)

Erich von Stroheim re-emerges in this film – now the loyal butler to an ageing and faded star of the silent movies, played by another legend, Gloria Swanson. Still dreaming of her return to the big screen, waiting in her folly of a mansion for a day that will never come. she is quickly losing her grip on reality. Nothing is quite what it seems in this bitter-sweet study on the transience and vanity of 'success' (indeed life) and the pain of rejection made by one of Hollywood's very finest craftsmen. Wilder employs the interesting device of a Narrator coming to us from beyond the grave, the voice of a young unsuccessful writer (William Holden) who becomes co-opted by this forgotten star to 'script doctor' a project she has written with which she hopes to make her come-back. But he quickly finds that he is not only becoming the projection of her hopes, but also the misplaced object of her romantic affections and desires. Deluded by herself, humoured gently by others (it turns out her butler, Max, (von Stroheim), was not only once a celebrated director who made 'Madame' into a star, but also her husband), she is a pathetic but tragic figure. In one sequence, she visits the studios to talk about her script with Cecil B. de Mille(playing himself) and is recognized by one of the crew – a spotlight is turned onto her and for a few seconds, she is again the famous star she once was...It is moving to see. But when Holden rejects her and tells her the cruel truth about herself, it not only seals his own fate, but finally unhinges her altogether. Threatening to kill herself, instead she turns her gun on him, shooting him dead as he falls into the swimming pool. The famous final scene, lost in her fantasy word, as she descends the staircase ("Alright, Mr de Mille, I'm ready for my Close-up now") coaxed down by von Stroheim calling 'Action' to her, is perfectly judged and enormously poignant. The film became an instant classic – apart from Cecil B.

de Mille, look out for appearances from the gossip column dragon Hedda Hopper – but also for another small batch of Hollywood's forgotten silent stars – amongst whom you will see the inimitable Buster Keaton. In some ways, this is a cruel film – but then the film business itself can be as cruel and pitiless as anything on earth.

22. "TO BE OR NOT TO BE"

(1942 – Director: Ernst Lubitsch)

This is an outrageously funny film – outrageous inasmuch it chooses high comedy as the tool with which to talk about nothing less than the Nazi persecution of the Jews. But Lubitsch, himself another Jewish exile from Nazi Berlin, knew what he was doing – and his comedy bites and hurts where it is meant to hurt. Brilliantly deadpan Jack Benny, and zany, bubbly Carole Lombard (in her very last role before her tragic death in an air disaster) play the two leading lights of a theatre company in Poland(?), continually bickering and endeavouring to upstage one another (Carole Lombard appearing in glittering evening dress to rehearse a scene set in a concentration camp is absolutely shameless! And shamelessly funny!). After the Nazi invasion, the entire company use their talents to fool the Nazis and plot their escape to freedom. How they achieve this – by both dressing up and playing the roles of their invaders AND also using "The Merchant of Venice" – (Shylock, of course – the "Do we not bleed, etc" speech here addressed to a group of German officers is outstanding and hilarious) – as the means of outfoxing them, is executed with a sure and dexterous touch (in fact this stylish wit became known as 'the Lubitsch Touch'). The result is very, very funny indeed – and Lubitsch sends up the Nazis for all its worth. Yet the aftertaste, however, is curiously sobering. Rudolf Maté offers some interestingly stylized photography to tweak the underlying point. Lubitsch is better known now for his "Ninotchka" with Greta Garbo, (co-scripted with Billy Wilder) but "To Be or Not to Be" will always remain my personal favourite…It's a classic! Not long after he had a massive heart-attack and, although he lingered on until after the war, Lubitsch didn't really manage to do much more…

23. "SULLIVAN'S TRAVELS"

(1941 Director: Preston Sturges)

Some of the themes of "Sunset Boulevard" and the power of comedy explored in "To Be or Not to Be" sort of come together in this picture, written and directed by the maverick and iconoclastic *auteur* film-maker,Preston Sturges, here at the top of his game. The Sullivan of the title is a successful director of escapist films, played by Joel Mcrea, basking in renown and money during the Depression era. But, despite his Studio's reluctance, he wants to make a 'serious' film, titled "Brother, where are Thou?", dealing with the social issues of the times and decides to go on the road as a hobo and see what life is really all about in order to research it. Initially followed by all the paraphernalia of the Studio's back-up publicity crew, he quickly abandons that and gets stuck into the altogether different reality of soup kitchens and life on the road. He meets up with the lovely 'peek-a-boo' Veronica Lake, an out of work and failing actress, who mistakes him for a genuine tramp and treats him to a plate of fried eggs. When she discovers his true identity, she is less than amused and throws him into his own swimming-pool – not quite rejection, but certainly a strong warning signal not to mess about with life. Identity confusion develops further when the death of another tramp is mistaken as his own and, through a series of fluke mix-ups, finds Sullivan being mistakenly arrested and wrongly convicted for assault. Sent off for 6 years to the penitentiary and shackled to the chain gang, Sullivan's subsequent attempts to get himself cleared and freed become increasingly hopeless and his despair of ever returning to the life he has led before deeper and deeper. He has dug himself into a hole from which escape seems impossible. But this is a cautionary tale – Sullivan has to learn he is no better, no worse than other mortals and open his eyes to the common lot of man and see also that, at best, his own 'experiment' is nothing less than patronizing ....One day Sullivan, along with his fellow convicts, is taken along to a Baptist church to attend a film show. A cartoon, Mickey Mouse and Pluto, comes onto the screen and, for all their sad misery, suffering and loneliness, the prisoners can laugh. Despite himself, Sullivan finds that he, too, can join in with the laughter and in it find relief and a degree of freedom from his sorrows: it is, quite literally, an 'escape'. A chastened Sullivan begins to understand that perhaps he should have stuck at doing what he was good at and see the value of it – making so-called 'escapist' films, and forgo the vanity of his lofty artistic pretensions. All's well, (well almost), that ends well – and Sullivan does return to his former life, lovely Peek-a-boo Veronica is there (is she?) and there are smiles and laughter all round....but the taste is bitter-sweet.

Preston Sturges was an intelligent and astute observer of the human condition, and this is a memorable film which manages to combine different *genres* – comedy,social realism, even slapstick – into one unified whole. It was finely photographed by John Seitz (who went on later to do "Sunset Boulevard") and Sturges himself was a fascinating character, a perfectionist and one of the first *auteur* directors. He made only 12 films, achieved enormous success, but managed to fall out with pretty well everyone – with Paramount to begin with, then Howard Hughes with whom he formed a short-lived production company, all of his many wives and many others beside. His own mother had been a friend of Isadora Duncan, and one of her many lovers (she sometimes had two or three on the go at the same time of both sexes) was the infamous occultist, prophet, libertine and all-round creepy Alesteir 'The Beast' Crowley, so it could be said her son grew up in a distinctly bohemian atmosphere which might partly account for his own iconoclastic leanings. Before becoming a writer, then writer-director and finally writer-director-producer, he had started out life as an inventor, at which he failed miserably. Fortunately, however, his very considerable talents found their outlet in Cinema where his powers of invention were put to altogether more fruitful ends. He died in 1959 – I fear rather alone – in the Algonquin Hotel, and probably not too far away from a bottle and aged only 60....the legendary and beautiful Louise Brooks, herself no stranger to the bottle, recalls coming across him in Paris – and even she found his drunkenness intolerable…Sad…

* * *

"Sullivan's Travels" came out in 1941 before the Japanese attack on Pearl Harbor in December, which finally brought the United States into the war, and, perhaps reflecting American sentiment at the time, the conflict going on in Europe is not even inferred obliquely in Sturges' movie. Not that the Americans were not very much aware of the perils of Nazism and the grim shadow being cast by the swastika. And à propos, the year before The Boultings had made "Pastor Hall", directed by my father, which opened in New York with an added introduction presented by none other than Eleanor Roosevelt, warning the Americans of the dangers Hitler posed to the entire world, not just Europe. Based on a play by Ernst Toller, (another Jewish exile who ended up committing suicide in 1939)the film tells the true story of a pastor(played wonderfully by Wilfrid Lawson) in a small German town who preached against the Nazis from his pulpit and ended up being sent to die in Dachau concentration camp. The film caused quite a stir – didactic and politically engaged, it was a salutary and heartfelt plea which troubled the consciences of many Americans. Coincidentally also, the year after "Sullivan's Travels", the Boultings made "Thunder Rock", adapted from the 1939 play by Robert Ardrey. Starring Michael Redgrave, James Mason, Barbara Mullen and Lilli Palmer, the film warned of the dangers of appeasement, of turning your backs and running away from a threat which had to be confronted and fought against head-on. Again directed by my father, the film played for over 3 months in one theatre alone in New York and won public as well as critical acclaim. Both these films were photographed by the gifted Mutz Greenbaum, yet another Jewish exile, who continued working with the Boultings (now under his anglicized name, Max Greene) well into the 1960's: in the art of black and white photography, Mutzi was something of a master – and I, personally, learnt a lot from watching him at work during my adolescence. The following year, 1943, Roy went on to make "Desert Victory", the Oscar winning documentary about the

battle of El Alamein. The sequence of the artillery barrage which opened the battle has been used in countless films since and indeed shows Roy's tremendous gifts as an editor. By this time, of course, the Americans were up to their neck in the war – and were slightly miffed that their own role in El Alamein had not been sufficiently featured to their liking in Roy's film. It didn't take long for them to send in Frank Capra to set the record straight with "Tunisian Victory", but Roy's film remained the template for a certain documentary approach and Capra was not shy in consulting my father – so much so that in fact they ended up co-directing. There was always an edge of competiveness between the Yanks and the Limeys, wasn't there..?

An anecdote concerning Winston Churchill and the making of "Desert Victory" might not go amiss at this point. Originally, Churchill had wanted to end the film with shots of him giving his speech to the troops after the battle. Roy had different ideas – and, although merely a young and lowly Captain, did not hesitate to tell Mr Churchill so. Surely, Roy persuaded him, wouldn't the effect of his speech be even greater if played over shots, not of him, but of all the different troops who had fought and won the battle? The people? Slightly taken aback at first by this impudence, Churchill had the good grace to agree. When it came to recording his words down at Chequers, with all the business of setting up the lumbering equipment and cables involved in those days, Churchill interrupted the business of running the war to come in and do his bit. Having delivered the speech into the microphone he got up to leave and return to more urgent matters – and was far from pleased when Roy suggested they should do it again and do it better. What? Take 2? Churchill? With a war going on? I beg your pardon!...But he did....And when Churchill saw the finished film, it is said he wept openly – with Roy sitting at his side...

But back to the List...and back across the pond...

24. "HIGH NOON"

(1952. Director: Fred Zinneman)

I return to Fred Zinnemann and this film of his which is one of the very best in the genre. I was brought up on a diet of Westerns and war films – as was all my generation – but I have always loved Westerns most for their portrayals of the timeless struggle of the Good against the Bad. You know where you stand with a Western from the very first frame – right is right and wrong is wrong! Gary Cooper plays the Sheriff who, on both the day of his retirement and his very wedding day to Grace Kelly, must decide whether he will do the right thing and take a stand against the Baddies heading into town by train at noon that day or cop out of it. In choosing to do the right thing, as his duties as a Sheriff and his conscience demand of him, he puts not only his life but also his marriage on the line – and, against all the odds, abandoned with one excuse after another by the very townsfolk he is defending, faces the menace all alone. Zinneman builds the tension up and lays out the arguments for the 'pros' and 'cons' quite beautifully. The sweat dripping down Gary Cooper's face, the suggestion of a real tear being wiped away by him are caught in surgically intense Close-Ups. The repeated Low-Angle shot up the railway line as everyone waits for the train cross-cuts with the increasingly fading hopes of Gary Cooper to get anyone in town to stand beside him. More than that, the film is almost shot in 'real time' – in the 90 minutes or so between the threat being known and the arrival of the 'baddies' at high noon. Like Wilder, Zinnemann was a terrific craftsman also – spare classical camerawork and excellent editing accompany an intelligently structured script by Carl Foreman. Some people have suggested that the townsfolk abandoning their Sheriff, while they all wait for the train to arrive down the tracks bringing in the 'baddies', is a veiled metaphor for the cloud of Macarthyism descending over America at the time. Whilst it is clear from his films that Zinnemann was morally concerned with the oppression of individual freedoms by collective, ideological forces, I am not at all convinced that the extremely disagreeable witch-hunt Macarthy pursued was at the forefront of his mind when he made "High Noon", (although it might have been so for his screenplay writer, Carl Foreman, with his known left-wing sympathies). Dimitri Tiomkin wrote the score, but there is also a great theme song "Do not forget me, oh my darling , on this our wedding day" by Tex Ritter with an underlying percussive menace which really works a treat…. But I'm not sure I have ever really completely forgiven Grace Kelly for deciding to get out of town before the bullets started flying and leaving Hubby to face them on his own…

25. "REAR WINDOW"

(1954. Director: Alfred Hitchcock)

...On the other hand, I could forgive Grace Kelly for just about anything in this masterful work in which she plays the beautiful high society girlfriend of photo-journalist and rugged outdoor man of action, James Stewart, currently confined to a wheelchair with a broken leg in the sweltering heat of a New York summer. Hitchcock, another supreme craftsman, sets himself the problem of how to shoot the film entirely and exclusively from the viewpoint of Stewart's room and it's window overlooking the backyards and into the lives of all the others living in the apartment block. The result is a master class in film craft. By making his protagonist a photographer, Hitchcock can move us closer to all their lives by the simple device of the telephoto lens Stewart uses to watch the goings-on around him – yet without ever breaking the rule of moving outside the room. Pertinent and very effective, it also makes us complicit in his voyeurism. The murder he thinks he has seen committed by one of his neighbours (played by a sinister Raymond Burr) provides the suspense plot and narrative drive overlaying the sub-text – which is really about 'the battle of the sexes'. All the characters in the film – the lonely woman, the young newly-weds, the pert and gymnastic dancer, the retired couple with their dog, the composer struggling with a composition, etc, including the murderer himself – offer different facets of the relationship between men and women. It goes without saying – being a Hitchcock film, that there is suspense aplenty and flashes of the Master's genius(Grace Kelly's first appearance is pure cinematic magic), but the film is also surprisingly tender and touching at times. Thelma Ritter plays the down-to-earth no-nonsense nurse who cares for Stewart, and Wendell Corey, a skeptical detective who ostensibly doesn't believe a single word of his friend's suspicions of foul play...But Grace Kelly is more convinced and sets out to do something about it – at nail-biting risk to herself.... Look out for the moment when Hitchcock breaks his rule and steps outside for the one and only time...Its clever! Hitchcock originally wanted to shoot it all on location – but in the end built the whole set on a Paramount lot where, having started life as an Art Director, the Master could also resort to some very clever 'cheats' indeed – if you can spot them! ...One of my favourite films of all time.

26. "VERTIGO"

(1958. Director: Alfred Hitchcock)

Brooding, moody, despairing and obsessive, this is one of Hitchcock's darkest films. Once again, his early training as an Art Director is apparent in his use of colour here – at times swamping the screen with reds...with greens...with misty gardens of pink. The vertigo of the title is suffered by James Stewart, a detective who has been forced to retire after being unable to prevent a colleague from falling to his death during a rooftop chase (thus bringing on the vertigo), and is achieved by the novel technique of the Camera tracking backwards, whilst simultaneously zooming forward – creating a dizzying and nauseous effect. But the heart of the film is his anguished attempt to try and re-create his lost, dead love in a woman who appears and is her spitting image. Kim Novak plays the blonde – both the dead lover and the doppelganger Stewart tries to replace her with, moulding her down to her hair style, her dresses, every detail of her looks. Enhanced by one of the very best scores Bernard Hermann, Hitchcock's long time collaborator, ever wrote, there is a sense of how doomed (and sick) Stewart's dreams are bound to be. The fact he has been duped all along and led into an elaborate ploy doesn't dawn on him until it is almost too late....The outcome is painful, the whole story disturbing and doesn't make for comfortable viewing – although mesmerizing and suspenseful it most certainly is. Barbara Bel Geddes, as a painter friend of his, appears in her studio – shot on location at Russian Hill, San Francisco, in a building, part of which now just happens to be owned by a friend of mine...She tells me "Vertigo" fans are forever popping up and clicking away with their cameras... "Vertigo" has become a classic and is certainly vintage Hitchcock, psychologically complex, reeking with the anguish of loss and haunted by the follies the dark daemons of memory can drive us to. Yes, vertiginous...

＊ ＊ ＊

Great craftsman as he was, Hitchcock was not known for his respect or indulgence of his actors in their various searches to understand the meaning of the characters there were playing: like all the other elements in a film, they were ciphers, parts of a jig-saw puzzle which he had designed and knew how to put together. Ingrid Bergman once told him she didn't understand what was meant to be motivating her part in a certain scene – and, so she recounts, he is said to have replied, "Don't worry – just fake it!". She claims she saw his point – after all, so much of film is made up of artefact, 'cheating', technical manipulation and deception – like Picasso's "I paint lies in order to show the truth". There is no guarantee that a profound "method" understanding of your role will necessarily end up as a better or truer performance on the screen. However, there are some directors who can draw out the most extraordinary results from their cast which go way beyond what craft and technique alone can supply. One of the most influential, in this respect, was by origin a Cappodocian Greek, another migrant who came to America and whose talent and creativity with actors is responsible for introducing the world to the likes of Marlon Brando, James Dean, bringing Natalie Wood from childhood into mature roles, and even helping Warren Beatty into stardom as well. Elia Kazan (born Elias Kazantzoglou) was very much "an actor's director", who had come out of theatre and into film, a one-time Communist deeply concerned with social issues, and another enormously gifted film director. Controversy and condemnation may have surrounded his decision to give in and become a 'friendly witness' when he was hauled up before Mcarthy's House for UnAmerican Activities, but I believe only the most po-faced and puritanical did not forgive him in the end or fail to recognize that he and his films had their heart in the right place and that he was, in every sense, one of the best…

27. "ON THE WATERFRONT"

(1954. Director: Elia Kazan)

I was barely 11 years old when I was taken to see this film – and I am far from sure that it had the Censor's certificate "U", allowing someone of my age to see it. The impression it made on me was enormous – not simply because it introduced me to Marlon Brando, as the ex-fighter turned longshoreman up against the union bosses, the mob and the racketeers, but because I don't think I had ever seen before such gritty realism and such a tough a portrayal of working life: the film is unflinchingly brutal. It was a real eye-opener. I don't remember now too much of the details – but apart from Brando, I remember Rod Steiger as his corrupted brother; Lee J. Cobb, mobster and de facto 'boss' of the longshoremen; Karl Malden (he of the amazing proboscis) as the fiery priest who encourages Brando to stand up against the corrupt union bosses and to testify against the crimes and murders they commit. Eve Marie Saint makes her debut, as a pure and lovely girl who sees the good in Brando, even though he has been responsible for her own brother's death, and provides a delicate foil for his inarticulate, stumbling efforts to come to terms with his conscience. The tenement buildings, wharehouses, the slightly putrid atmosphere of the waterfront itself – all these are superbly evoked: this is a hard and unforgiving world for anyone to live in. At the end, when Brando having finally testified, has been shunned and ostracized by his fellow-workers for breaking the rule of silence, been beaten pretty well to a pulp by Lee J Cobbs' henchman, he still staggers up the pier to resume his place in the work-force – and his fellow-workers, at last learning from his example, quietly close ranks behind him. The power of the mob has been broken ... they all go back to work and the door of the wharehouse closes behind them. And now it is the power of the people taking over. Apart from seeing the use of Hand-held Camera in this final sequence for the first time I can remember; and apart from being bowled over by Brando's portrayal of this slow-witted, semi-illiterate man who nevertheless wants to do what is right, I remember being very moved by what truly felt like an heroic moment in which the world had, against all the odds, become a slightly better place.

It's a political film as well as a socially realist one – and its worth reflecting that, although it comes 2 years after Kazan had been up against Mcarthy and his committee and turned in the 'friendly evidence' for which he was so roundly criticized (and indeed ostracized by many also), the politics of Kazan's film could hardly have appealed to the horrid Mr Mcarthy or anyone else on the paranoid right: because clearly it challenges self-serving cronyness and the ruthless manipulation of power in whatever ideological colours they present themselves. I hadn't realized that Leonard Bernstein wrote the score(the only one he did which wasn't a musical) or that Budd Schulberg(also collared by Mcarthy's witch-hunters) wrote the script. And I certainly had no idea that the cinematographer was one Boris Kaufman – but I certainly did know it was amazing photography, whoever did it. Made as a low-budget film, it was nominated for 12 Oscars, won eight (including one as Best Supporting Actress for newcomer Eve Marie-Saint, whom I next remember as a very different character in Hitchcock's "North by Northwest") and was both a critical and box-office success. And how well it stands the test of time! Kazan then went on to make "East of Eden" which brought us another legend – close on the heels of bringing us Brando, then, hey presto, up he pops with James Dean! No wonder actors loved to work with him – Kazan was a genius *non pareil* with them.

28. "RAGING BULL"

(1980. Director: Martin Scorsese)

This follows on neatly, if only because Brando's famous speech to his brother, Rod Steiger in "On the Waterfront", ("I coulda been a contender") becomes a kind of mantra for the emotionally self-destructive middleweight boxing champion, Jake LaMotta (Robert de Niro) on whose turbulent, violent life in and out of the boxing ring Scorsese's film is based. Although I could just as well have picked another of his films, "Raging Bull" seems representative of all that marks out this exceptional director as a master of his craft. Superbly shot in black and white by Michael Chapman (who also shot "Taxi Driver") who had to cope with the demands of some of Scorsese's most breath-takingly complex and brilliant camera set-ups, LaMotta's ups and downs in the ring are paralleled by his decline as a man and human being. Fights are fixed, won and lost; his marriage to a teenage girl goes from bad to worse; he alienates (or beats up) everyone around him; is finally sent to prison and emerges, at the end, as an overweight has-been doing a stand-up routine about his life ("I coulda been a contender") in a tacky night-club in Florida. Apart from having some of the most brutally realistic depictions of boxing in cinema, (bloody water dripping from the sponges between rounds, clotting on the ropes, sweat showering from the faces with the impact of the punches), it is also a searing portrait of a man tearing himself apart and wounding everyone else around him in the process, physically as well as emotionally. The unknown 17-year old Catherine Moriarty plays his much younger and put-upon wife, endlessly the target of his all-consuming jealousy; and the wonderful equally unknown Joe Pesci his brother, confidant and quasi-manager whose efforts to temper his brother and somehow keep his life on the rails are rewarded by suspicion, antagonism and finally brute violence. The shady underworld controlling boxing and fixing the fights, the shabby world of the Bronx in which LaMotta lives all contribute to a picture of a world losing its moral compass. As LaMotta slowly destroys his marriage and himself as brutally as he demolishes his opponents in the ring, his life spirals downwards into a sickening abyss before our eyes – yet Scorsese manages to make sure we never completely lose some grain of sympathy for him. Eventually, having lost wife, championship title, trust and respect, he ends up alone in prison punching the walls with his bare fists in a desperate act of self-immolation it is painful to watch: enveloped by a very dark night of the soul indeed.

Having survived a close shave with death from a drug overdose, and possibly being something of a tortured Catholic himself, Scorsese allows for redemption of sorts at the end…much to my, (and everyone else's I imagine) relief. Co-scripted by Paul Schrader(also of "Taxi Driver") and with a towering central performance by De Niro (who had to go on a food binge around France and Italy in order to gain a prodigious amount of weight to portray the flabby LaMotta of his late years, during which shooting was suspended for 3 months), the film is also fantastically well edited by the legendary chain-smoking Thelma Schoonmaker (see the delicious parody of her in the Coen Bros' "Hail Caesar") – and both she and De Niro quite rightly won Oscars for their work. A terrific film by a terrific film-maker… and how interesting that, for a long time, Scorsese was reluctant to make it (no interest in sport, loathed boxing); yet, after his scare with drugs, he began to think the project might be his 'swan song' – fortunately not, and he has gone on since, as we all know, to make some of his most brilliant films…Perhaps, like Jake LaMotta, he was going through his own dark night of the soul at the time, Jacob wrestling with his Angel…or a boxer taking all that terrible punishment in the ring…

29. "KUNDUN"

(1997. Director: Martin Scorsese)

The disturbed sociopaths, gangsters, morally adrift individuals we usually associate with Scorsese's restless, frenetically charged films tend to mask the very real spiritual/religious side to the man. "Kundun" is about the life of the Dalai Lama from his childhood and discovery as the 'Kundun' to his flight from Tibet into India in the 1950's. It is a beautiful and thoughtful film, compassionate and tender – and clearly respectful of Buddhist beliefs. Although the menace of the Chinese invasion and the violence it implies is clearly present, there's hardly a drop of blood in sight and, for the most part, the violence remains invisible off-screen, or as brief almost prophetic visions. This restraint allows Scorsese to explore a more poetic side to his own sensibilities – the spiritual in him, perhaps, the mystical even, grappling with the timeless questions of faith and belief and indeed the nature of vision itself. Starting with the search for and then discovery of the new 'Kundun', incarnated in a happy little child from a simple peasant family, swept gently away from them to learn about and grow into his pre-ordained destiny as a spiritual leader, the film never falls into the trap of false reverence – on the contrary, the humanity of this child growing up into a man and the Dalai Lama we all know today is very much at the core. The visions of a traditional Tibetan shaman (an extraordinary sequence of him in frenetic trance), the flashes of projections which can foretell and physically see the future are not presented as magical, super-human powers so much as gifts liberating the mind achieved through centuries of tried and tested knowledge. There is a simplicity and a humility – but both in service of a deeply held belief. Wisdom perhaps… Beautifully photographed by British cinematographer, Roger Deakins (and you can hardly look at an important American movie nowadays without seeing his name up there), this quiet and basically gentle film would confirm Scorsese as a major talent even if this were the only film he ever made.

* * *

…Since we have got as far as an American director in Tibet/India, and find ourselves more or less in that neck of the woods, let's travel on further North-East and look at a Japanese director, one of the true Titans of Cinema, making a truly beautiful film, not in the land of his birth, but in Siberia…

30. "DERSU UZALA"

(1975. Director: Akira Kurosawa)

This is an epic story on an intimate scale – the story of the friendship between a Russian Captain on a geological mission in the wilds of Siberia and an ageing local hunter, one of the last of a local indigenous tribe, shapes the intimacy of the story ….but it is Nature – the forests, the vast wilderness, the elements in all their varied manifestations – together, in particular, with man's relationship to it, which provides the epic size to the film and which is the real star. And what a huge and hugely moving work it is. Dersu has lived alone all his life and survived by his skills as a hunter and his deep knowledge of the environment in which he lives in a perfectly balanced harmony and respect. But now, in his advancing years, he has accidentally shot and killed a tiger – and fears the retribution of his spirit gods …for he has transgressed the proper natural order of things and will surely have to pay the price (a salutary warning for our own times). With his eyesight failing, upon which he depends for his own survival as a hunter, Dersu is grateful for the 'technology' the Russian Captain can offer him and, in return, uses his own knowledge and skills to save the Captain from the perils he faces in the wild. But, touching and affectionately heart-warming as their friendship is, Dersu knows he is essentially alone to face the judgement of his own gods. The end is painfully beautiful – and I left the cinema to feel the world outside almost as alien and weird as it would have felt for Dersu, had he been at my side.

* * *

It is not irrelevant to point out that this was the first film Kurosawa had made in 12 years. Rejected in his own country, he had been driven to such despair that he had attempted suicide. It was the intervention, I believe, of 'Star Wars' George Lucas and friends, which gave Kurosawa this new lease of cinematic life, leading to his late and glorious flowering after "Dersu..." with the magnificent "Kagemusha", "Ran" and finally the much undervalued "Dreams" which, in the last section, has the seraphic serenity of a Zen garden. Today, restored to the pedestal from which he should never have been removed, there is even a studio in Tokyo named after him. More than admire Akira Kurosawa-san, I almost revere him and, in accordance with Nipponese custom, when I stood at the gates of the Kurosawa Studios myself, I bowed deep and long from my waist in honour of his memory.

31. "SEVEN SAMURAI"

(1954. Director: Akira Kurosawa)

On more than one occasion during production, the Toho Studios threatened to close this picture down. We are lucky Kurosawa persuaded them to think again – for this is rightly recognized as one of the cinematic masterpieces of all time. Set in a 16th century Japan, torn apart by warring factions, an impoverished peasant village pools together its meagre resources to employ the services of 7 equally poor samurai to defend and rid them of the bandits who have been ruthlessly stealing their crops, raping and killing, and leaving them at the point of starvation. All they can offer as payment is a pathetic 3 meals of rice a day. Led by an ageing but masterly samurai, Kambei (Takashi Shimura), each of the selected warriors has distinct qualities and skills, but all of them are bound together by the same lofty Samurai codes of honour, service and discipline. That is, with the exception of a maverick outsider, Kikuchiyo(Toshiro Mifune), on the surface something of a buffoon and cynic who insists on attaching himself to their band: he has a personal score to settle. He is also the down-to-earth realist amongst them who knows that these farmers they have come to save are no saints either, but, the result of ages of oppression and injustice, fearful human beings every bit as scheming, cunning, deceitful and suspicious as anyone else.

Interestingly, the bandits themselves are hardly given any characterization – they are simply a force, energy, a blind destructive power. Although heavily outnumbered, the Samurai use their prowess, intelligence and ingenuity to win back the freedom of the village. The set pieces are thrillingly choreographed and executed, but this is much more than a mere 'action movie' – it contains many insights into the human condition and behaviour; into the nature of honour and duty; into the fragility, prejudices and corruptibility of social fabric. The village regains its freedom, but 4 of the samurai are sacrificed to win it – and the *ingénue* romantic amongst them elects to choose life and love with a village girl, rather than the high codes of the samurai tradition he previously so worshipped. At the end, as the villagers happily start to plant their rice fields, Kambei ruefully remarks to his one surviving companion, "We have lost again…"

At almost 3.5 hours, it was meticulously planned (each samurai, for instance, was given a dossier by Kurosawa detailing his life style, right down to what he would eat for breakfast!) and achieves an extraordinary sense of realism, transporting us back with, not only our eyes, but almost all our other senses into a palpable, sensory world from a very different culture and making it feel as if it belongs to the here and now. Kurosawa was a gifted painter with an acute eyes for design and composition, as evident here as it is in his last films over 20 years later. To what extent this also shaped Asaichi Nakai's cinematography of the film I can only guess at – but I would imagine it did and in no small measure. Above all, however, Kurosawa knew how to design the shape as he was shooting, where to cut – not surprising, therefore, that he takes the Editor's credit as well. Many years later, Hollywood snapped up the basic storyline and came up with John Sturges' "The Magnificent Seven" – pretty good stuff, too, but there's a difference, is there not, between 'pretty good stuff' and the sublime and brilliant…

* * *

26 years lapsed before this next film, one of the finest in the glorious later flowering of Kurosawa….and I must include it.

32. "KAGEMUSHA"

(1980. Director: Akira Kurosawa)

Instructing a young Prince in the attributes of leadership he must one day assume, his ageing Tutor tells him "The Mountain does not Move"... In the final, bloody battle scene of Kurosawa's late film, that same prince, now warlord of his clan, sits unmoving on a stool while he watches his army being slaughtered...the mountain does not move. Behind the mask of his helmet, he watches with eyes aghast with horror – but he does not move, anymore than we, the audience in our seats can move either. For the depiction of the sheer futility and senseless carnage of warfare, Kurosawa's picture is hard to better and I include it here, my 3rd Kurosawa film on the list, as not only such a wonderful example of his late mature work but also as one of his most poignant in showing us "the sorry and the pity of it all". It is immensely moving.

A *'kagemusha"* is a kind of double, a look-alike impostor used as a decoy to fool one's adversaries. Set again in 16th century Japan, ravaged by feuding clans endlessly at war with one another, it is the story of one such "kagemusha', a common criminal with an identical appearance to a warlord, who is spared his life so that he can deceive a rival clan into believing the warlord is still alive after his death. He goes further than that, however, slowly assuming both the mantle and also the personality of his dead lord: he transforms in himself to become almost a reincarnation of his Shingen. Thus, quite apart from fooling the rival clan, he also fools everyone else around him – from the wives and concubines of his late lord to his closest advisers and friends. It is only when it is discovered that he does not bear the same battle scars as the dead warlord that the deceit is unmasked and the 'kagemusha' sent packing. By this time, the young Prince, now head of the clan, is taking the decision, against better advice, to go into battle. The folly of this becomes apparent all too quickly when he sits atop a hill to watch wave after wave of his troops being mown down by musket fire in one of the most vivid and ghastly battle scenes ever filmed: this is not simply violence – it is sheer horror. The *'kagemusha'*, loyal to the dead lord whose being he has so closely adopted for himself, re-appears to throw himself single-handedly at the enemy only to meet his own inevitable and senseless death…It is terrible and very sobering to watch.

There is an extraordinary stillness at the heart of Kurosawa's late works – it can sometimes feel like sitting in the serene and balanced tranquillity of a Zen garden. Yes, there is a wisdom present, evident in both his assured mastery of the craft and the depth of the compassion he shows for humanity. Yet apparently, like many great artists, he could be an exacting and extremely demanding taskmaster. On more than one occasion, however, in moments of crisis or panic, I have found myself repeating the words of that wise old Tutor to his charge …"The Mountain does not Move"… "Kagemusha" won the Palme D'Or at Cannes …and was it on that occasion, following Japanese tradition when accepting the prize, that Kurosawa apologized and promised he would try and do better next time..?

33. "TOKYO STORY"

(1953. Director: Yasujiro Ozu)

Ozu is the other great master of Japanese cinema, and, back in 1953, a year earlier than The "Seven Samurai" had created his own masterpiece as well. And what a very different animal it is! An ageing couple have travelled by train to see their family in Tokyo. Busy with getting on with their own lives, their children have little time to pay attention to their parents whom they receive with an indifference bordering on the callous – and it is only their widowed daughter-in-law who shows them the kindness they seek and deserve. As a study of family relationships, and of the shifting of old social traditions in post-war Japan, it is remarkably insightful and emotionally extraordinarily deep. Delicately understated, Ozu never hurries and always allows time for a scene to develop to its full. The camera never moves and he always shoots from round about waist level and always using a lens of the same focal length (I think, but am not 100% sure, 25mm or 50mm). Lean and spare, the film is as stripped of the extraneous as a Japanese tatami and paper-screen bedroom, but charged with electric attention to detail and nuance. Never wearing its heart on the sleeve,(as we tend to do too readily in the West), Ozu's film is brimming over with humanity and compassion. Beautiful! Absolutely beautiful! I will say no more about this undoubted masterpiece.

34. "FIRES ON THE PLAIN"

(1959. Director: Kon Ichikawa)

I don't want to leave Japan without including a film by this director. Although perhaps he cannot rank with either Kurosawa or Ozu (and who can?), he is nevertheless a remarkable talent. When I saw this film I was pretty shocked and even sickened by its brutal depiction of how low and vile man's behaviour can become in wartime and it has stuck in my memory ever since as one of the most vivid and telling 'anti-war' films in the canon.

In 1945, The Imperial Japanese Army in The Philippines is quite literally falling apart on all fronts. Without supplies, morale or food, they are starving in every sense, and harried by both the advancing Americans and the Filipinos themselves. One of a bedraggled platoon, sick with tuberculosis, tries to seek help in a hospital but is rejected as not being sick enough. The alternative, to commit suicide with a grenade, is an option he declines. His ensuing journey to find safety is a series of increasingly shocking encounters of a descent into brutality, arbitrary violence, barbarism, betrayal and even cannibalism amongst his fellow soldiers concerned only with their personal survival. It is very bleak, very grim and unremittingly so. The "fires" of the title are never quite explained and only dimly seen, but I think they represent for Ichikawa a distant glimmer of hope that normality will return and man will lift himself out of the barbaric depths into which the war has sunk him. As a portrayal of how easily the social fabric we construct for ourselves can unravel and disintegrate, there are few films to equal it. Strong stuff.

* * *

War, of course, in all its colours and terrible paradoxes has been explored forever and a day in all the Arts, inevitably including Cinema. Its horrors, futilities and sheer waste of human life has been as much a subject for film-makers as have its very debatable heroics. But, since we are on the subject, I want to cite 2 other 'anti-war' films, both notable for their great cinematic skills as well as for their message...

35. "PATHS OF GLORY"

(1957. Director: Stanley Kubrick)

Made 2 years prior to Ichikawa's film, "Paths of Glory" propelled Kubrick at the age of 29 into the limelight as a major film-maker where he remained ever since until his death in 1999 at the comparatively early age of 71. Beautifully photographed and acted, it has a formalism almost as elegant as the 18th century chateau in which much of the action takes place and has all the hallmarks of Kubrick's developing style. Set in WW1, a fluid camera leads a Captain (Kirk Douglas) through the French trenches as he prepares to take his command "over the top". The attack he leads is a complete disaster, no thanks to the incompetence of the commanding generals, (Adolphe Menjou at his most suave and George Macready at his most rasping). Because of this failure, it is decided 3 men should be picked out as an example and tried for cowardice and desertion from their duty. The Sergeant ordered to select the 3 uses the opportunity to settle a grudge against a fellow soldier (Ralph Meeker) and picks out the 2 others simply because they are social misfits. The Captain, a lawyer by training, becomes their defence but the trial is a mockery and the sentence a foregone conclusion: the men are condemned to be shot. Appalled by this injustice, and aware that the responsibility for the failure of the attack lies directly at the feet of George Macready, Kirk Douglas pleads their case to Adolphe Menjou and blows the whistle. The General listens, all civility and charm, but suggests that the Captain would be wiser not to upset the apple cart and destroy his own promising career by muddying the waters. However, although the execution goes ahead – a harrowing sequence shot with cut-glass precision, ritualized death which we watch with helpless anguish – Menjou does summon his fellow General and George Macready is dismissed from his command with the same cold-blooded, pragmatic charm Menjou has shown throughout. At just under 90 minutes, "Paths of Glory" is a masterly essay on the crass futility, bungling indifference and sheer inhuman stupidity of war. It is very, very good. Look out for the German girl serving in the bar where Douglas' soldiers gather to unwind after the execution. In a very moving scene, she breaks into a faltering song which slowly and thoughtfully they all join in. She is played by Susanne Christian ….a.k.a Mrs Kubrick…

36. "WESTERN FRONT 1918"

(1930: Director: G.W.Pabst)

Long before Kubrick, and made in the same year as Lewis Milestone filmed his "All Quiet on the Western Front" over in America and bearing many similarities in theme, Pabst's German film is an altogether bleaker and darker study of war, as well as being so pacifist in tone that Goebbels was later to have it banned. The story of a group of Germans fighting together in the trenches is told with a cool objectivity Pabst favoured, but is no less moving for all that. It is so long since I saw it and I remember little of the details, except to know I was watching a very special and heartfelt film, crafted with great skill and sensibility. It was so different from the 'gung-ho' depictions of war I was so used to seeing on film that it jolted me into realizing what a horrid and bloody business it is. German Cinema of that era is best known for its Expressionist films – G.W.Pabst was much more of a social realist and has, by and large, been rather ignored of late except for his powerfully unsettling "Pandora's Box" with the extraordinary and magical beauty, Louise Brooks. This is a pity – he was an exceptional and innovative director who deserves a long-overdue revival.

* * *

Since we've stumbled into Germany, let's stay there awhile, continuing with Pabst before turning to the more remembered Expressionists.

37. "KAMERADSCHAFT" ("Comradeship")

(1931. Director: G.W.Pabst)

When I saw this film as a teenager, I was struck by how realistic was its setting in a coalmine caught up in a terrible disaster and assumed it had been all shot on location. How wrong I was – it was made entirely in a studio and the meticulously convincing set was the work of the Art Directors : an early and important lesson for me on the nature of film language. This was – is still perhaps – an important and political film in which Pabst continues his pacifist plea and call for international friendship through the story of an actual huge mining disaster in which Germans and French rescuers worked alongside each other to rescue those who had survived. Some might think that, by today's standards, the film's call for mutual understanding and rejection of warfare is somewhat sentimental. I would disagree – although an impressionable teenager at the time I saw it, it moved me and moved me for all the right reasons, I think. It inspired me too with its muscular camerawork and harsh contrasted lighting: it had a disturbingly present sense of realism I found hard to put out of my mind. It was Pabst's second "talkie" and important also for a technical innovation which he had experimented with a year earlier in "Western Front 1918". In those early days of sound movies, Hollywood had opted to build clumping great sound booths to house the camera and hide the sound of its motor. Pabst, however, wanted to liberate his camera so it was free to track and travel and so invented a casing for the camera itself – today we call it a 'blimp' and don't give it a second thought…But it began with Pabst who refined it on this film which was once considered a classic – and should be so again.

* * *

But to the Expressionists of German Cinema, whose stylistic influence has crept down to us still today, like the tentacles and sinister finger-nails of some of their monster creations peering out of the mists to tap us on our shoulders...Horror!

38. "THE CABINET OF DR CALIGARI"

(1920. Director: Robert Wiene)

Along with Murnau's Dracula film "Nosferatu", this is one of the great German Expressionist horror films. Scary, unsettling, weird – all of those, but extraordinarily prescient too. Dr Caligari is a hypnotist who controls a somnambulist and gets him to commit murders at his command. It really is the stuff of nightmares – but Wiene seems to be using his story as a metaphor for what he saw were the dangers of blind obedience to authority in whatever shape it presented itself. Did he see what was coming in just over a decade later? Or was he referring to something he saw as an inherent danger in the German psyche itself? Hard to know – but the film remains sinister, powerful – with its extraordinary Expressionist sets, on which the shadows were painted and the twisted perspectives constructed to create a surreal and abstract sense of time and place. The invention and creative artistry are unique – and, despite being genuinely really creepy, it blew my mind away – but I often wonder what audiences made of it at the time…and what it is in our psyche which draws us all towards it?

39. "METROPOLIS"

(1927. Director; Fritz Lang)

This is, of course, one of the great futuristic films of all time. Like Wiene's film, it also concerns itself with control, manipulation, oppression of the human soul in service of a uniform state. It is puzzling as well as intriguing that, years before there was very much more than a sniff of Hitler's National Socialism in the air, so many German artists, as well as Wiene and Lang, somehow had caught the scent even before it became manifest. Lang constructs a vision of a world in which the workers, like automatons, carry on their lives solely for the benefit of their élite bosses, reduced and shaped to be no more than obedient cogs in a state machine, dehumanized and stripped of their individual free will. The son of one of these privileged few bosses finds himself falling in love with a girl from the oppressed majority. Moreover, she is endowed with the gift of seeing a dream of freedom....What is remarkable about the film, however, is its visualization of this dystopian world – the sets and photography, sci-fi visions of Lang's de-humanised world, are a triumph of expressionist design and thinking, and, despite the technical limitations of the time, incredibly modern. The film was highly successful and established Lang as a kind of Uber-director. The complete original version was destroyed, I believe, by the Nazis – but some years ago a badly damaged copy was discovered in a museum in Argentina, painstakingly restored and now saved for posterity. Even today it exercises a considerable power over the modern viewer – perhaps uncomfortably reminding us, as Orwell would do later with '1984', how insidiously easy it can be for any of us to be sleep-walked out of ourselves and into blindly obedient automatons.

40. "M"

(1931. Director: Fritz Lang)

Heavens, what a disturbing and frighteningly dark film this is! But how compelling too. The story of a child murderer being sought by the police and the criminal underworld alike at the same time, it is a classic of its genre and a savage, visceral portrait of what Lang saw as a diseased society. A baby-faced Peter Lorre plays the murderer(and how clever to cast this seemingly innocuous, timid little man as the psychopath),his presence always heralded by him whistling the same tune from some popular operetta. It is chilling stuff, but compulsive viewing – foggy streets, smoky bars and brothels, ugly and misshapen faces, brute and filthy bodies pile up on the screen like scenes out of Bosch – or perhaps Lang's contemporaries, the artists Otto Dix and George Grosz – to paint a vision of a world in terminal decay and rot. The grotesque made manifest in highly atmospheric black and white imagery – all shadows and contrasts and expressionist distortion. When Lorre is finally cornered and captured he makes a speech to explain he cannot help himself from doing what he does…"Think what it is to be me?", he pleads pathetically. This hint of sympathy suggests that Lang is able to see him almost as much a victim of a rotten, grotesque society as the children he has murdered. But the children are the future – and Lang saw the beginnings of the ugly rise of Nazism taking place around him and didn't like the future he saw coming either. He was to make only one more film in Germany, "The Testament of Dr Mabuse", before he, too, skipped town and jumped on a train to save his skin, fetching up in Hollywood where he continued to make his provocatively dark films … and earn himself the reputation of being a bit of sadist on set as well. A unique filmmaker, touched by greatness nevertheless, if not necessarily the nicest of human beings…

41. "TRIUMPH OF THE WILL"

(1935. Director: Leni Riefenstahl)

...And this is precisely the kind of spectacle from which Lang, and many others, had fled: Nazism and the swastika showing itself off to the world. Whatever one may think about it's message, Leni Riefenstahl's film about the 1935 Nuremberg rallies was – and remains so today – one of the most powerful propaganda films ever made. It was admired at the time, not only in Germany, but all over the world – and its influence on many subsequent films, commercials, promos cannot be denied (see even the latest "Star Wars – The Force Returns" movie).

Still banned in Germany today, it is a spectacularly brilliant piece of filmic choreography, a hymn to the glory of the new emergent German dream of its own Aryan superiority – and it is all the more scary to think of such talent being employed to promote such a dangerous ideology, (I was slightly reminded of it when watching Zhang Yimou's production of the opening ceremony of the Chinese Olympics – the massed precision of all those drummers, perfectly drilled and synchronized, however brilliant to look at was also a little sinister). Not to admit the virtuosity of it's technical achievements, however, would be foolish and myopic – few films demonstrate so well just how powerful a tool the language of film can be. So, although I loathe what it stands for, I cannot but admire the manner in which she shows it or ignore the troubling questions about the responsibilities of film-making that come along with it. Leni Riefenstahl has been roundly criticized by some ever since – and equally roundly has defended herself: and, in the process, her name has almost become a synonym for the word propaganda itself.

* * *

I want to leave Germany behind now – besides, after the war German film-making, not surprisingly, went into a dormant decline as the country struggled to put itself back together again and re-establish its identity.... Hardly surprising, given both the terrible destruction of the war and the significant amount of major talent which had already fled the persecution of their faith well before and taken up the tools of their respective trades in the altogether sunnier climate of California...And in 1960 one of the very best of these exiles made one of his very best: and it remains to this day an absolute gem.

42. "THE APARTMENT"

(1960. Director: Billy Wilder)

Movie-wise, to use the corporate-speak so amusingly employed throughout, this is one of my favourite films of all time, written by the delightfully named I.A.L. Diamond and directed by the man who gave us "Sunset Boulevard" 10 years previously and the delicious "Some Like it Hot" just before this one. Career-wise, C.C. Baxter(Jack Lemmon) is just another cipher, an anonymous cog in the wheel of a giant corporation, spending a life of drudgery churning out meaningless figures, accountancy-wise. Hoping to get promotion and eventually be given "the key to the executive washroom", the bachelor Baxter has been lending out his own key to his own apartment to his superiors in middle-management, so they can carry on – extra-marital affairs-wise. The fact this means at times he has to spend the night on a park bench catching a stinker of a cold before he can get back into his own home doesn't seem to matter to any of them – just so long as "buddy boy" keeps handing across the key, they might put in a good word for him one of these days – promotion-wise. In the same skyscraper, Miss Kubelik (Shirley Maclaine) works as an elevator girl for whom the unfailingly respectful Baxter has more than a soft spot, romantic-wise. What he doesn't know is that she is in the midst of having an affair with the heavily married Chairman of the company (Fred Macmurray). The inevitable happens – the Chairman hears about Baxter's key and soon is using his apartment for the same purposes as everyone else-wise. But this time it goes wrong – on Christmas Eve, left alone and abandoned in the apartment after their tryst by the Chairman while he goes home to his wife and children, Miss Kubelik realizes that, love-wise, he is a complete shit and she is no more than a 'bit on the side' for him. In a moment of desperate unhappiness she takes an overdose of sleeping pills there and then, and Baxter returns home to find her pretty well comatose. He is left with the task of rescuing and caring for her over the Christmas break... For this, he indeed is rewarded with promotion and "the key to the executive washroom" but he, too, realizes that he is just being used, convenience-wise – and that there has to be more to life than just being an insignificant "yes-man" to the corporation and all it stands for. He stops handing over his own key, returns the one "to the executive washroom" and promptly gets fired for his ingratitude. Too bad – "that's the way it crumbles ...cookie-wise"... How it all works out in the end on New Year's Eve is gloriously poignant and heart-warming, with a terrific musical score by London-born, Adolph Deutsch, working in lovely harmony with Joseph La Shelle's finely judged black and white cinematography, accompanying the *denouément* we've all been hoping for . Beautifully restrained to the very end, up to the last 2 lines of dialogue over a game of unfinished gin rummy, (Baxter: "Miss Kubelick – I love you" – Kubelik:"Shut up and deal"), there's not a kiss in sight in what really can call itself a true love story! Witty, beautifully performed, faultlessly constructed, Wilder and I.A.L.Diamond take a healthy dig at big corporation values, probe wryly into the reality of hypocritical American male attitudes and behaviour towards women and show us what is entailed to be a real "mensch". Very funny, very touching and indeed perceptive, a delight in every way, it thoroughly deserved the 5 Oscars it won. Wilder at his very best – and, something-wise, that's saying something!

* * *

Like Zinnemann, Billy Wilder also lost close members of his family, including his mother, during the Holocaust. I wonder whether the pain and suffering this inevitably involved shaped the sensitive compassion which quietly shines through in his films...after all, comedy sits side by side with tragedy on the same face and Wilder's brand of comedy was always branded by a humanity which has sorrow lurking in its heart and then joyfully averted ...(He was, incidentally, like the great actor Edward G.Robinson, also a lover and compulsive art collector – with a magnificent collection – and I dearly wish I could have met him). The kind of comedy of the following film on the list is of a very different order, however – and steps straight out of vaudeville onto the screen, and unforgettably, even brilliantly so...

43. "A NIGHT AT THE OPERA"

(1935. Director: Sam Wood)

Zany, anarchic, irreverent, totally loopy – I don't think I could get through life without a dose of The Marx Brothers to keep me going from time to time. They are so absurdly wonderful and downright silly that I could forgive them for anything. The plot of this my favourite film of theirs'? God knows – there is one of sorts, of course, but who gives a damn!? Because from the start Groucho is too busy fleecing the much put-upon and long-suffering (and wonderful) Margaret Dumont (Groucho to Dumont: "I was only with her because she reminds me of you – on second thoughts, you remind me of you"). He and Chico are artiste's managers of dubious probity, armed with endless contracts ("The party of the first part...") for opera singers ("He's the finest singer since Caruso") and the usual mix-ups and thwarted love affairs are thrown into the mix. Plus the endless interferences of Harpo Marx, dropping sandbags and mallets on the heads of all and sundry when not using his scissors to cut off their beards. The action hurtles all over the place including onto an ocean liner where, crammed into a cabin the size of a matchbox with a huge trunk already containing Chico, Harpo and the 'Romantic lead'("the finest singer since Caruso"), Groucho orders a dinner of everything on the menu – plus two hard-boiled eggs(honk-honk from Harpo inside the trunk -"make that 3 hard-boiled eggs") and are joined by an endless succession of the crew staff, including a manicurist, and finally a line of stewards delivering the supper itself (honk-honk -"make that 3 hard-boiled eggs") as if it were a competition to see how many people you can fit into a telephone box. When Margaret Dumont knocks on the door, they burst out like water from a dam that has been breeched, landing like fish dynamited out of the river at her feet. Outrageous! The whole thing is mad – and the final sequence of a performance of "Il Trovatore", with Harpo and Chico creating mayhem in the gantries pursued by the police, ending with the audience booing and pelting the self-important tenor ("He's the finest singer since Caruso") with rotten tomatoes is just glorious. Appropriately, the film ends with Groucho and Chico drawing up yet another contract ("The party of the fifth part..")…Bonkers! And essential viewing for those with constipated minds…or just commonplace constipation – miles better than prunes! (and "make that 3 hard-boiled eggs!")

* * *

The Marx Brothers sit up there with the immortals, of course, having doubtless made a suitably outrageous deal with St Peter ("the party of the heavenly party…")and continue to appeal across the generations and to all age-groups. As does the following director, another genius for all times and a very much more subtle film-maker than perhaps meets the eye at first glance…

44. "LES VACANCES DE MONSIEUR HULOT"
("Monsieur Hulot's Holiday")

(1953. Director: Jacques Tati)

The sticky inner tube of a tyre rolls down the hill, collecting leaves on the way to become a wreath where it joins the mourners at a funeral. The hapless Hulot has to join them as he tries to retrieve it, but as it is solemnly hung with the others, it punctures and deflates with an embarrassing hiss....Hulot, on the tips of his toes, can only politely raise his hat in apology... Who, but the most churlish and mealy-mouthed, can fail to rejoice in the good-natured, clumsy, pipe-smoking figure of Monsieur Hulot? I first saw this French classic – French national treasure even – during my own holidays when I was a kid boarding at prep-school. I loved it then and have loved it ever since. Hulot's holiday in a modest seaside boarding house hotel is a series of well-intentioned mishaps from start to finish. Tati never derides but he does take an affectionate dig along the way at some of the pomposities and pretensions of his own people, in particular the new 'holiday classes' and the niceties of their conformities. Charmingly funny from start to finish, it is also the work of a director with an acute and affectionate eye for the details and foibles of human behaviour. But, of course, the special thing about Tati is that he uses sound and sound effects to point up and punctuate the comic moments – the wind whistling in from the sea every time someone steps from outside into the dining room; the clatter of cutlery and slurping of soup; the exaggerated 'tock' of a tennis ball when Hulot serves one of his eccentric underhand deliveries. There is no discernible dialogue and the film is exclusively carried along by its visual narrative. And don't be fooled – Tati constructs his *mise-en-scène* with great economy, but it is complex and disciplined in its apparent simplicity. A good subject for study, therefore, for aspiring would-be film-makers, and also an exemplar of comedy at its finest.

45. "PLAYTIME"

(1967. Director: Jacques Tati)

In my mind, there is a probability that this is a masterpiece. I first saw it in the summer of 1970 at the Svenska Film Institutet in Stockholm in it's original 70mm form and have since re-visited it on several occasions. As Truffaut astutely remarked "Tati comes from another planet – where they make films differently" and this 'difference' may account for the hugely expensive film's disastrous failure at the box-office. It drove Tati into bankruptcy where he was treated extremely harshly and unfairly by the banks: they really knew how to break a man, and break him they did – it was disgusting and they should be ashamed.

Appearing intermittently in his Hulot persona, Tati builds a complex panorama, set in a huge modern office block he had constructed for the film (which came to be known as Tativille), of what he perceived as the sterile conformity of the times and the cold heartlessness of modern 'efficiency'. People have become robotic sleep-walkers, walking only in straight lines, turning only at right angles. Where has all the old humanity gone? Where the curves? Bumbling Hulot brings a little of them back, as does a young girl, part of a group of American tourists, who is continually stepping out of line…The restaurant preparing its opening night next door to this huge office of glass and steel is also beset by a string of minor disasters which bring back a few 'curves' into life as well. There is so much going on at the same time in the different offices that it is like watching all the details of an elaborate ballet – different vignettes taking place simultaneously on the same screen. Again, it is the use of sound effects alone that are used to punctuate the gags and dialogue is consigned to a background blur. It is certainly a film which needs more than one viewing but which is densely rich in human detail and tinged by a hint of melancholy and regret at the fading of a world as much guided by the dictates of the heart as by the exigencies of the balance-sheet and the god of technology which seemed to be replacing them with an altogether more sterile world. Prescient – or the lament of every generation? Perhaps a bit of both...

* * *

Zany, wise-cracking, fast one-liners from The Marx Brothers; the more modest observational Gallic charms of Tati – it is extraordinary how comedy, despite its national variants, can manage at its best to cross all boundaries and touch some universal chord. Humour has always been one of the most effective ways of establishing communication between seemingly very different cultures and dip into a common pool to bring people together. Be it in Africa, India, Brazil, the Philippines – and even in Japan I have been surprised again and again by how it can break the ice and bond us in our common humanity.

Apart from Jenning's little jewel, there has been no mention of British Cinema so far and, upon reflection, I can see this may be a bias on my part but also must confess that British films have not played such a decisive role in shaping my personal sense of what film is all about. However, at their delightful best, the comedies that came out of Michael Balcon's Ealing Studios do seem representative of something we Brits do rather well: poking gentle fun at ourselves without ever quite completely taking our gloves off. We like the wry, we like the absurd, but we also like it to be modest and softly spoken. It's a little bit quaint and old-fashioned – but terribly good-mannered...perhaps less so now, but in the 50's and '60's a degree of decorum was expected – even when murdering your aunt or thieving the Bank of England. Think of Robert Hamer's "Kind Hearts and Coronets" ...or think of the following film which still has the power to delight...

46. "THE LAVENDER HILL MOB"

(1951. Director: Charles Crichton)

Racing by foot, round and round down the dizzying spiral staircase of the Eiffel Tower in mad pursuit of a class of English schoolgirls descending in the lift, Alec Guinness and Stanley Holloway finally regain *terra firma* with the world spinning around them and in a state of giggling, vertiginous hysteria, as if they had been inhaling balloons of laughing gas…while the schoolgirls they are chasing, for the booty they are unwittingly carrying, pull sedately away in their bus. At another moment, in hot pursuit of these two apparently dangerous criminals, Guinness and Holloway, a squadron of police cars converge and crash into one another, their radio aerials braiding together like rope and all crackling to the tune of 'Old Macdonald had a Farm – Eeeye, eeye – oh!'… Welcome to the world of Ealing comedy, in which the hi-jacking of a bank van and robbing it of the considerable amount of gold bullion it is carrying is treated with rather less gravity than such a crime might receive and merit in a court of law or under the sterner eyes of some 'M'lud' at the Old Bailey. Ealing was never shy of the whimsical…

Alec Guinness plays the meek, unassuming bank clerk who has conscientiously fulfilled his duties over the years supervising the transport of his bank's gold bullion from one vault to another. No-one would suspect that such a loyal and dull servant of the bank would have the imagination to be secretly dreaming and plotting over the years the ways and means of robbing all that gold and treating himself to a rather more exciting life. His problem, however, is not so much how to steal the gold (which he has planned down to the last detail), but how to get it undetected out of the country and disappear to enjoy it. But when a new lodger arrives at his dreary boarding house in Lavender Hill, in the shape of the rumbustious

Stanley Holloway, Guinness has a little 'eureka' moment: for the new lodger runs a foundry casting trinkets and souvenir models of this or that, some of which he exports – in particular a metal paperweight of the Eiffel Tower, gilded with a fake gold finish. Might this not be the way..?

The film starts in Rio de Janeiro, where a smart, cigar-smoking Guinness enjoys dinner with a fellow Englishman in a fashionably elegant restaurant (and watch out for that girl in the walk-on part – yes, it *is* Audrey Hepburn) where he recounts the story of his heist. Roping in not only Stanley Holloway as a willing partner and accomplice, but also two petty criminals, Sid James and Alfie Bass, the robbery is executed perfectly and the gold melted down to be turned into miniature Eiffel towers, crated up alongside others made of cheap base metal which are all shipped off together to Paris to be sold to tourists in the very tower itself. Things begin to go wrong, however, when the crate of real gold towers, which they have marked 'not for sale', inadvertently gets mixed up with the fakes and half a dozen of them bought by a class of visiting English schoolgirls. Hence the giddy chase down the Eiffel Tower to get them back – which continues across the English Channel and onto their school. Through shameless cunning and duplicity, the offer of a generous swap plus a small cash reward, Guinness manages to retrieve all but one of the real gold paperweights (talk about stealing the toys out of a baby's pram!) but one girl refuses to swap her's back – having promised it as a gift to a friend …who just happens to be a policeman as well. Guinness and Holloway have no option but to snatch it away and make their escape in a stolen police car. Hence also, therefore, the chase after them – during which Guinness uses the car radio to mislead and misdirect the other police cars so that they converge upon one another in an almighty pile up all tuned into 'Old Macdonald had a farm' with which Guninness has jammed their radios. In the end, however, everyone is rounded up except Guinness who makes his escape to Rio de Janeiro with six of the gold paperweights to indulge in a life to which previously he had in no way been accustomed. Nevertheless, justice must prevail – after all good manners dictate there should be English fair play. At the end of recounting his story, Guinness and his dining companion rise from their table to make their way politely out of the Rio restaurant.... and we see now that Guinness has been discreetly handcuffed: he's been nicked!...Well, it was fun while it lasted he seems to say...

Its all charmingly silly and amusing and inoffensive. And, above all, polite. Guinness, who played in so many of the best Ealing comedies, (including 8 roles in "Kind Hearts and Coronets", "The Man in a White Suit")shows yet again his extraordinary versatility in creating nuanced characters – the meekly subservient bank clerk, who has a slight problem pronouncing his 'r's, masks a scheming mind and almost malevolent glee in pulling the wool over everyone's eyes (watch him switch a real gold paperweight for a fake one from under the eyes of an innocent schoolgirl – he's sharper than a 3-card trickster on Oxford Street!). Stanley Holloway makes a splendid partner in crime and Sid James with Alfie Bass suitably dim-witted representatives of the villainous fraternity. Like many of the Ealing comedies, it was photographed with a fine sense of realism by the redoubtable Douglas 'Dougie' Slocombe whose long and equally versatile career would find his talents being employed by Spielberg on "Raiders of the Lost Ark" as well as "Indiana Jones and the Temple of Doom" as late as the 1970's. Apart from Audrey Hepburn, look out for Robert Shaw making an appearance at the beginning of his career...Light-hearted, lightweight, it is nevertheless a fine piece of filmcraft and undeniably great fun to watch.

* * *

In 1988, almost 40 years after this film, the elderly Charles Crichton was hauled out of semi-retirement by one John Cleese to direct "A Fish Called Wanda" and show the world that the Ealing Comedy 'formula' could still work: and it did. Whether this is solely due to Crichton's own directorial talents and skills or a considerable amount of Cleese's own input is open to debate – but, if nothing else, Crichton must have brought the spirit of Ealing with which the film is imbued along with him, and, for this alone, he must be credited. Michael Balcon's Ealing nurtured some remarkable talents, and almost became synonymous for English comedy generally (on occasion as much an irritation to the Boulting Twins as to their being sometimes confused with the makers of the "Carry On..." series – which really got up their nose) – but, for me, one talent in the Ealing stable was particularly gifted and brilliant, as shown in the following film he made in 1955.

47. "THE LADYKILLERS"

(1955. Director: Alexander MacKendrick)

Alexander Mackendrick's film, which is superbly crafted, could be described as being both quintessentially Ealing and quintessentially English. Curious, therefore, that it should have been written by an American(William Rose) and directed by an American born Scots …

Posing as a Professor of Music, criminal mastermind, Alec Guinness(complete with prosthetic protuberant teeth and muffled in a long woollen scarf) persuades a gullible, trusting little old lady (Katherine Johnson) – a genteel, lace-gloved, God-fearing model of propriety with a house at the end of a cul-de-sac – to rent out one of her rooms so that he and his group of 'musicians' can practice in peace and quiet. You'd have to be either blind, a complete idiot or a total innocent not to realize that the bizarre individuals he has assembled for his 'quintet' have other rather less musical matters on their mind – but, being the latter, Katie Johnson is delighted to invite them in and goes happily about her housework to the sound of Boccherini floating down from upstairs. Of course, the music is being played on a gramophone whilst Guinness and his gang of gentleman con artist 'Major' Cecil Parker (pricelessy seedy and impeccable), gangster Herbert Lom, spivvy Peter Sellers and heavyweight punch-drunk, brain dead Danny Green plot the last-minute details of a bank robbery. Having successfully pulled off their heist they retreat to their hide-out to gloat over their spoils while Boccherini plays on. It is only when they take their leave of the little old lady that things go wrong. The strap of the cello case, containing the stash of loot in convenient paper notes, gets stuck in the door and opting to employ brawn rather than brain, when Danny Green attempts to wrench it free, the case flies open and the money spills out in front of the little old lady's very eyes.…Mother is not pleased AT ALL – they have been very naughty boys indeed and have a lot of explaining to do before she will allow them out of the house! As the only witness to their otherwise perfect crime, they decide there's nothing for it except to get rid of her. The unenviable task of performing this unpleasant deed is decided by the drawing of the shortest matchstick...The comedy unfolds as, one by one, they fail to bump her off and, one by one, get bumped off themselves instead. This being 1955 there is no question of crime paying off but every one of virtue being rewarded. And so it proves to be...with the bemused little old lady ending up being advised by the indulgent police at the station, where, as a good and honest citizen, she had reported what has happened, that she best run along home, make herself a nice cup of tea and hang on to the 'loot' herself...

The film hangs on the credibility of this sweet, little old lady – dressed and bonneted as if she had last bought her wardrobe in the Edwardian era – believing that gentlemen were simply incapable of the kind of dishonesty she is now encountering in her music-loving guests. Katie Johnson convinces us completely in this respect and very touchingly so. She is an innocent from bonnet to boot, and its impossible not to love her.

The prolific and versatile, Czech-born Otto Heller photographed the film to give it a slightly stylized look and together with the studio sets the overall feel of the film is that of one slightly and politely removed from reality-as-we-know it. The performances and direction throughout are vintage and it is no wonder that it has become a classic of the genre. Some years back, the Coen Brothers made their own version – but the story didn't quite translate into the American idiom, but their film can be deemed a near-miss and an honourable failure, as well as a well-deserved homage to Alexander Mackendrick himself.

48. "OH, BROTHER, WHERE ART THOU?"

(2000 . Director/Writer: The Coen Bros)

The same cannot be said of the Coen brother's terrific take on The Odyssey. Their title is the same as the film the director in "Sullivan's Travels" is planning to make before he ends up in a chain gang – and, like Sturges' film, theirs' is also set in The Great Depression and its three heroes are in a chain gang.

The Coens have a singular style and a singular sense of comedy. They tread a fine line between the real and surreal, often blurring the edges. Their wit is mordant, ironic, absurdist at times and, for me utterly captivating and mostly very telling. It is typically cheeky of them to post the credit " Story written by Homer" and then to add their own as co-writers. George Clooney plays their Ulysses as perhaps not the brightest apple in the basket, who, together with two fellow convicts – a scary near psychopathic, John Tuturro, and the simple minded Tim Blake Nelson – escape from the chain gang and go in search of their freedom and a fortune Clooney claims he had buried before being imprisoned. Acting as a kind of seer and chorus, a blind black American comes in and out of the action, trundling up and down a rail line on a hand-propelled cart. Clooney's ultimate goal, however, is to win back his wife, Penny (Holly Hunter) from her current suitor but to do that, as in Homer, there are many obstacles he must overcome and past wrongs to be put right…

Without ever becoming didactic or preachy in any way, the film does take us nevertheless also into the dark world of the Ku Klux Kan; to the strange fervours of religious belief and practices in the Bible Belt; to the bigoted attitudes and prejudices of lawmen and townspeople alike. How the Coens manage to balance this with the overall comedy of the piece is a credit to their skills and unique talent. It really works! It is also one of the first films to use digital colour correction to create a slightly sepia look and set it back in time in an almost mythological hue, as befits. The film was finely photographed (yet again) by that ubiquitous Brit, Roger Deakins. Original talent and original film from two of America's most original talents: long may they thrive!

49. "MEN WHO STARE AT GOATS"

(2009. Director: Grant Heslov)

This film made me smile, then laugh and finally giggle aloud in delight like some silly teenager. The story of a special US military unit being developed to use paranormal and psychic powers, as opposed to conventional weaponry, to defeat 'the enemy' would be preposterous – were it not for the fact that the US military did (and perhaps still do), indeed, have such a programme and took/take it mighty seriously. So that makes this wonderful comedy just a little bit spooky too and it uses farce as its own weapon to tilt at an US institution so frighteningly brainwashed by its own sense of power and self-importance that it lives in a foggy, paranoid and humourless world unable to see beyond the tip of it's own regulation nose. Dangerous.

Ewan Macgregor plays the writer/journalist who, jilted by his wife, sets out to prove to her the man he really is by going off to Iraq to bring back a story which will bring her back too. To get into Iraq from Kuwait he falls in with a soldier (George Clooney) who reveals that he is part of special elite command known as the New Earth Army – the modern day Jedi's of the military and masters of paranormal and psychic powers. These include a demonstration of 'cloud-busting'(elementary level), running through solid objects like walls(advanced) and even the claim to be able to kill a man just by staring at him (currently, however, they are confined to practicing on goats). This secret unit, set-up some years previously by an enthusiastic if possibly deluded general, had originally been under the command of a Vietnam veteran whose own epiphany saw him returning from war as a long-haired New Age hippy, armed not only with his own superior paranormal powers but also the conviction they could be used for the purposes of securing world peace. Played with consummate skill by a drawling, benevolent Jeff Bridges at his very best, the creation of his army is told in neatly interspersed flashbacks – but whatever substance there may be to the powers possessed by the New Earth Army, they don't seem to have helped George Clooney from avoiding getting himself and Ewan Macgregor into a series of increasingly dangerous scrapes. But is their deliverance from these life-threatening perils the consequence of Clooney's psychic interventions – or just bloody good luck? The film plays on this ambiguity with mischievous relish: nothing is empirically sure.

In the years following it's creation, the command structure of this New Earth Army has changed radically and, by the time Clooney and Macgregor manage to reach its secret desert location, it is now being run by an officious, self-satisfied Kevin Spacey. Poor old hippy Bridges has been reduced to the ranks and his original 'Peace and Love' vision consigned to the dustbin. He wanders around the base of no further use to anyone, mostly drunk, while Spacey trains up his boys to be what the US military want them to be : a killing machine. On the compound is a large hangar – and in it are herds of goats, the practice targets for the lethal psychic machine Spacey is developing. It is all rather sorry and disagreeable. But Bridges is not finished yet – he gets his own back by spiking the camp's food and water supply with LSD, and in the hilarious final sequences the complete command, including Spacey, crashes around stoned out of their tits. Bridges and Clooney, equally tripped out, hijack a helicopter and lurch off into the skies ("like true shamans do") never to be seen again.

Back in the States, Macgregor writes up the story but, predictably, none of it is believed apart from a small clip, mentioning the mistreatment of goats in the desert by the military....A rueful Macgregor gets up from his desk – and runs across the room and straight through the wall...a new Jedi and believer is born....

I hadn't heard of this director before, but I notice that he is part of George Clooney's own company, Smokehouse Productions, who developed and made the film. He's done a good job and I'm sure I.A.L (Izzy) Diamond would have approved – there are some very good lines indeed.

* * *

I was 18 when this next film was being shot at Shepperton Studios, where I was working in the Stills Department to get my all-important union ticket, without which you simply couldn't work. So I was lucky enough to be able to spend a lot of time on the set and get to ask a lot of questions and receive a lot of answers (including those from Kubrick himself) about the nature of film-making which have influenced me for the rest of my life. It was clear to everyone on the film that we were working in the presence of a director who, apart from his obvious creative talent, was also a ferocious master of innovative technology. To a young man of my age, it was nearest I had come to seeing genius in the flesh. I have no shame in saying I hero-worshipped him at the time and have admired him ever since.

50. "DR STRANGELOVE"

(1964. Director: Stanley Kubrick)

Comedy doesn't get much blacker than this, but perhaps comedy is the only way to approach a subject as terrifying and as mad as the nuclear threat (Frankenheimer's "Seven Days in May" dealing with the same subject as a 'straight' drama doesn't have half the bite). The Cold War was very much on at the time – and Kubrick's highly plausible scenario makes one shudder, even as, in the blackest possible terms, it also makes one laugh.

Insane General Jack.D.Ripper (quite superbly played by Sterling Haydn) launches an unauthorized all-out nuclear attack on the Soviet Union whom he believes are poisoning "our precious bodily fluids". Can they be recalled before they reach their targets and trigger the nuclear holocaust? Not without the recall code, they can't – and the only person who knows that is crazy General Jack. In the Pentagon War Room (a powerful set design by Ken Adams), the progress of the planes is tracked on a large electronic map watched by all the chiefs-of-staff including gung-ho General Buck Turgidson (George C. Scott excelling himself with a virtuoso performance) as well as President Merkin Muffley (Peter Sellers, carefully restrained in one of the 3 roles he plays). The hotline is opened to his counterpart in the Kremlin and the President pleads his excuses ("No of course we didn't do this on purpose, Dimitri – Dimitri, listen to me – Dimitri, will you listen to me – Dimitri, calm down…"). Much to everyone's relief, a RAF Captain Mandrake (Sellers again with handlebar moustache and English 'old boy' accent) embedded on General Jack's base does finally work out what the key figures in the recall code are likely to be …. and the planes are brought back in the nick of time. Except one – piloted by a rootin' tootin' rodeo cowboy, played by Slim Pickens, his damaged aircraft, flying low beneath the radar screen, continues its mission (watch out for the young James Earl Jones as one of his crew – even in this minor role he excels) and eventually releases its bomb which flies towards earth with Slim Pickens straddling it, whooping it along with his stetson like a bucking bronco… And that's it! Bang – the world goes up in smoke. Back in the War Room, the sinister, wheelchair- bound scientific adviser Dr Strangelove (Sellers once more with mad blonde wavelets of hair), muses, in his strangulated German accent, on life after Doomsday and finds, to his amazed delight, that the result of this catastrophic obliteration of most of mankind is that suddenly he is able to get to his feet again. His and the film's last lines are "Mein Fuhrer! – I can walk!"…

Terry Southern (he of "Candy" fame) wrote the very black script, but Kubrick encouraged both Sellers and Scott to improvise some of their speeches. It was electrifying to stand on the set and watch them do so. In editing, Kubrick was as ruthlessly disciplined as he was on set – an entire custard-pie slapstick sequence in the War Room, shot over more than 2 weeks and involving hundreds of freshly-made cakes from Harrods being on call every day, promptly ended up on the cutting-room floor. Just as stimulating and instructive for me, however, was witnessing Kubrick's complete technical control over every aspect of the filming – from camera to sound, set dressing to wardrobe. His experiments with different film stocks (for instance, Ilford HPS at 800 ASA inside the plane) even included tests of infra-red film, fascinated me and I was amazed at just how little conventional studio lighting he needed to achieve his effects… and so, I believe, was his veteran cinematographer, Gil Taylor also – Kubrick was simply streets ahead of everyone. With his next film he was to go yet further and break every rule in the book to usher in a completely new set of cinematic possibilties…

* * *

It was 1968 – while everyone was running around Paris getting a whiff of tear gas and hurling cobblestones and petrol bombs at the CRS police as revolution took to the streets during "Les Événements du Mai", Kubrick was tucked away in the Boreham Wood Studios, making a cinematic revolution all of his own, and spending very large amounts of MGM's money in so doing. My father told me that the indignant studio big-wigs were so concerned by the huge flow of their lucre, that they decided to come across from the States in force and 'sort that bastard Kubrick out and, if needs be, shut him down'. Their indignation pretty well boiled over when, on arriving at the studios, Kubrick declined to come and meet them personally, saying he was too busy 'working'. Instead, through his assistant he invited them to view some of the material he had assembled. When they emerged some time later from the theatre after the screening, dazed and blinking into the daylight, Kubrick was ready to meet them – and they, in a state of shock and amazement at what they had seen, far from wanting to close him down anymore, were ready to meet his every demand...Let's not forget, Stanley Kubrick was a fiendishly good player of chess – he knew exactly how to have them eating out of his hand! How accurate this story is I cannot say, because my father enjoying embellishing his stories – but I'm sure the core of it is true and the studio bosses thankfully cut down to their proper size...

51. "2001: A SPACE ODYSSEY"

(1968. Director: Stanley Kubrick)

A year ahead of Neil Armstrong's "one small step for man", Kubrick took us and Cinema into the space age way beyond the Moon and on as far as Jupiter – smashing through all previous technical conventions with this great giant of a film epic and landing cinema right in the 21st century 32 years before it arrived – a moment from which it has never looked back. For this reason alone, it must be considered one of the most important and indeed visionary films ever made. So many of the technological accessories we take for granted in our lives today were foreseen in this film – (God, what a shock to remember that back in 1968 there was hardly a Fax machine in sight, let alone laptops or smart phones) – and incorporated into both it's fabric and also the process of making it. Shot for projection on the massive Cinerama screen which had previously been limited by a 3-camera system which led, rather like a badly made wig, for the seams where they joined to be visible, Kubrick filmed on Super-70mm Panavision and cut out any 'join' altogether and made it seamless. And then off he set, like a magician, to pull one rabbit out of the hat after another as he led us deeper and deeper into space – portraying weightlessness, artificial space gravity, complicated docking manoeuvres of spacecraft involving the use of models inset with multiple matte effects, etc, etc – all executed with a credibility and precision never seen or attempted before. Moreover, defying conventional thinking which also advised avoiding Close-ups, partly because no-one dared take the risk on such a huge screen, and partly because of the focal problems presented by it's pronounced curvature, Kubrick basically said 'to hell with all that' and audaciously proceeded to fill the screen with a massive Close-up of no more than the eye of a computer. It was altogether dazzling!

But this is Kubrick, after all, so there's much more substance to the film than a mere display of technical virtuosity. At the Dawn of Man where the film starts, a strange black obelisk or monolith appears amongst our Ape forefathers (again an incredible use of the combination of prosthetics and behavioural patterns make them utterly convincing). Its presence seems to trigger new thought processes, evolution through the quest for knowledge. What before was just an object, a thing, such as a bone on the ground, can now be perceived by our distant ancestors as also a tool…and the tool as a weapon …Apeman rises to his feet…a bone is thrown triumphantly into the air….and becomes effortlessly, thousands and thousands of years later, a spaceship sailing serenely through space…

The same monolith has been discovered on the Moon and the deafening signal it suddenly emitted has led to an expedition setting out for Jupiter. Apart from the models made for this spaceship, Kubrick had Vickers Armstrong build a massive centrifuge in which the two astronauts manning the craft, Keir Dullea and Gary Lockwood, could literally move in 360 degrees around it. But the day to day operating of the ship is run by a massive and highly advanced computer named Hal, taking his orders from the astronauts. Kubrick plays the two astronauts with a languor, almost a fatigue, their words stripped of any emotion. Even in their videophone calls back to their families, there is barely any evidence of feeling…of their human qualities: it is as if the very advances of technology have had the effect on man of reducing his ability to behave on a sentient level. By contrast, Hal the computer suggests, even with his resolutely neutral, electronically generated voice, a certain melancholy that lies behind his artificial intelligence and the seeds of a thinking, feeling entity with its own autonomous life. The theme of machines taking over the masters who have invented them is, of course, as old as Frankenstein, but Kubrick looks at this fragile relationship through a quietly glittering prism, compelling in its imagery and magnetically creepy. Hal does indeed begin to malfunction and more than that he begins, apologetically, to refuse to obey his orders. When this includes also engineering the death of Gary Lockwood, Keir Dullea realizes he must shut Hal down and escape in a space pod from what will now become a crippled ship. As Keir Dullea slowly disables the computer, Hal becomes more and more 'human', ending up with his own rendering of "Daisy, Daisy, give me your answer, do" with his voice, like a wind-up gramophone running down, getting deeper and deeper, slower and slower until he/it is no more.

Keir Dullea's escape into remote and unknown space leads into the famous, mind-blowing Light Trip, a whirlwind of images, hurtling us through Time and Space into another dimension in which all things are relative. He confronts himself in the Now, but also in the Future and the Past. Beyond Self, he becomes a Timeless moment … and out of this a new Dawn of Man presents itself in the vision of an embryonic child rolling across Space to be born…Metaphysically as well as scientifically, Kubrick concludes this roller-coaster of a film with the image of Hope…

The film is truly epic and I would hate to see it again in any other format than the one for which it was designed; and the idea that it might be watched these days on something as reduced as a Smartphone fills me with dismay. Giants should not be dwarfed – and this is a giant.

52. "SOLARIS"

(1972. Director: Andrei Tarkovsky)

Some consider this to be greatest of all sci-fi films ever made and a masterpiece of Cinema. It is easy to see why – it really is an extraordinary, densely wrought and original piece of film-making. Coming out 4 years after "2001", Tarkovsky's film does not rely on Kubrick's technical pyrotechnics to weave its special magic, but its imagery as well as its psychology is certainly as powerful albeit on a different scale. Solaris is a distant planet around which a space station has been orbiting and monitoring its unusual activities. The reports coming back to Earth from the two remaining astronauts on board(the third has died mysteriously) are increasingly bizarre and confused, so it is decided to send up a psychologist to see what is going on. What he finds on arrival is a ship and its crew in considerable disarray – unwelcoming, unhinged and with reality unravelling around them...Stranger still, there appear to be other people on board – who are they? Figments of the imagination or manifestations of something else? Most incomprehensible of all for the psychologist, though, is the appearance of his own wife, who killed herself years before...How can this be? Has it in some way to do with the activities of the planet Solaris they are orbiting? Is it transmitting a power to make memories become manifest and 'real'? For what purpose? And is this benign or not?

Nothing in Tarkovsky is ever straightforward or easy – his imagination is always oblique, but he does seem to be exploring in his own hallucinatory and truly poetic way the nature of not only reality itself but also of love. I cannot pretend to say I fully understood it at the time, nor now, some 40 years later. Nevertheless, with its haunting imagery, at times almost hypnagogic, it sucked me into its own universe and then sent me back to earth with parts of it destined to float around in my head forever. Tarkovsky is a poet of Cinema, stretching and testing the language of film beyond his own personal limits and always commanding from us our very real and humble respect. What a loss it was when he died at too young an age from a brain tumour.

53. "GRAVITY"

(2013. Director: Alfonso Cuarón)

I confess I am a complete sucker when it comes to anything to do with space, the stars, the planets – child-like in my awe of the sheer vastness and incomprehensible wonder of our Universe and blown away by the images of planets and stars sent back to us from craft like Voyager 1 or Rosetta or the Hubble Telescope. I am a sitting duck, therefore, for this kind of film and, until I saw Cuarón's brilliant 3-D blockbuster movie, I had always thought how fantastic it would be to blast-off into space and float around a bit myself in its wonders. Now, though, I don't want to be anywhere near it: Cuarón's vision has stripped space exploration of any romance for me: its too damn scary!

"Gravity" follows on from where Kubrick left off almost half a century ago – before the advent of CGI and the advanced 3D technology Cuarón employs. It could be also said that, in one respect, it owes something to Tarkovsky too. Certainly it is a stupendous technical achievement, visually outstanding in its depiction of a cold, silent, inhospitable and remarkably lonely Space. George Clooney and Sandra Bullock play the two astronauts menaced by the impending arrival of a veritable storm of 'space debris' which tears through their spacecraft, leaving both of them with the distinct prospect of the loneliest extinction to life imaginable. Protected only by the vulnerable armour of the spacesuits which stand between them and the pitiless, silent, airless cold of space, their chances of saving themselves and getting back to Earth seem very remote. Indeed, George Clooney has to sacrifice himself in order that one of them might survive, floating off to wait for the inevitable moment his oxygen runs out. It is a gruesomely horrible moment, all the more pitiless for the deep, deep, deathly silence of space enclosing it.

How Sandra Bullock, having succeeded in reaching the slender hope offered by another abandoned spacecraft, overcomes one threat and setback after another to reach the safety of Earth provides the bulk of the action narrative. Her indomitable determination and will to live are pitted against the huge implacability of all the space hazards imaginable. But her journey is also one through memory and past trauma towards a rebirth...And is there something of Tarkovsky and "Solaris" when she hallucinates the presence of George Clooney(now dead) beside her in the capsule to encourage her and lend her advice?

When she finally hurtles back into Earth's atmosphere, like a sheet of fire, and crashes into a lake, there is something of Man's (or Life's) emergence onto land from his primordial watery amphibian origins as she drags herself out of the soupy lake – now a lithe sinewy creature no longer clad in a bulky spacesuit – and clambers onto land, lying there with her toes squelching the mud before rising to her feet, like our ancestors did at some moment in time, and walking away ... And how precious our planet Earth felt at that moment. How glad I was to be back from space – alien, cold, cruel in its total impartiality.

Many find the film rich in spectacle and effects, but thin on story and substance. To my own way of thinking, I think that is to miss the point – as with the medium being the message, so too all these stunning effects are parts of the story and the questions they pose in themselves – and I do not find the film half as slight as some critics do: "Gravity" has gravitas. It is photographed by Emmanule Lubezki, fast becoming elegible for the title of the most exciting and innovative cinematographer of our times, with the same genius as he had already shown on Iñárritu's "BirdMan" and now again for the same director on "The Revenants".... Cuarón, Iñárritu, Guillermo del Toro and Lubezki...all Mexican, all friends and all major creators (perhaps Mr Donald Trump would like to build another of his famous walls to keep them out as well? Maybe out in space?). Finally, it is a matter of some pride, too, to know that this "Hollywood" film, directed and photographed by Mexicans, was 99% designed and executed almost exclusively by British technicians. *Chapeau* …! (but then Brits have always excelled in this department, haven't they?... after all, who put together Kubrick's odyssey for him, if it wasn't a British team of technicians too…?)

* * *

But now that we are firmly and safely back on Earth, I want to dig further back into my memory to my own childhood and fish out the early influences which began to shape my imagination and indelibly plant the magic of Cinema in my young and impressionable mind…So I have to include the next film on this list if only because it's the first film I remember ever seeing – and "firsts" tend to take up a permanent, if fragmented lodging in our memories. I was in Switzerland at the time I saw it, recovering from tuberculosis, and I guess I must have been around 4 years old…

It was 1949 and, not that I was or could have been even remotely aware of it, back in Britain "those bloody twins", my father and uncle, had finished their (pretty good and now accepted classic) "Brighton Rock" with the young Richard Attenborough and were turning their attention to the perils of nuclear weapons and preparing "Seven Days to Noon". Carol Reed had triumphed with "The Third Man", as had Robert Hamer with "Kind Hearts and Coronets". I have no idea what David Lean or Michael Powell were up to at that time, but I assume Jack Hawkins and John Mills were to be seen somewhere wandering around in duffle coats with mugs of cocoa in their hands, standing on the bridge of some warship or other and saying exciting things like "Hard 20 degrees starboard – and give her all the steam you've got, Chief!" or "I don't like the look of this, Number One, I don't like the look of this at all" … or even more philosophical musings such as "Funny thing, sir – war…don't you think?"…As for the rest of the world, who knows what they were filming in 1949, but John Wayne was sure to be around somewhere in front of a camera for John Ford and busy sorting out the West…It was the heyday of Cinema and people still went to 'the pictures' in their many millions before television came along and changed the landscape forever…a time when the very idea of a DVD, or of streaming onto a lap-top computer to watch a movie were the stuff of sci-fi fantasy also…unbelievable.

For me, up in the Alps, though, someone called Snow White entered my life…well, to be more precise, two Snow Whites….one was a woman who could boast a moustache that would have done credit to Errol Flynn and the physique of a lumberjack who was Nanny's 'friend' , called Blanche Neige/Snow White (yes, all a bit confusing for a three, four year old) – and the other was a little girl in a bright blue blouse and a golden yellow skirt who wasn't quite real either ….

54. "SNOW WHITE & THE SEVEN DWARFS"

(1937. Directors – Walt Disney stable)

For a long time, until I watched it again with my daughter when she was about 4 years old, all I can really remember about this world-famous animation film was how hypnotically scary the Wicked Queen was, and how absolutely terrifying the sequence in which Snow White escapes through a forest of extremely menacing trees which assumed eyes and faces and generally devilish forms. And that sinister, oh so shiny poisoned apple! I shudder still. It reduced me to quivering jelly – and my infant daughter didn't fare much better some 50 years later when watching this same section of the film (although she kept her best tears for Disney's "Bambi" which we had to see over and over again, pitiful sobs and all when Bambi's mother is shot, until sheer emotional exhaustion brought the curtain down on both of us).

But now I recognize "Snow White" for the grim Grimm fairytale it is – overlaid with Disney's sugar-coating does not prevent it from also being the stuff of dark nightmares, and Freudian complexities. But it is also a real triumph of technical and visual animation. In this day and age we have got used to the highly sophisticated and often brilliant animation techniques computers have made possible. And I readily own up to being quite a fan of this curiously anthropomorphic genre and have been all my life. But when you stop to consider the sheer size of the undertaking of old-fashioned cel animation in 1937, the achievement is all the more impressive. Running 83 minutes at 24 frames per second, that involved preparing individual hand-painted cells for no less than some 120,000 individual frames – of people, plus their backgrounds, objects, all the while animating them to walk, talk, run, dance and express character and emotions of all kinds; colouring each frame to give light and shade, mood and dynamic –

in short to make them *live!*. It's a mammoth and painstaking task. Disney knew how to make a shape (Mickey Mouse, after all, is not much more than two circles put on top of one another) and his palette – bright, saturated primary colours, vivid blues, reds, yellows, greens and blacks – is boldly delineated. Perhaps it is because they imprinted themselves on me at such an early age, but I sometimes regret that they have been replaced by today's brilliant computer-generated effects and their altogether subtler, more 'realistic' hues of colour.

"Snow White"(and I think I'm right) was the first full-length animated picture ever to be made. A veritable beacon which has maintained an almost universal appeal, gripping children from all over the world and holding sway over their young imaginations, for not far short of 100 years. And Snow White herself, in her bright blue blouse and golden yellow skirt, has been absorbed into that huge brand invented by Walt D., along with Mickey M, the Sleeping Beauty and the rest of the gang – BIZARRE! What would the grim Grimms have made of it all? And I wonder if this film has anything to do with my slight hesitation and wariness now of shiny apples and anyone offering them…?

55. "THE RED BALLOON"

(1956. Director: Albert Lamorisse)

I have no such trepidation when it comes to shiny balloons, however: in no small measure, this is thanks to Lamorisse's charming and lyrical film about a small Parisian boy and the red balloon he finds one day. It becomes his friend, a being with a mind of its own, following him wherever he goes – home, school, along the streets, behind him when he travels on a bus. The envy of his schoolmates, perplexing and sometimes alarming to adults, the little helium balloon expresses the ingenuous joy and innocence of childhood and the loveliness of its dreams. Too often, of course, this cannot last – and in Lamorisse's film, both boy and balloon are hunted down by a gang of bullies – and the balloon punctured and destroyed. It slowly deflates and crumples on a patch of wasteland. The cruelty and pain of the moment is heart-wrenching. Consolation is at hand, however – like "all the birds in the air" coming to lament the death of Cock Robin, one by one, all the balloons of Paris come together to comfort him in his loss, lifting the little boy up and floating him away across the skies of Paris to live on with his dreams. Lovely, tender, gentle!

At only 33 minutes, this poignant fable went straight into my heart when I saw it at the age of 11. There is little dialogue and the story is composed of some beautiful imagery and accompanied by a wistful music score. It made me yearn to see this elegant city of blue-grey buildings, stairways and alleys of streaming light. Shot in and around old Belleville, it shows a Paris that is no more, but there was just about enough of it remaining when I first got there 5 years later for me not to be disappointed and to fall quietly in love with that city, not only of Truffaut's Antoine Doinel, but also of the little boy and his pet balloon.

Lamorisse's son, Pascal, plays the boy, and together father and son won the Palme D'Or for Best Short Film and an Oscar on top of it. It went straight into the canon of classics and remains one of the loveliest children's films ever made.

56. "SHANE"

(1953. Director: George Stevens)

"Shane – come back!", desperately pleads the young homestead boy, as Alan Ladd rides off into a glorious sunset and an uncertain future just as mysteriously as he had ridden into the boy's life at the beginning... "Shane – come back!", the sunset, Alan Ladd on his horse ...that's about all I can recall of this classic of the genre. But, yes, I do also remember that the boy was played by Brandon de Wilde – and I only remember that because I couldn't help thinking at the time, aged all of 8, what extraordinarily bizarre names some Americans had.

The rest is a blank. But I must include "Shane" here because, despite being unable to recall more than just the basics of the plot, it seeped into my unconscious and stayed there. If asked to name 10 of the best Westerns, therefore, I would still cite "Shane" as one of them – recalling it more as a series of flickering sensations, of feelings I had experienced when I watched it, than as a story, but knowing nevertheless it was bloody good stuff A subliminal memory which cannot be erased. Such is the power of conditioning film can have...

My generation was pretty well brought up on a diet of Westerns and war films, and I have always had a fondness for the former – the good and the virtuous pitted against the bad, the Law against anarchic lawlessness, all set against the vast magnificent landscape of the mythical American West – with its frontiers, covered wagons, saloons, honky-tonk pianos a-playing while alluring ladies of questionable virtue with lots of ruffles and plenty of *décolleté* wandered about with names like Dutchie or Frenchy able to spot a card sharp at 100 yards and soften the hearts of the heroes by revealing the soft underbelly of their hidden goodness. And, of course, although usually heavily outnumbered, we all knew Good would win out in the end – because Good always does, doesn't it?! That's part of the American parable and Heavens forfend if we should think otherwise.

"Shane" is no exception to this formula. Ex-gunfighter and baddie turned goodie comes to the aid of some simple, honest folk trying to make a living for themselves and their young son on their modest homestead in a valley. The boy, the said Brandon de Wilde, is in awe of the ex-gunfighter and his fancy tricks with the pistol to the point of hero worship, but his mother (Jean Arthur in her last role) is not about to allow her boy to be influenced into believing the rule of the gun is the path to take in life. Oh, no, siree! Nevertheless, she and her husband, Van Heflin have a dilemma – the local big shots and barons are intimidating them and trying to force them to give up and get out. Ex-gunfighter Alan Ladd is not about to let this happen to these decent all-American folk and, although he has put his days with the gun behind him, its time to strap on his holster again and go out and do what a man must do. And do it he does: the valley is cleansed of guns and the power of the avaricious 'baddies' broken – order and virtue prevail. Mother is mighty happy – but the boy not so…"Shane – come back!", a plea from the heart….yet Alan Ladd rides away into the sunset forever… Oh Shane, oh Shane – did you have to go? Not a dry eye in the house…

* * *

A stagecoach, flanked by a posse of whooping cowboy outriders shooting their pistols into the air, thunders down a driveway, reining up in front of a ranch. An ageing man, with a black patch covering one eye and grumpy jowls , steps forward from the ranch porch to the stagecoach door – but it is the door on the other side which now opens and from out of which tumbles an individual who, if we're not mistaken, is at least three sheets to the wind, – in short, having clearly tied on one too many, blotto! The man with the black patch is not at all amused, in fact he is vexed and his displeasure very evident as he barks an order for them all, cowboys, stagecoach and its korkified passenger, to return up the drive and make their arrival again – and, dammit, get it right this time! Oh – and, by the way, the pie-eyed gentleman in the coach is also unmistakably dressed as Father Christmas – mind and eye boggle! But no,this is not a scene out of some extremely bizarre Western, but a moment from an altogether different occasion. For it is 1967 and the man with the black patch is the legendary film director, John Ford, and we are witnessing the opening ceremony (Take 1) of the children's Christmas party he gave at his ranch each year. Take 2 – and the stagecoach arrives again and this time, inebriated or not, Father Christmas manages to open the right door to be greeted by Ford, stepping forward through the throng of children surrounding him...(but, by the look on his face, whether he would be casting the same actor as Father Christmas the following year is extremely doubtful).

During World War II, Ford was, if I'm not mistaken, made a Rear Admiral in the US Navy and given a command. The wisdom of this is open to debate, for it is far from certain that Ford was as good a sailor as he was a film director. I don't know if his ship was shot out of the water or sunk beneath him, but clearly some misfortune was visited on him – for these Christmas parties were given for the children of his crew members who had become paraplegic victims under his command – and they were more than just a handful. It was Ford's way of showing his gratitude to them for their loyal service...and, who knows, perhaps a way of expressing his remorse for his shortcomings as an Admiral too. I simply do not know. In the glory days of his career, all the stars would come to these parties at his ranch and the children got to meet the stars, the likes of 'Duke' Wayne, Maureen O'Hara, Vera Miles, Harry Carey Jr,(and maybe old silent star Harry Carey and his wife Olive too with whom Ford made so many movies), Richard Widmark, Carroll Baker, Ward Bond and other well-known stalwart character actors whose faces would have been so familiar to them, while all around them other cowboys and cowgals performed tricks with horses, lassoos and all the other paraphernalia of the Wild West.

But by 1967, Ford's star was not shining so brilliantly in the Hollywood firmament anymore and his career as a film-maker was reluctantly coming to an end. His last big film "Cheyenne Autumn" had been made 3 years previously and, although he did make a couple of pictures after, it was essentially the end of the line for this giant of cinema who had made his first picture as far back as 1917: his own autumn was giving way to winter…So, by the time I was lucky enough to be taken that year to meet him at his Christmas party, it was a distinctly more subdued affair, lacking the lustre it must have had in his heyday … no sign, therefore, of 'Duke' Wayne, the man he had made into such a star, or others whose careers owed him so much – but, yes, there was Richard Widmark…and I glimpsed Eleanor Powell, both loyal to the last, and there were still tricks with lassoos and cowboys and gals…and, of course, Father Christmas, unforgettably in the grips of seasonal good cheer providing an image I will cherish forever. But something was missing… Ford had not been abandoned as such (that would have been impossible) but I did get the feeling he had been sort of left behind to wave good'bye as the stagecoach went on its way. I found it all a little sad….."Shane!...Come back…!"… Six years later, he died…but, unlike Fellini in Italy, he wasn't given a State funeral…well, after all, he was only a film-maker, wasn't he..?

Whatever you may think about the content of John Ford's films, there's surely no denying that he REALLY knew where to put the Camera. He is rightly regarded as the Big Daddy of the Western – but beyond that also a Grand Master of his craft. A legend in his lifetime, he straddled each and every era of Cinema, being part of its growth from infancy and the early silent movies to talkies to colour, widescreen, and stereo, with the literally dozens and dozens of films he made. Born in the 19th century he also went through two World Wars, the Korean War, Vietnam and the so-called Cold one – "Oh earth what changes hast thou seen!"… By the time he made the following film on the list he was at the top of his game – while I was still in short trousers at a prep school and pondering 'Turkey' Odell's "Well, Boulting Minor – do you think you can do any better..,?" He was a colossus.

What is it about Ford that sets him on top of the mountain, black patch on one eye and chewing a handkerchief like a child's comforter, all jowls and growls and scowls?(well, that's how he appeared to me when I was taken to meet him back in 1967). Possibly its not simply what he does but what he doesn't do that makes him so exemplary. Ford eschews effect almost as much as he chewed that handkerchief of his. There is no "look at me and see how clever I am being" – he doesn't want his skills to be noticed, he just wants to get on with it and tell the story. As a director, therefore, he is not an auteur with a necessarily distinctive style – he is the opposite: almost invisible. And this 'invisibility' paradoxically is what gives him his style: judicious placement of the Camera, an astute sense of pace to drive forward the narrative yet retain the appropriate 'mood' and a wonderful feel for landscape and the individual(s) placed within it. Once asked why he made movies, Ford growled "Because it gives me 2 hours to play poker with the boys – 2 hours to try and make the leading lady behind the covered wagon – 2 hours in the most goddam beautiful scenery on the face of the earth – and 2 hours to run film through the camera!" ...Stop to think about it and that's a pretty fair description of how a day works on any set of any film, but also gives an insight into his no-nonsense approach to film-making. There may be sentiment galore at times IN his movies, but none whatsoever in how he MADE them.

57. "THE SEARCHERS"

(1956. Director: John Ford)

Of all his films, I have chosen to include "The Searchers" because it is in many ways his most unsettling film as well as one of his finest. Again, relying on my memory, I recall that it made me feel quite uneasy when I saw it – because at times I wasn't at all sure which side of the fence Ford had positioned himself, or whether, in fact, he was on neither side but actually sitting on it. The story tells of a man (John Wayne, of course) coming home from The Civil War to find his brother's family have been killed and his niece (the lovely Natalie Wood) abducted by Comanches, and it follows his obsessive search over the years to track her down and bring her 'home'. There is an ambiguity about its attitude towards the American Indians which is occasionally disturbing at first viewing. But perhaps that is precisely what Ford intended to show – the ambiguity of attitudes and opinions in us all and the uncertainties of the posture of absolute moral Rights and Wrongs. Certainly, in this film, pretty well everyone will have blood on their hands before the 'Duke' will get his niece 'home'... Or will he?

The surprise – shock even – that Wayne has to take on board is that when he does finally track her down, is that she doesn't want to come 'home'. Natalie Wood has adopted the Comanche way of life, embraced it and is perfectly happy where she is, thank you very much. This is a hard pill for Wayne to accept, let alone swallow – and relentlessly intent of both avenging his family's suffering and also getting her back to where she belongs, he won't give up. His obsession only gets deeper – blood is spilt, scalps are taken(not by the Comanches but by one of Wayne's own) and only at the very end can the 'Duke' haul up Natalie Wood onto his horse and say "Right, let's go home"...

Vengeance, justice, obsession, prejudice, racism – "The Searchers" touches on them all. Gloriously shot in VistaVision, largely in Ford's favourite Monument Valley, the film has long been considered by many as Ford's masterpiece. I'm not so sure….but it is most certainly beautifully crafted and a classic of the genre. And John Wayne, Ford's long time collaborator, turns in one of his best performances…

* * *

À propos the 'Duke's' talent, I was once told by another famous actor, not unknown for being seen in the saddle himself, but who shall remain nameless here, that when asked how he directed John Wayne, Ford replied drily "Syllable by syllable!"….I suspect that may just be a bit of mischief at expense of the 'Duke' but it made me chuckle and I can't quite watch his performances in the same way ever again… nor without feeling another quiet chuckle rising in my throat every time he opens his mouth… In the '70's and '80's the appetite for the traditional Western began to wane (if you'll excuse the unintentional pun) as the realities of the Vietnam War, the "hippy" revolution, and social mores generally were shifting the public sensibilities. The old formula of the homey, black and white frontier homestead virtues, the simplistic lore of the West no longer seemed to appeal as they had in the past. The world had moved on. Strangely enough, for all the 'Peace and Love' in the air, the Westerns still being made became more violent and the codes of honour altogether less noble. Quietly and slowly, however, the Western genre fizzled out… and seemed to leave the stage…Then, in 1992 ….

58. "UNFORGIVEN"

(1992. Director: Clint Eastwood)

… along came Clint Eastwood with this modern classic. Dubbed a 'revisionist Western', in fact I don't think it could be more traditional if it tried – but what a good piece of film it is! Although he dedicated the picture to his mentors, Don Siegel and Sergio Leone, I think the influence of John Ford on this film is altogether more evident. I would even go so far as to venture that Eastwood, as a director, is the Elisha to Ford's Elijah…and has taken on the mantle to very good effect. He has made some very good films.

Yes, its true he de-mystifies the Western lore, de-romanticizes it's heroic pretensions, but at its heart it remains a good old-fashioned story about Good versus Bad. Set at the end of the 19th century, Eastwood plays an ex-outlaw/gunfighter who, having renounced both violence and alcohol on the death of his wife, for whom he is still grieving, is now struggling to bring up their two children, barely able to subsist on his small farm-holding…and the picture of him flailing around in the mud trying to catch his hog is hardly that of the heroic gunfighter of yore… Elsewhere, in a town ruled by a ruthless sheriff, a bully and a sadist, with a strictly no-gun, no vigilante policy, (a flawless performance by Gene Hackman), a girl in the brothel-saloon has been cut up and her face disfigured by 2 cowboys for daring to laugh at the size of one of their pricks. The biased leniency with which they are let off by Sheriff Hackman disgusts the girls and they pool together their resources to post a bounty reward of US$1,000 for anyone who will avenge them properly. It comes to the attention of a young, would-be tough-guy, Jaimz Woolvett, ambitious to emulate the deeds of the legendary gunfighters he has heard about. Aware of Eastwood's past reputation, he endeavours to enlist his support. Reluctantly, he agrees – quite simply he needs the money – and sets off. On the way he picks up his old friend, also an ex-gunfighter (Morgan Freeman really shining in this role). Unlike their young companion, a Boy seeking fame and glory and boasting his skills with the gun (in fact, he is so short-sighted he can barely see further than the end of his finger), for them it is just a job for which neither has much relish...they know all about the hollowness of gun glory...

The offer of reward has also brought fancy-dressed Richard Harris as a self-promoting English gunslinger into town, accompanied by a sycophantic journalist who is chronicling his feats and perpetuating his myth in cheap 10 cent novels. In fact, he is a lot of hot air – known as such to Sheriff Hackman(himself a man with a past) who, after humiliating him very publicly, locks him up and then throws him unceremoniously out of town. This is an eye-opener to his amanuensis and biographer who promptly switches loyalties to stay in town and write up the life and deeds of the Sheriff instead.

Riding through a torrential downpour and into town, a fevered Eastwood and his companions are gratefully received by the girls they have come to avenge, but not so by Hackman who metes out yet again his own brand of justice on Eastwood...

Suffice it to say that, once recovered from fever and being beaten-up. Eastwood and Freeman do corner their quarries; that one of two cowboys is killed with agonizing slowness in a gulley; the other one shot at point-blank by the Boy while he is in the shithouse; that Freeman can no longer stomach this violence and decides to go home; that the Boy also owns up that, despite all his boastings, he has never shot a man in his life and realizes that there is not an ounce of glory or heroism to be found in this sordid killing business. Suffice it also to say that the Sheriff's deputies intercept Freeman on his way home and bring him back to town where Hackman can then proceed to take immense pleasure in bull-whipping him to death and posting his body outside in a coffin as a warning to all....No wonder, then, that Eastwood breaks his years of temperance, uncorks a bottle of whiskey and also rides back into town and the saloon-brothel where

Gene Hackman – in a terrifically staged show-down – finally meets his nemesis.

Filmed with admirable economy and restraint, finely acted, beautifully shot and edited, Eastwood succeeds in showing us an inglorious world in which the often arbitrary business of both exercising the law and meting out revenge is mostly a grubby, sordid, protracted and messy affair, stripped of any glamour. In many ways, it is a melancholy piece – and the score by Lennie Niehaus (who went on to work with Eastwood again) gently underlines the sadness and pity of it all. "Unforgiven" scooped up the Oscars and, had there been any lingering doubts before, showed the world that our Clint of spaghetti-western and Dirty Harry fame was a formidable director to be reckoned with. I could watch this film again and again….and sometimes do …but mostly just in my head…

* * *

…Yes, in the head with all those synapses popping and neurons colliding as memories race in and out at maybe as fast as 1fps or faster(I believe part of Kubrick's 'light trip' at the end of "2001" was made up of thousands of images of 1 frame only, whizzing subliminally past us at 1/24 of a second – God knows what we were looking at) … to the early memories of Snow White and the other Snow White, Nanny's 'friend' with the Errol Flynn moustache (and was it Flynn or Burt Lancaster who was "The Crimson Pirate" and how old was I when I saw that, for God's sake?)… to the Red Balloon (heavens, how my infant daughter loved to have a shiny red helium balloon as we raced through the streets in her Japanese push-chair; and, oh, what dismay in the look on her face when her tiny fingers let go of the string and it floated away, to be replaced again and again by the nice man in the Bermondsey shop close to where we lived)… and onto Shane – "Come back Shane!" (Come back who? Who were we all calling for, who did we miss so much?)… and on and on until there was suddenly this period of so-called "epic" films, when 'big' was somehow meant to be 'better' .And 'big' usually meant Charlton 'Chuck' Heston. Why? I have never understood why Charlton Heston – there he is again and again,

with that strange all-American set of odontological ivories and those weird pectoral muscles a-twitching as Moses, as Ben Hur, El Cid, there in Peking at the centre of the Boxer Rebellion – hero in them all and usually shining from head to toe in some oily unguent (was this a mandatory requirement in his contract, do you think – that he should always be seen to glisten?) If 'Duke' Wayne had to be directed "syllable by syllable", then our 'Chuck' wasn't far behind him with the added impediment of always coming across (to me at any rate) as a man frequently straining to be relieved of a terrible and extended bout of constipation. But, to be fair to him, he was not alone, was he – Richard Burton went 'epic' too, wooden as a door-frame in "The Robe" alongside the even more wooden and total-immersion-oil-drenched Victor Mature in its sequel "Demetrius and the Gladiators" (and who in the hell is ever called Victor Mature?? Archibald Leach becoming Cary Grant I can understand, but Victor Mature??). God, they all glistened in olive oil and sweat as they embraced the Christian faith to face persecution and martyrdom at the hand of extravagantly mad, over-the-top Caligula's, hamming it all the way to Camp Ham, or wherever Ham resides. (To be honest, though, it really could be amusing at times). And since I have brought up the name of the 'Duke' Wayne again, let's not forget either his immortal nine syllables in another well-meaning stinker, starring that fine actor Max von Sydow as Jesus Christ (did Jesus really always wear perfectly washed white?) in "The Greatest Story Ever Told" in which the 'Duke' plays the Good Centurion at the foot of the Cross. His delivery of the line "Surely this man was the Son of God" led his director to suggest he should do it again with more... 'awe'... leading to Take 2 which thus came out as "OR... surely this man was the son of God". One of those unforgettable film moments when either, like Judas, you want to go out and hang yourself, or alternatively wet your pants with uncontrollable mirth. Or maybe both.

Why did they all do it? Such fine and talented directors such as William Wyler, George Stevens, Nicholas Ray, Anthon Mann – even Kubrick, who was brought onto "Spartacus"(and made a better fist of it than most of the others, maybe helped along by 'leftie' Dalton Trumbo's script, although Kubrick disassociated himself from the film later). When I saw Wyler's

"Ben Hur", for instance, at the Odeon Marble Arch, there was a full symphony orchestra in black tie playing the theme tunes (slowly sinking out of sight into the pits as the lights went down, the curtains parted and the film itself began). There was also a glossy programme itemizing just how many metres of metal tubing, gallons of paint, tons of plaster, yards of cloth, etc had been used to create the mammoth sets and so on: as if the sheer quantity would guarantee the quality of what we were about to watch. Well, it didn't... for all the directorial and acting skills at hand, the majority of these often pious, biblically themed films never seemed to rise above the mediocre. They were Reader's Digest and, for all the money and effort which went into making them, never managed to convince me that they were anything other than what they really were: lots of people dressing up in costumes, painting their faces and slapping on the olive oil to play a 'pretend' game.

However, to be fair, it must be allowed that they all had their moments – and one of these 'epic' films, indeed, stands out as an honourable exception to the rule. I went to see it at the Odeon Leicester Square one Sunday afternoon with my father, his editor of the time, Anthony Harvey (who went on to direct "A Lion in Winter")and an old family friend and painter, Enslin duPlessis. Suddenly, here was an epic film worthy of that name – as vast and majestic as the desert in which so much of it is set. It is, of course, "Lawrence of Arabia", and besides impressing me as a beautifully made and unusually intelligent film, I remember it also for two other salutary lessons I learnt that day – firstly, that film-makers themselves can never really experience watching films with the same immersive connection as the general public and that's part of the sacrifice you have to make if you wish to be a film-maker; and that, secondly, one really has to watch out very carefully about how you employ music in a film. I was 17 and the wool was slowly being pulled away from my eyes ...

59. "LAWRENCE OF ARABIA"

(1962. Director: David Lean)

Lesson One: the huge Super-Panavision 70mm screen at the Odeon Leicester Square is filled with a shimmering desert. A mirage of trembling shapes, a vision through which some thing or person is very slowly approaching us out of the distance. Only the faint jangle and chink of metal come to us on a quiet desert breeze across the vast silence. Breathtaking. Out of this blur of light Omar Sharif finally materialises on his camel, it's tackle and saddles gently chinking, to confront Lawrence. A beautiful and magical moment....that's what the audience see. But I am seeing something else at the same time – two men standing in front of a microphone in a small sound studio. One is a short, chubby, cheerful Italian Cockney and the other, his partner, tall and melancholy: they are two Prop men, the infamous duo of Chuck and Bobby. Both dangle a small bundle of keys in front of the mic – chink, chink, chink they gently go ...and there you are – the jangle of Omar Sharif's camel appearing out of that mirage.... Pop! – there goes another illusion...

Lesson Two: Held between thumb and forefinger, in big close-up filling the 70mm screen, the flame of a match burns down towards Lieutenant T.E.Lawrence's fingers. At the last moment, just as it is about to burn him as well, it snuffs itself out – and the image cuts effortlessly from this Close Shot to a wide panorama of endless desert, dunes rolling upon dunes. A beautiful edit, another beautiful moment – and up swells Maurice Jarre's grand theme tune to cover it. "No, no, no!", groaned editor Anthony Harvey during the Intermission, "no music – SILENCE – he should have let it breathe!". I could see 'Uncle' Tony's point – (and everyone who came into my father's house was dubbed either an honorary 'Uncle' or 'Aunt' – and should it ever come to it, God forbid, to writing my father's biography

I should probably have to call it "My Father and Other Uncles") – at times the images are already so grand and powerful in themselves that the addition of music is in danger of not adding, but subtracting from their impact : leave them alone to speak for themselves. Let them breathe!

Of course, David Lean was a master craftsman and there are many other profitable lessons to be learnt from watching his films. "Lawrence of Arabia", although criticized for its historical inaccuracies, was also widely acclaimed by critics and public alike as a film masterpiece: understandably so, because it *is* truly big and does have epic stature, possessed of an emotional depth and complexity so often absent in other 'epics' which rely more on spectacle than on the intimacy and ambiguities of character and plot. And, in this latter, with Robert Bolt's thoughtful script, Lean's film excels – his portrait of Lawrence is of a man as tormented as he is also narcissistic, 'walking backwards into the limelight of history' even as he sought to avoid it in anonymity. A man who discovers, contrary to his better instincts, that he had a taste for killing; whose sado-masochistic sexual inclinations battled with his intellectual sense of moral probity; but above all, a man with a genuine affinity with and understanding of the Arab peoples, through which he could eventually marshal the different (and often mutually antagonistic) tribes to rise up in revolt against their Ottoman masters during the First World War. To what extent this made a significant contribution to the Allied efforts or the awakening of Arab nationalism remains, with historical hindsight, uncertain – but one has only to look at the Middle East today to know that his dream of Arab unity remains very far from being realized.

Lean starts his film with the death of Colonel Lawrence(who, after the war, had assumed the anonymous identity of Ordinary Airman Ross) in a motorcycle accident and, as befitted a national hero, the ensuing Memorial Service at St Paul's cathedral – where there is perhaps a thinly veiled sense of relief amongst the great and the good who had gathered to honour this somewhat enigmatic individual that he was no longer around to create any more awkward trouble for them. The film then goes on to plot his journey from being an insubordinate Intelligence officer to the heroic instigator of the Arab Revolt culminating in the taking of Damascus and the so-called Arab Council which, far from unifying them, became a forum in which the different tribes could air their differences and which collapsed under the weight of their endless bickering. By which time, Lawrence had served his purposes for General Allenby and his staff, been promoted to the rank of colonel and shipped out of the war arena: his triumph was also a failure...

Along the way, Lawrence has formed alliances with both the wary Faisal (Alec Guinness) and the even more suspicious head of another clan (Anthony Quinn) and lead them both in the attack and capture of the strategically important Turkish garrison at Aqaba; executed the very same young Arab he has previously rescued from certain death in the desert; sabotaged and massacred a Turkish troop train; been captured, flogged and probably raped by the Turks under the command of their Bey(an excellent Jose Ferrer); saved by the loyal friendship of Omar Sharif; and argued his case with his not altogether convinced superiors and 'handlers', headed by Allenby (Jack Hawkins) with Claude Rains, Anthony Quale as his colleagues both for and against Lawrence's schemes. The big action set pieces evolve smoothly out of the more intimate and personal moments, of which there are many, and are superbly and convincingly handled. At the centre of it all is the blue-eyed, blonde and magnetic Peter O'Toole as Lawrence, turning in a tremendous performance which shot him into stardom. So attractive was he in the role, skitting around in his white djellaba and admiring himself amongst the dunes, that it led Noel Coward to quip rather wickedly "If he had been any prettier, they would have had to call the film 'Florence of Arabia'"...

It was filmed in Jordan and Spain – with absolutely stunning photography by the great Freddie Young. Anne Coates, the *grande dame* of English editors, cut the film with equal brilliance and, despite 'Uncle' Tony's reservations, Maurice Jarre's score was and is unforgettable. Lean's talents as a director were many and prodigious as he had shown from "Brief Encounter" onwards up to "The Bridge on the River Quai" – also with Guinness and Jack Hawkins and also produced by the wily Sam Spiegel – but while his work is sometimes touched by brilliance, I have always felt he fell short of exercising that extra visionary flair which would set him in the pantheon of the gods. What is it? A certain English restraint? Perhaps, but admire him I most certainly do.

* * *

I referred to the infamous duo of Chuck and Bobby, the two prop men recording with key-rings the sound effect of Sharif emerging through the mirage in that stunning shot, and I can't resist another digression here for an anecdote or two about them. Chuck, round-faced on round short body, was a chirpy, cheeky Italian Cockney much of whose early life had been spent at His Majesty's pleasure in a Borstal. When it came to the moment of his release, he was interviewed to assess what trade might be suitable for him. Various possibilities were put to him – plumbing, electrician, building, etc – for all of which Chuck felt himself to be eminently unsuitable. In the end, throwing up his hands in despair, the Careers Officer said "Well, its hopeless and there's nothing for it – you'll just have to join the film industry". We already know that Wardour Street was the only street in London which was 'shady on both sides', but Chuck's talents as a chronic pilferer were a thing of wonder and a certain beauty. Nor was he shy, much to his prop partner Bobby's disapproval, of showing me as an adolescent, how to snaffle a lobster or two from MacFisheries or as many cigarettes and chocolates that could be crammed into the airline bag he always carried with him while the shopkeeper's back had been turned by him to find an article on the top shelf. Among the countless films he worked on was Kubrick's "Dr Strangelove" and you can be sure that not all of the fresh cream cakes, ordered each day from Harrods for the custard pie sequence which never made it to the final cut, went to waste – but found their way home with Chuck. After the demise of Shepperton, he found work as the backstage doorman in a West End theatre. After some time, the management noticed that more and more goods were disappearing from the hospitality suite – and when they raided Chuck's flat in Covent Garden, they found it stacked with enough stuff to fill a quartermaster's store. Hauled before the Beak, he was only saved from going back to prison again by his age and the testimony of a certain witness called Roy Boulting who was prepared to swear to the blameless record and upright character of the prisoner in the dock, who had been so many years in his employ at Shepperton. A forgivable economy with the truth for a very forgivable man. Bobby, who was hopelessly and faithfully in love with Judy Garland, and he made an odd couple, but were much loved by film-makers and stars across the world. The last time I made an unexpected visit to Chuck at his little flat he greeted me with "Lord-a-fucking-bove! Its the fucking guv'nor's fucking son!". Something of poet with the word "fuck" was our Chuck... I was very fond of him(and the snaffled lobsers were pretty good too...)

In my teens, now I was no longer a child and not seeing through a glass quite so darkly, I was also asking myself what were the key films which led me to understand that Cinema, at its best, really could be and was the art form I believed it to be. To answer that now I have had to go back in time but not quite so far back in the recesses of my memory – because the four examples I have chosen still sit close to the surface...

60. "INTOLERANCE"

(1916. Director: D.W.Griffith)

One. D.W.Griffith was one of the great innovators of Cinema, and this epic film is considered by many as a masterpiece of the silent era. He made it in indignant response to the criticism and censorship levelled at his previous film, "Birth of a Nation" (which was pretty damn epic too), in which his portrayal of black Americans really was a disgusting stereotype and his lauding of the Ku Klux Klan a mind-boggling folly! Great film-maker that he undoubtedly was, Griffith nevertheless held some really dubious, if not downright deplorable views.

Mandatory viewing for any student of film, I saw "Intolerance" in my 'teens and was suitably impressed: it's a behemoth of an achievement! Huge sets, thousands upon thousands of Extras (those were the days!) God only knows what the budget would have been by today's standards. Four separate stories of 'intolerance' in 4 different centuries (Belshazzar in Babylon, Jesus up against the Pharisees in Judea, the St Bartholomew's Day Massacre and a modern day story of capitalist exploitation in America) are linked together by the recurring image of The Eternal Mother(the great Lillian Gish) rocking a cradle through the passage of time. Forget about the sentimental, sometimes mawkish titles – Griffith had a penchant for giving his characters rather coy names (The Mountain Girl, The Boy, etc) – and concentrate on the imagery.

Griffith reserved most of his budget for the great Babylonian sequence – and, to be perfectly honest, I have reserved most of my memory of the film for that sequence too and it really is unforgettable. Not simply for the spectacle of thousands of all carefully choreographed Extras, (plus a troop of elephants), or for the massive set of the great walls and gate of Babylon, but also for Griffith's novel use of aerial photography (he used a hot-air balloon) allowing him to track the Camera into the action. Equally radical for its time was the intercutting of the 4 stories – which, as the film advances, becomes faster and faster, almost blurring the lines between one story and another. Quite simply, it was very bold. Finally, and as important, Griffith was experimenting with ways to make a Close Up(strange as it may seem now, Close Ups did not exist then) – and by closing down the iris to isolate one area of the screen, he was groping towards a solution and laying the foundations for what today we would call montage editing...

His influence was almost as huge as his sets – and, in particular, his work played no small part in developing the theories of one young man in the Soviet Union, a certain Sergei Mikhailovich Eisenstein... And it was he, of course, who was going to catapult the language of film into the modern day...But that would be nine years later in 1924...

*　*　*

Griffith didn't so much fall out of fashion as out of favour. There is a sad story of Eisenstein meeting him in New York in 1931 when the Russian was embarking on his own doomed adventure in America, which was to end so painfully with the disaster of "Que Viva Mexico", his ambitious portrait of that country financed by the left-wing American author, Upton Sinclair. By this time Griffith couldn't raise a dime from the Studios and ruefully confessed to Eisenstein that he was reduced to courting wealthy widows in the hope they would finance his films...It was all rather tacky and demeaning...."My name is Ozymandias, king of kings – Look upon my works, ye mighty, and despair"...

61. "BATTLESHIP POTEMKIN"

(1925. Director: Sergei Mikhailovich Eisenstein)

Two. If Griffith exercised a significant influence on Eisenstein, then, with "Battleship Potemkin", Eisenstein was going to influence pretty bloody well anyone and everyone else who has ever seen it! It was a cinematic earthquake – and its aftershock has been felt by everyone from successive film-makers to painters like Francis Bacon, quite apart from the millions of ordinary cinema-goers who saw it then and since. Not only for the power of its imagery, but also for introducing montage editing into the dictionary. A + B = C, Eisenstein would teach his film students – two images put together produce a third, the meaning and dynamic of the two, Put another way, he showed how a 'cut' inside a scene could and would produce the drama, the intended effect. Let's just say he invented 'editing'…

The story of the mutiny on board the Potemkin was, and was meant to be, an inspirational piece of revolutionary propaganda for the Soviets. In this it succeeded admirably – and how incredible today to think the film was actually banned in Britain until as late as 1954 for fear of its revolutionary influence inciting violent insurrection, and continued to be 'X' rated until the end of the 1970's (!!); whilst conversely, in Nazi Germany Goebbels would recognize it as a masterpiece and a model for all propaganda films (and the influence of that 'model' would be seen in Leni Riefenstahl's "Triumph of the Will" a decade later).

It is the famous 'Odessa Steps' sequence for which the film is most remembered. The lines of Cossack soldiers descending the steps to the port, their boots moving in unison, stopping step by step to fire on the 'people'; the recurring image of the pram bouncing down the steps; the screaming bloodied face of the old woman and her broken spectacles – all these have gone into history. The cutting, the rhythm, the dynamics of movement – all of these are hauntingly seared into my mind and they make for one of the most memorable and powerful sequences in Cinema. At the time of its release, many found the degree of violence unpalatable, although it is small beer by comparison to the depiction of violence we are used to seeing today. This may account for the film enjoying less success with the public than its rave reviews suggested it might receive. Not that this matters in the long run, for there it is today, right up there with the gods on Olympus.

* * *

Like Griffiths, Eisenstein was to fall out of favour too – his adventures in Mexico not only upset the Mexican and US authorities but also incurred the displeasure of Uncle Joe Stalin himself: Sergei Mikhailovich was chucked out of the States and sent home in disgrace. But, unlike his American mentor, he was eventually to be allowed back into the fold and would triumph again – with a film which also contained one of the most seminal pieces of film-making and which I must include as one of the four exercising a lasting influence upon me...

62. "ALEXANDER NEVSKY"

(1938. Director: Sergei Mikhailovich Eisenstein)

Three. There was no lack of spite and *Schadenfreude* towards Eisenstein from his fellow Russian film-makers, and they managed, by and large, to close him down for the best part of a decade after his return from The States after his ill-fated venture in Mexico. But grudgingly they had to admit – despite his 'formalist tendencies' and other political errors in portraying the socialist ideals – he was a formidable intellect and a unique creative talent. Nevertheless, this didn't stop them from attaching a co-director to this film as a 'minder' just to make sure none of those 'formalist tendencies' popped up out of the bag again. Hahaha – they might as well have delegated a donkey to do the job!

Alexander Nevsky was the great Russian hero who drove back and defeated the invasion of the Teutonic Knights of the Holy Roman Empire at Novgorod in the middle ages. Clad in menacing iron helmets, with white tunics and crosses, the Teutonic Knights are shown as a formidable and merciless killing machine. At their hands infants and babes are tossed to their deaths, others are hanged from towers, as they make their relentless advance into Russia....Yes, of course, the film was made in 1938 – and everyone knew what was coming and from where. Their ground troops, the infantry, also wear helmets so obviously similar to those worn by the Nazi troops that there is no room for any doubt. Their war machine seems unstoppable and the Russians in disarray, badly lacking in leadership. And then Alexander Nevsky (played by the great Nicolai Cherkassov) takes up the baton and makes a call to arms to save beloved Mother Russia. The decisive confrontation takes place on a frozen lake, in the great Battle on Ice sequence, during which Nevsky outwits the Teutons and sees them vanquished, their horses and the weight of their armour breaking the ice and sending them down to an icy death. Stirring stuff indeed!

Eisenstein started life in experimental/ revolutionary theatre (with Meyerhold) and I don't think he had much time for "naturalism" or "realism" *per se*. He was much more interested in composition, of the dynamics of frame and movement and, of course, their Montage. There is, therefore, a touch of theatricality in the way he treats his performances (Oh, dear – here come those 'formalist tendencies' again, I fear), but it is a style which works perfectly for this film – lending a grandeur and nobility to Nevsky and a frightful sense of menace to the Teutons. The Battle on Ice is thrilling – with great blocks of almost abstracted groups of the armies moving this way and that, culminating with the fatal horseback charge of the Teutons and their armies' collapse into an icy watery grave. It was filmed at the height of a sweltering summer, presenting a real challenge to Eisenstein's long time and faithful cameraman, Eduard Tisse, and how he overcame these obstacles is a fascinating story in itself.

Prokoviev wrote the magnificent score, working closely with Eisenstein all the way through production. It is a truly real film score, integrally involved in the action and way beyond being the usual wallpaper to hide a thousand cracks that many film scores end up being. The last time I saw the film must have been some twenty-five years ago when it was screened at The Royal Festival Hall – with a full symphony orchestra and chorus playing the score live! Goosebumps galore – a glorious experience which made me wish for the return of the silent days... and a time when going to 'the pictures' was still an *event*...

63. "THE PASSION OF JOAN OF ARC"

(1928. Director: Carl Dreyer)

And Four...Falconetti in Close-Up...head shaven, eyes sorrowing... Falconetti in Close-Up after Close-Up as a saintly simple country girl, Joan, called by God to deliver France, being slowly martyred at the hands of her ecclesiastical Inquisitors... A film of Close-Ups...A poem of Close-Ups searching, studying, revealing the innermost, invisible heart and emotions of its heroine, leading her all the way to her inevitable death at the stake. For France, for faith, for truth..?God, what a film!

Quite a few French chauvinistic feathers were ruffled when it was announced that Dreyer, a Dane, would make a film about France's national icon (well, they do that from time to time, the French, don't they – get all anally retentive about their national treasures), but I don't suppose that bothered Dreyer a single jot. His script was based on the actual transcripts of Joan's trial at Rouen when she had been captured by the English and follows her ordeal through to her death at the stake. The trickery, hypocrisy and malice employed by her 3 inquisitors (including one played by mad-eyed Antonin Artaud) more intent on proving they are right by getting her to recant than on finding the truth is matched by the patent sincerity and simplicity of Joan's belief in her visions and her mission. It is made all the more poignant because everyone in the audience already knows how it will end – and this leads us to share more keenly in the anguish of her ordeal. The continued, repeated Close-Ups of Falconetti's refusals to give in; the Low-Angle Close-Ups of her tormentors combine to make it all seem like some terrible ritualistic piece of theatre... which, in some ways, is exactly what it was. The effect, however, is immensely powerful – the Camera scrutinizing the faces with such surgical detachment to show warts and all, every flicker of emotion, that the film builds to such intensity that you rather wish they would just get it over with and kill the poor girl there and then.

I first saw it, or a fragment of it, by proxy, as it were, through Godard's 1962 "Vivre Sa Vie" in which Anna Karina playing a prostitute is watching it and identifying with the suffering of Joan. For the life of me, however, I cannot remember where or when I saw the film itself – but I do remember that it knocked me sideways and that I could never look at a Close-Up ever again without some part of my brain and heart stirring with the recollection of that amazing face of Falconetti (photographed, incidentally, by the same Rudolf Maté who would later shoot Lubitsch's "To be or Not to Be"). To achieve the effects he wanted, Dreyer used no make-up and Falconetti had to endure hours kneeling on a hard stone floor – the pain we see was very real.

The film cost a lot of money to make. It was hailed as a masterpiece on release but was an almighty financial flop! Cuts were made to it by order of the Censors and the Archbishop of Paris and over the years several different versions appeared. The original negative was destroyed by fire and it looked like the film was lost forever. Then, some years ago, a copy of Dreyer's original cut was discovered In Oslo – ironically and perhaps appropriately in a hospital for the mentally insane....Funny, isn't it, where films turn up – Fritz Lang's "Metropolis" resurfacing in an obscure museum in Argentina, and Dreyer's Joan in a lunatic asylum....The great Henri Langlois of the Paris Cinematheque was forever nosing around in dustbins and pulling out film cans of lost treasures ...I wonder where he would find them today..? And how many have been lost forever..?

* * *

If these 4 films influenced my thinking as a teenager and contributed to the process of honing my own sensibilities, keystones, as it were, then I also realise there are many others which, although less significant in their impact, nevertheless have made such an impression on me that they have stuck in my mind forever...The teen years are impressionable, of course, but they are also formative – a tremendous clash between the personal dream awakening and the outside world surrounding it. The Jesuits want the first seven years of a child's life to catch him or her forever, but perhaps that's because they also knew that there is nothing you can do to control the battleground that starts with puberty – try as you may, it's a lost cause. I was lucky (or unlucky) enough to enter adolescence just as everything in society was being questioned and the appetite for 'new' and 'experiment' was voracious – only to gradually discover that, of course, it always had been…We just didn't know…

'Surreal' has become one of those over-used words which has lost some its currency along the way. André Breton and the Surrealists laid out their ideas and concept of surrealism back in their 1930's manifesto, which I haven't read, but I do know that the next director was invited to join them only to find himself kicked out almost before he had got in through their revolving door. Well, purists can be a pretty earnest bunch and maybe, like General Jack. D.Ripper in Kubrick's "Dr Strangelove" they felt their "precious bodily fluids" were under threat from this maverick film-maker. If 'surreal' also allows for the absurd, for social criticism also to involve a wickedly morbid sense of humour, then the director they expelled from their Parisian group must surely qualify as surreal as surreal can be…He also happened to be bloody good at making films as well…

64. "VIRIDIANA"

(1961. Director: Luis Buñuel)

After years in exile in Mexico, Luis Buñuel, the "bad boy surrealist" of Spain who had so upset the establishment with "Le Chien Andalou", "L'Age D'Or" and his damning documentary "Land without Bread" was allowed to return to the country of his birth, where he promptly proceeded to upset Franco and the Church all over again with his film "Viridiana". Mischievous, irreverent and some would say (and did) blasphemous, its humour is caustic, its symbolism crude and vulgar, a deliciously iconoclastic film and altogether a tremendous swipe at the hypocritical pretensions of the country which had rejected him so many years before. Franco, maybe celebrated for his truly remarkable bladder control, was never noted for his sense of humour though, and must have cursed the day he ever allowed Buñuel back to Spain, as much as Buñuel probably relished reducing "the dwarf of Salamanca" to an apoplectic froth of puritan outrage. Vintage Buñuel – but also, look at it carefully, very Spanish, a country rich in the dilemma of paradox and a dark cynicism!

The silver-blonde, chaste novice nun preparing to take her vows (Sylvia Pinal perfectly cast) visits her only living relative on his run down farm, an ageing uncle (the immaculate Fernando Rey) who has been supporting her and now living alone with a housekeeper. He is struck by his niece's resemblance to his late wife and persuades her to dress in her wedding dress (Buñuel could never resist a fetish or two). Having drugged her drink, he then lays her out on his bed with every intention of deflowering her, but thinks better of it. Nevertheless, in the hope it will persuade her to stay, this doesn't stop him from telling her that he has in fact taken her virginity and thus she can no longer return to the convent. But then stricken by moral conscience he confesses that this, too, is a lie and, before she can return to a life dedicated to God, promptly goes out and hangs himself. She, together with an illegitimate nephew (worldly-wise Francisco Rabal) inherit the property.

Rather than return now to the convent, instead she takes in a very motley bunch of paupers, waifs and stray individuals, with the noble intention of dedicating herself to morally reforming and educating them through the virtues of faith, hope and charity (mostly the charity). Her cynical cousin, however, is altogether more impressed by her potential voluptuousness than by her lofty ideals, but any attempts to insinuate himself are in vain. Frustrated in his desires, he simply takes up with the only too willing housekeeper instead.

Taking advantage of the two cousins' absence on business, the waifs and strays grab the opportunity to let themselves into the main house and have themselves a party, helping themselves to anything they can lay their hands on. So much for charity! The sequence ends with them having a banquet – set around the table in a direct parody of Da Vinci's 'Last Supper'… When the owners return, Francisco Rabal gives them short shrift and chucks them all off the property… And his chaste cousin has her eyes quietly opened. The film ends with her discovering her cousin in bed with the housekeeper … he invites her in to play cards with them – and this time she says 'yes', entering the room and closing the door behind her…and on us…

Buñuel has a direct, almost matter-of-fact style. The Camera does not move, and improbable, illogical events are made plausible through his confidence in just showing them happen and then moving on. He doesn't play them up – he makes them ordinary – The Uncle feels guilty remorse, so he hangs himself – so what, end of story, move on! This is what gives them their power and impact, possibly also the 'surreal' quality Buñuel is famous for. In fact, "Viridiana" is more naturalistic than many of his other films. The "dwarf of Salamanca" and The Church between them had the film banned and Spain would have to wait the best part of 15 years for Franco's death in 1975 before it was released. It won the Palme D'Or as Best Film at Cannes, and enjoyed a critical and commercial success worldwide.

Its not my favourite film of one of my very most favourite directors, but it strongly impacted me at a time when I was discovering my own attachment to the frequently paradoxical Spanish sensibility – you can see it all the way on from Cervantes, in Goya, in Velasquez,…and later in the terrible contradictions of the 1936 Civil War on into our times. Earthy, carnal, cruelly satirical at times …yet also so capable of such dignity and honour, of reaching into the ecstatic…

65. "THE DISCREET CHARM OF THE BOURGEOISIE"

(1972. Director: Luis Buñuel)

Dreams, of course, are part and parcel of the surrealist dictionary – especially anxiety ones, dreams of the morbid, of decay, of unspecified guilt and uncertain fears – and they play an important and recurring role in Buñuel's work. There is no shortage of them either in this delightful and often very amusing story of 6 upper middle-class friends trying to get together to have a dinner and forever being thwarted by one absurd or bizarre obstacle or another. In some ways it harks back to his "Exterminating Angel" in which the guests at a party suddenly find themselves unable to leave. "The Discreet Charm…", however, is lighter and altogether less nightmarish in tone. Mature Buñuel, Buñuel with his ever mischievous tongue in his cheek…but nevertheless still taking a bloody good tilt at the hypocrisies of the 'bourgeoisie' and digging into the darker recesses of the human soul at the same time.

He assembled a really superb cast for this film – Fernando Rey as a Latin American Ambassodor, in fear of a real or imaginary revolutionary girl; Delphine Seyrig at her most elegant with her husband, Paul Frankeur and her petulant, spoilt younger sister, Bulle Ogier, in tow; Stephane Audran and Jean-Pierre Cassel, all polished charm and manners and taking on a Bishop as their gardener. But there's also Michel Picccoli and Claude Piéplu doing their bit too, plus a whole gallery of excellent character actors. Together they make the ingredients for a wonderful dish – if only the 6 friends could finally sit at a table to eat it!

From their first aborted attempt when they turn up to find they are not expected and nothing prepared; to arriving *chez* Audran and

Cassel who escape through their bedroom window, more intent on having sex than serving dinner, and leaving their hungry guests alone downstairs; to the interruption of a Colonel and his officers commandeering their home to conduct some military exercise just as it looks they might get their dinner at last, the 6 friends all behave with impeccable manners throughout, their mounting frustration masked behind their good breeding. At times it is absurdly hilarious – the improbable and illogical breaking through the veneer into the cracks of their civilized universe.

The dreams come in and out – sometimes even becoming a dream within a dream. They sit down at a dinner only to find that they are in a theatre and the curtain rising. Cold sweat and anxiety overcome them as they realize they do not know their lines. A young soldier is asked by his Colonel to tell his story and we are led into a world of the ghostly dead. Ambassador Rey dreams of being mowed down by the guerillas threatening his country only to awake in another cold sweat and urgently stuff himself with comfort food from his fridge....And throughout the film, a scene is intercut of all of them seen walking down a country road towards...toward what..? Its irresistible stuff and, whatever you think of him, Buñuel certainly knew how to have fun!

The film duly won the Oscar as Best Foreign Film and went on to make considerable amounts of money for its Producer, Serge Silberman... which he promptly re-invested in the Spanish master to give us the satisfaction of two more films before Buñuel drank his last favourite dry martini and went to give St Peter a headache in that other place...

* * *

Don Luis' love of a finely made dry martini is legendary but there were only a few places in the world where he believed they could make a good one. One of them was the monastery/hotel of San Paular, outside Madrid, up in the Guadalajara mountains, where he would go to write his screenplays. I went there once with my then girlfriend, later wife for some years and mother of my daughter, together with another friend while I was filming a series for Channel-4. In the sombre gloom of the great big gothic bar (and how well the Spanish do 'gloom'!) I asked the old barman whether it would be possible for him to make us dry martinis "in the style of Don Luis Buñuel". With that immaculate dignity the Spanish also do so well, he replied "Don Luis is no longer with us – I regret, señor, that therefore this is not possible...". It was a chastening moment – and a touching show of loyalty and respect for the old master...

I suppose you could say that Buñuel was the father of Spanish Cinema – certainly his influence can be felt in the works of many of their directors, including Pedro Almodóvar today. I think it is also lurking there in the films of the next director on this list...or, equally possible, is it just that they all share in a common pool of sensibility that is peculiarly Spanish..?

66. "EL ESPÍRITU DE LA COLMENA"
(The Spirit of The Beehive)

(1973. Director: Victor Erice)

Victor Erice is a poet – I mean, a real poet: and this, one of his very few films, a poem of translucent beauty. Finely scripted (by Erice), an allegory rich in carefully observed metaphor, beautifully shot by the great Luis Cuadrado, the action pared down to the most delicate essentials, and acted with solemn grace by all the players, for me it is a true masterpiece of pure cinema, as simple as that.

The story takes place in a obscure little village on the arid, dusty plains of Castile. The Civil War has ended and Spain lies in the grip of Franco and the victorious Nationalists. A sensitive little girl of 7, (played by the extraordinary mournful-eyed Ana Torrent – the only name of the cast I can recall, because she was just too remarkable to forget), lives with her slightly older sister and parents – their father, and his much younger wife. Neither of the parents – in fact nobody – talks to one another around the family table – indeed the fabric of family seems to have broken down altogether. Their father devotes his time to the study of bees, while his wife writes endless letters to someone who might well have been her lover in the past. They – and everything – appear to be in a kind of quiet mourning for a past dream they had hoped for.

Into the village rolls a van with a mobile cinema to show the old classic "Frankenstein". Doubtless, for the Nationalists, Frankenstein's monster is the embodiment of the godless, atheistic socialism which they had so recently conquered and which must be destroyed whenever it shows its face. For impressionable and thoughtful little Ana, however, moved when watching how the Monster kneels down by the lake and so sweetly and tenderly offers a flower to the child he is about to unintentionally kill, she cannot understand why he must be killed too...her sympathies lie with him, not the vengeful society around him. Her elder sister, pragmatic and manipulative, tells her the Monster doesn't really die – that it's a film and films are only make-believe fakes. Moreover, she plants the idea in her sister's mind that, if she closes her eyes and wishes, she can summon back the Monster to her...The innocent dreamer child, Ana, takes this to heart... 1973 was a long time ago and I would be deceiving myself and everyone else to claim I can remember all the details since the time I saw it at George Hoellering's late and much lamented Academy Cinemas in Oxford Street, where so many of the finest "art films" got to be shown. But the memory is not lost, even if it is forgotten – it is there still, as a tone, as a sensation, as glimpses of the honeyed light and the melancholy hues of ochres, browns and blues of a sorrowful Spain, bereft of its life-blood. I can still just about recall the fugitive Republican soldier (the lover to whom Ana's mother has been writing?) also kneeling down gently by the little girl, just as the Monster had done in "Frankenstein" – and like him being hunted down and shot by the police. I see, too, the elder sister pricking her own finger to use the blood as lipstick; the bees and the question of what law, invisible to man, makes so many thousands of these creatures instinctually obedient to the same law and order. And I recall that at the end there is the sense of a beginning of wounds being healed, the past being put aside for the sake of the future, of family returning – and of Ana, the dreamer child, closing her eyes at the window and wishing...

Simplicity is not achieved by being simple – rather it is like steel that has been tempered again and again on the anvil. Erice's film glints like a sword and cuts silently through the air with an effortless grace shining with humanity. Truly wonderful! Spain has no shortage of original talents but, as quite possibly many of his peers might wistfully agree, Erice is one of those special creators who is beyond the reach of us all.

* * *

I cannot leave Spain without tipping my hat in the direction of its finest living film-maker, Pedro Almodóvar. But before I do – and whilst 'surrealism' is still in the air, I want to include a haunting film made by Georges Franju, a highly original French film-maker who has been sadly neglected today. I have included this 1960 film of his not only because it is an extraordinary film in its own right, but also because it so clearly influenced the film of Almodovar's I have chosen and which he made almost half a century later.

67. "LES YEUX SANS VISAGE"
("Eyes without a Face")

(1960. Director: Georges Franju)

Is this a horror film? You bet it is! Creepy, scary, psychologically disturbing, sprinkled with surreal symbolism, it is as mesmeric and haunting as Wiene's "The Cabinet of Dr Caligari" was back in 1920. Both live in a dream world where fantasy impinges upon reality to ghastly effect.

A brilliant Doctor (Pierre Brasseur) is riddled with guilt for being responsible for the car accident which has horribly disfigured his beautiful daughter's face. Cut off from the outside world and living with her father in a country chateau, her face covered by a mask, showing only her eyes, she looks as if she has just stepped out of a Magritte painting. Obsessed with restoring her to her former loveliness by grafting on a new face, the Doctor takes to luring in unsuspecting girls upon whom he can conduct his experiments. In this he is aided by his assistant (the wonderful Alida Valli) whose unquestioning loyalty derives from her gratitude to him for restoring her own previously disfigured face. Although the Daughter has a fiancé, the only real outlet for her human need for tenderness and affection are the caged German Shepherds and doves the Doctor also keeps for his lab experiments. Being slowly driven half-crazy by their confinement they readily reciprocate her gentle attentions, in no way disturbed by her mutilated appearance.

The graft he performs on his daughter, having lifted the face off his kidnapped victim – herself now so hideously deformed she kills herself – goes badly wrong and he is obliged to get his Assistant to lure in another unsuspecting girl in order to retry again...And so the whole gruesome cycle begins all over again...

But the Daughter, irrespective of her deformed appearance, is tired of being a guinea-pig – tired indeed of a loveless existence so far removed from the norms of humanity. Moreover, it has steadily been loosening her own grip on sanity…By the end, before another hideous graft can take place, she has freed all the caged animals, stabbed her father's assistant in the neck and witnessed him being savagely disfigured by one of the German Shepherds and then mauled to death by the others….Disfigurement is the key word for the film which closes with the Daughter, seemingly unmoved by her father's death, wandering off into the woods…a white dove perched on her arm…It could be another Magritte too.. The film was both praised and reviled as disgusting. I found it very unsettling, but was glued to the screen from start to finish. Franju knew his craft and knew how to balance this unpleasant story so that it never becomes gothic horror but more a moral fable – about obsession, guilt, misplaced affection and the fragility of sanity. Although 'realist' in style, it remains for me an essentially surreal experience – and no worse for that.

* * *

Certainly it is a film which prompts immediate comparisons with the next film on the list. Until I saw his wonderful "Volver" with Penelope Cruz, and "Talk to Her", I was never entirely convinced by Pedro Almodóvar – impressed, fascinated,yes, but nevertheless something held me back from giving him the outright acceptance his very unique talents deserve. I remained cautious, on guard…"Volver" changed all that and this next film confirmed for me what so many others had realized a long time before: that Almodóvar is an exceptional creative talent…well, I always was a bit of a late developer…

68. "EL PIEL QUE HABITO"
("The Skin I Live in")

(2011. Director: Pedro Almodóvar)

If Franju's film is spooky, then Almodóvar's is spine-chilling, the silent scream of an extended nightmare. As coldly precise as the work of the surgeon in his film Almodóvar succeeds in evoking horror without ever showing it explicitly. Instead, it is like being stood blindfolded in front of a late Goya, with someone whispering distantly into your ear to suggest what horrors the painting may or may not be depicting: reality becomes more frightening by remaining invisible. It also feels deeply rooted within that part of the Spanish temper which never strays too far from the morbid and the dark. In the same way that people slow down their cars when they pass an accident on a motorway, we are forced, despite ourselves, to *imagine* beyond anything we are actually seeing: extremely uncomfortable.

Antonio Banderas plays Robert, a plastic surgeon, haunted by the traumas of his past, now experimenting in the present on the body a young woman, Vera, (Elena Anaya) to both exorcise his demons yet also exercise revenge by turning her into an exact replica of his late wife. Working alone and out of the scrutiny of the public eye on his estate, he is accompanied and served by only an ageing servant, Marillia (Marisa Paredes), as, with the same cold, clinical precision Bandera practices his skills on Vera, Almodóvar peels back the skin, layer by layer, to reveal their background stories – Dr Robert's wife, hideously disfigured in a car crash, during an affair with a man who turns out to be Dr Robert's brother, and who has spent years in darkness before jumping to her death when accidentally catching sight of herself in a mirror; their daughter, suffering psychosis who has been raped by another young man, Vicente, and who has also jumped to her death; and Vicente, abducted and held in captivity by Dr Robert and on whom the plastic surgeon has been executing revenge over six years by re-assigning his gender and turning him into Vera. And it also transpires that Marillia, the servant, is mother to both Dr Robert and also the brother responsible for his wife's horrendous burns in the car crash. Convoluted and precariously close to melodrama, Almodovar navigates his way through and succeeds, as a mature film-maker, in steering away from the pitfalls which could have beset this story. Everything is conducted at a sedate pace, cool and detached, visually so elegant and surgically clean, a polished veneer screening the dark horrors beneath. As I said, very unsettling. In the end, Vera, now transformed into a beautiful young woman, shoots both Dr Robert and Marillia and flees back to her/his mother's dress shop in town where he announces himself to her with the final words of the film: "I am Vicente"...Terrifying!

Identity, gender, betrayal, revenge...all familiar themes in Almodóvar's repertoire, but, whereas in the past he might approach them with a nervous excitability tipping over, at times, into the shrill, he exercises here a restraint entirely appropriate to his story and its themes which makes the film even more disturbing and truly scary. Sumptuously photographed by Jose Luis Alcaín and with an equally elegant score by Almodóvar's long-time collaborator, Alberto Iglesias, "El Piel que Habito" seems to me to be a summation of all that is original, unique and even witty in this masterly director's work and confirms his place on the world stage as one of the very best film-makers.

***

Serendipitously, just as I was sitting down to recall this next film, a clip of my favourite scene popped up on television out of the blue – a timely and much appreciated aide-memoire. How strange to be sitting in my favourite room in my favourite Apartelle in Manila on the other side of the globe, writing about the movies in my life and for this one to show up right on cue. And how strange to jump from surreal, visceral Spain to the very different, but equally visceral humanity of India.

69. "THE WORLD OF APU"

(1959. Director: Satyajit Ray)

This is the last film in the "Apu" trilogy,(which had started 4 years previously with the wonderful "Pather Panchali"), made by the great Bengali director, Satyajit Ray. It is a tender, compassionate work, with a humanity which reaches out to us all. When we think of Indian Cinema, we tend to think of the great film dream factory in Mumbai, churning out a film a day – but, without disparaging Bollywood, the Bengali film industry on the other side of the sub-continent in Calcutta is rather more aesthetically inclined…or was during this epoch. Ray was without question its finest son, related more to the Italian neo-realists than to the extravagant song and dance fantasies of Bollywood and more concerned with the social complexities of his world.

Apu works as a minor clerk (and, by God, Calcutta teems with them!), but really he aspires to be a writer and is working on a novel. A friend takes him to a village wedding, where it is discovered the bridegroom-to-be is mentally deficient and the bride's mother calls off the ceremony. Hindu tradition dictates, however, that if the girl is not married off on that same auspiciously appointed day, then she must remain unmarried for the rest of her life – a fate worse than death. Reluctantly, Apu is persuaded to step into the breach, the wedding goes ahead and he takes his young bride back to a new life and world in Calcutta, living in the strange surroundings of his dingy flat overlooking the railway lines. He doesn't know her, she doesn't know him and the nervousness, uncertainty of both is handled with gripping sensitivity by Ray – how, we ask ourselves, can this union of two complete strangers possibly work? Then, in a beautifully judged scene, we see this lovely young girl rising one morning beside her husband, but with the corner of her sari caught beneath his body.

She pulls it away and then turns and playfully slaps his wrist: with this one simple gesture we know everything is alright – and when Apu then opens his eyes, smiles, gazing happily at his wife, we also know that not only is everything going to be alright but they have fallen deeply in love with one another as well. It is an immensely moving and tender moment – there in the grubby little flat with the trains rattling the windows, their happiness is almost palpable. All the more painful, therefore, when it is shattered when she dies giving birth to their son. Grief-stricken, Apu cannot help blaming the baby for her death and cannot bear to be near him. He hands the infant over to his wife's parents while he abandons both the city and his novel to wander the roads of India, half-crazed by his loss. It is some years before his friend can track him down and persuade him to re-unite with his son and resume his responsibilities. The child, of course, cannot recognize him as his father, but accepts him as a friend. Together, the child astride Apu's shoulders, they set off to return to Calcutta... and Apu smiles again...It is very moving.

The trilogy established Ray as a director of world stature and influence. The social realism of the films also gave the world a different perception of India, besides introducing us all to that other great Bengali talent, Ravi Shankar, who wrote the music. Ray sits up there with other such greats, like Renoir or Kurosawa for instance, whose works transcend language and nationality and are stamped with the universality of our common humanity. Indelibly so, in my case...

* * *

How I got to meet Satyajit Ray in Calcutta in the early 1970's might justify another digression with this anecdote. His films had played no small part in my decision to travel round India – not in search of a guru or spiritual enlightenment as was the 'hippy' fashion of the time, but because I was fascinated to explore a culture so completely different from my own European one. In Calcutta I wanted to get a permit to travel to Darjeeling, which meant a long trek round office after office, caverns piled high to the roof with paperwork and worthy of something out of Kafka. I finally ended up in a police station where I could get the appropriate stamp to a piece of paper which would then authorize my journey. When the Police Inspector learnt I was involved in film, he brushed aside all bureaucratic formality, called for the tea-wallah, and proceeded to tell me what a movie fan he was himself. Indeed, so much so, that the next thing I knew was that he had launched into a replay of the last few minutes of "Now Voyager", playing both Bette Davis and Paul Henreid's parts, word for word. His rendering, in that disarming accent the Indians have when speaking English, of the last line in the film "Oh, Jerry, don't ask for the moon – we have the stars!" was almost as surreal as anything in Buñuel, and as funny as a scene out of Woody Allen, yet at the same time astonishingly touching. At the end of this unique performance (watched with profound admiration from start to finish by the tea-wallah who doubtless had heard it all before), the Inspector told me that he lived in a compound and his home overlooked that of none other than Satyajit Ray's. So when I expressed my own admiration for Ray, the Inspector invited me to go along with him and try and meet the great man. Which we did – for all of 10-15 minutes, as our visit was unannounced and Ray rather busy. I remember nothing of what few words we exchanged – but was rather dazzled by his brilliantly laundered white shirt and the gracious courtesy that went with it... Having taken our leave, the Inspector then kindly invited me to his home for supper and entertained me and his family with a few more extracts from his favourite films....From the slightly strained smiles on their faces, I got the impression the family rather wished the Head of the Household would knock it on the head and give it a rest for awhile...but that "Oh, Jerry, don't ask for the moon – we have the stars, (isn't it!?)" In that Calcutta police station? With that accent? – Priceless memory!...

Those strained smiles stitched politely to the Inspector's family's faces, reminds me quite suddenly of a similar somewhat constipated smile on Woody Allen's face, playing a theatrical agent, trying as hard as possible to seem enthusiastic as he listens to the pitch of a particularly unpromising act. It occurs in one of my most favourite films of that prolific director...

70. "BROADWAY DANNY ROSE"

(1984. Director: Woody Allen)

What I liked so much about this film is its affectionate warmth and sense of decency towards the hapless characters whose lives run through this story of a theatrical agent, Danny Rose(Woody Allen) whose clients really are rather hopelessly untalented. But be they a couple with a balloon twisting act, or a lady playing musical glasses, or a gentleman with a sorry canary act, Danny is touchingly loyal to all of them and never deflates their hopes that one day big success will come their way. It is very funny, but never at their expense.

Danny's story is told in retrospect by a group of comedians gathered together in a Broadway Deli where we learn one of Danny's clients is a singer whose career is on the rebound (Nick Apollo Forte); who is having an affair with a girl (Mia Farrow); who, in turn, has a jealous ex-lover who is a member of the 'mob'. Fearful for his own safety, the singer persuades Danny to take his place and masquerade as Mia Farrow's lover to divert attention – while he goes along to a big gig in front of Milton Berle which might lead to even greater things. So jealous is the Ex that he orders a 'hit' on Danny – and threatens him and the girlfriend at gunpoint with their lives. Danny only saves both their skins by convincing the Ex he is just a front – and that the real lover is another of his clients, currently away playing the cruise ships...

His singer, revived by Danny's secret formula from a complete alcoholic stupor, does indeed get to perform in front of Milton Berle – and indeed sees his fortunes revive. So much is his gratitude to Danny that he promptly fires him on the spot (encouraged by his girlfriend) to take on a more prestigious manager. And the poor client on the cruise ships who Danny has ratted on to save his own skin gets badly beaten up for his pains. Danny does the decent thing and pays his hospital bills. At the end Danny gives a party for his sorry, but decent bunch of clients – to which a contrite Mia Farrow comes to ask forgiveness…Loyal to a fault, Danny is never going to make the 'big time' – but, as the group of comedians gathered in the Deli reflect, he gets rewarded with the highest accolade of them all: a sandwich named after him in the famous Deli…and no greater praise can be better than that.

Woody Allen is one heck of a craftsman and a masterly director of his actors. This very funny and touching film was shot in black and white by the excellent Gordon Willis (who also shot "Manhattan" for Allen) and has a real feel of the slightly grimy world of Broadway. It is perceptive too in its observations of the down-at-heel dignity of these very minor players in show-biz. They are the little people and Allen does them proud, gently giving them their moment in the sun. I love the film: its has a beguiling and charming modesty.

71. "MANHATTAN"

(1979. Director: Woody Allen)

From the extensive canon of Woody Allen's work, it is difficult to choose a favourite – "Crimes and Misdemeanours" perhaps, for Martin Landau's knock-out performance, and much more besides? "Hannah and her Sisters"? Or even the more recent and delicious confection "Midnight in Paris"? Uneven as his work may be, there's always something in his films to enjoy and appreciate – and I don't suppose there's a living actor left on the face of the earth who hasn't and hasn't wanted to work with him. Its amazing! And on he goes – pumping them out year after year. Admirable.

I have settled for "Manhattan" because it is in many way quintessential Allen and also a tremendously witty and affectionate portrait of a city he clearly loves. Beautifully filmed in wide-screen black and white by Gordon Willis, the city is as much a protagonist as the characters moving through the story he has placed within it as if it was almost part of their DNA. Gershwin's 'Rhapsody in Blue' effectively accompanies and enhances Allen's romantic attachment to the city and shows his more sentimental side so often hidden behind his comedic wit. Perhaps this, too, is part of his Jewish sensibility and humour – so frequently wracked by angst and doubts about his feelings and thoughts on pretty well anything and everything in life.

Being part of the American liberal intelligentsia *and* New Yorkers, as you would expect in an Allen film, the relationships in the film are fairly convoluted and their meaning openly debated at every twist and turn. It amuses my slightly reserved English sensibility to see hearts worn so openly on the sleeve, but Allen portrays it all as if its almost a compulsion or social necessity, a sign of your 'liberation', to discuss your relationships as well as your sexual life and proclivities in as public a way as possible – in one delightfully funny scene at a smart socialite gathering, a lady earnestly declares that she has no problem in having orgasm, but that her therapist has worried her by advising her that they are the wrong kind! Allen looks on in polite dismay and mutters, almost apologetically, that, personally, for him it had never been a problem…weren't orgasms – well, just orgasms.? There's the inevitable amount of snobbish NY posturing and phoniness going on all around, but Allen makes light of it and it come across as almost endearingly naïve.

He plays a disillusioned TV Producer in his '40's, whose wife (Meryl Streep) has not only left him for another woman, but is also threatening to publish a 'warts and all' account of their marriage. With a fairly high dosage of existential angst coursing through his veins, he is currently dating a very much younger 17-year old Drama Student(the statuesque and husky-voiced Mariel Hemingway). In our own times, this is dangerous territory to step into and I wonder if Allen wouldn't think twice about depicting such a relationship if he set out to make the same film today. Although it worries him, she doesn't seem the least bit bothered by their age difference – refreshingly free from any cant or posturing, she just follows her own feelings without complicating matters. But this is a Woody Allen film, so of course its going to get complicated. So when she tells him she is thinking of going to do a Drama Course in London, he actively encourages her, seeing it as a way to extricate himself from a relationship about which he has so many anguished doubts. And pretty soon he has started an affair with the more suitably aged mistress(Diane Keaton) of his married best friend (the solid and amiable Michael Murphy) – she riddled with doubts and he riddled with guilt And so it goes on, like a merry-go-round, with much soul-searching and sparkling with that brand of Jewish New York wit which Allen is so good at…

The fact is that he is having a hard time of it all working out what is real – so at the end decides to make a list – certain bits of music… literature come to mind…and finally the smile of young Mariel

Hemingway. In a final sequence (echoes of Shirley Maclaine at the end of "The Apartment", glimmers of Jean-Pierre Leaud's long run in "Les Quatre Cents Coups") he dashes through the streets to find her. He arrives to find she is already packed and ready to go to London – and now it is his turn to try and dissuade her, to plead she stay with him in N.Y. But its too late – she's going. This doesn't mean she has stopped loving him – but shouldn't he learn to accept that not everyone has lost their integrity…shouldn't he learn to trust? Cut to Manhattan night skyline. Cue Gershwin. Light up the sky with fireworks…leave the cinema with a warm glow in one's heart…

72. "A SERIOUS MAN"

(2009. Writer/Director : The Coen Brothers)

The reasonable percentage of Jewish blood I can claim naturally attracts me to Woody Allen's brand of humour, as it does to this excellent film by the Coen Brothers about a decent Jewish family man (Michael Stuhlbarg) who wakes up one morning to find his world is falling apart, without rhyme or reason. Out of the blue, his wife is asking for a *get* (Jewish divorce) so she can marry some ghastly banal widower full of salesman-sincerity; his jobless brother has moved in and spends his time drawing maps of 'universal probability' or in the bathroom "draining his sebaceous cyst"; his teenage daughter is either being bolshie or endlessly washing her hair; while his son, who is preparing for his barmitzvah, appears to be permanently stoned and in debt to a thug of a schoolmate who is the local dope dealer. To compound his sorrows, the minor state university at which he works as a professor, is insinuating that they are receiving poison pen letters which, if proven to be true, might well mean his tenure will not be renewed ...What has he done to deserve all this? Conscientious at home and at work, he is a good man – blameless. What has he done wrong, how has he offended God? Its just not fair. Echoes of the Book of Job...?

Set in the 1960's in a faceless Minnesota suburban town, with row after row of identical houses, his is a life about as bland as you could imagine. The only excitement he can derive is by standing on his roof and having vicarious (and guilty) erotic daydreams by peeping at his comely neighbour's private sunbathing. Michael Stuhlbarg plays his part superbly with an air of baffled, mutely pained resignation. Accepting whatever is thrown at him without a murmur of protest, nevertheless he has a good deal of inner resentment towards the God of his faith. Wanting to understand how he has somehow earned the castigation of this God, he consults his Rabbis from whom he receives advice as bland as the town in which he lives, leaving him none the wiser and even sadder. But the Chief Rabbi – known for his deeper wisdom – and whom he really wants to see, is never available…

Certainly concerned with faith, with the idea of fate, with sin and guilt – the whole gamut of Jewish (human) anxieties – the film is also wickedly funny, as you would expect from film-makers as intelligent as the Coen Brothers. As in all their films, the casting – down to the most minor role – is impeccable and their direction finely measured to include their usual observations of the quirky idiosyncrasies of human behaviour. They really know how to make us *look* and *think*. The twists and turns of their plot are immensely clever – Fate or accident intervening to balance out the scales of justice…So, towards the end, albeit in a haze of marijuana, his son does get through his barmitzah without a hitch; his wife does kind of come back to him; and his tenure at the university is secured; even the loopy brother has some form of rehabilitation – with or without his "universal probabilities" maps and "sebaceous cyst"! The Coen Brothers, however, won't let us off the hook so easily with a conventional happy ending: after a routine medical check-up, our serious man receives a phone call urgently requesting him to come in to discuss his X-Ray results. It doesn't bode well. And the town itself prepares to batten down its hatches as a furious typhoon is seen approaching…These things happen…they just do…where is the hand of God?...In a delightful little scene, just right before the end, the son is ushered into the presence of the elusive Chief Rabbi after his barmitzvah and returned his confiscated transistor radio(in which, incidentally, he has hidden his stash of dope). The wise old ancient is as near to being in a catatonic trance as is possible but there is a glint in his rheumy old eyes as he pushes back the radio across his desk and advises the young man to "be a good boy". He is either as sharp as his whistling impaired odontological prosthesis (a.k.a dentures – an awful word I detest using) or can think of nothing better to say….On points, I think the Coen Brothers are telling us that there is nothing else to say – your wife leaves you over breakfast one morning, or you are killed in a car accident, fired from your job, told you have cancer…The typhoon comes… You do your best to "be a good boy" because what else can you do?…These things happen…they just do…

"A Serious Man" is a serious film and obviously a very personal one. It shows a side to the Coen Brothers which sometimes I wish they would show more often. When receiving an Oscar for one of their films I remember them thanking the Academy for allowing them "to continue playing in our own corner of the sandpit". I hope they keeping digging with their bucket and spade in that corner of their's for a long time to come – but it would be interesting to see what they came up with if they dug a little deeper… (And, oh, before I forget – yes, it was photographed, yet again, by that gifted Mr Roger Deakins!)

* * *

To leap from a small town community in Minnesota today to the Warsaw Ghetto during World War II might seem a leap too far, were it not for the thread of the Jewish themes connecting them. The subject of The Holocaust and the obscene horrors of the "Final Solution" has been and continues to be one of the most important one of our times. It has been explored on film many times, of course – from Alain Resnais' brilliant short "Night and Fog" to Spielberg's "Schindler's List", but, to my mind, Polanksi's 2002 film(alongside Lazlo Kemes' more recent and brilliant "Son of Saul") stands out as one of the most powerful, and probably one of the most honest to have dipped into and tackled that dark stain on 20th century history, whose implications have permeated all our consciousnesses and resonate onwards into today ….

73. "THE PIANIST"

(2002. Director: Roman Polanski)

He has been dogged by so much scandal in his life that one sometimes forgets what a bloody good film-maker Polanski can be at his best – and "The Pianist" really is him at his very best.

Long-faced and melancholic Adrien Brody plays the pianist of the title. Drawn from the true life story of a celebrated Polish pianist, the film follows him from 1939 when he is playing for the radio as Britain declares war, to 1945 when Poland is finally liberated. It takes us on from him and his privileged family's initial misguided optimism at the outbreak of war to the cruelties and deprivations of the Warsaw Ghetto; on through his time as a slave-labourer for the Nazis; to his escape and life on the run, starving and struggling to keep alive in the ruins of Warsaw. Hiding away in one such ruin, he discovers a piano and finds some consolation miming his fingers over the keys. He is discovered there by a Wehrmacht Officer who, moved by hearing him play Chopin, brings him enough food to stave off complete starvation. It is a friendship of sorts. As the German retreat begins, the officer bids farewell to the pianist and promises to listen to him again on the radio after the war is over. He gives him his greatcoat to protect him from the terrible cold – but it can't protect him from the advancing Poles liberating his city – mistaking him for a German in this greatcoat, the pianist is almost shot dead just at the moment he is being freed....A little later, a group of Jewish inmates liberated from a concentration camp pass a huddle of German prisoners amongst whom is the same Wehrmacht officer who has saved the pianist's life. As they pass, they pause to spit verbal abuse at the Germans. One of these Jews turns out to be a violinist who knows the pianist. The Wehrmacht officer now begs, through the violinist, for the pianist to return the favour and get him freed. However, it is too late to do anything…and the German officer has disappeared by the time the possibility of help arrives. At the end of the film, the pianist sits down again in the radio station and once more begins to play Chopin. A title tells us that he continued to play successfully until his death in his '80's. Another title also tells us that the Wehrmacht office died in a Soviet gulag.

Much of the power of this film is achieved by its absolute lack of sentimentality. Unlike Spielberg's perfectly respectable "Schindler's List", Polanski eschews any temptation to milk our emotions by playing up the degradations and horrors – he stands back and shows them with a cold eye and without a teaspoon of sugar in sight to sweeten the pill . The result, of course, is that he succeeds in moving us more profoundly and more shockingly. He should know what he is doing better than most, shouldn't he, having seen as a child his own father being marched away by the Nazis to his death. There are no heroics, therefore, nor moments of emotional grandeur: Polanski understands only too well that the unspeakable depths to which man can sink cannot be approached politely or circumvented – you have to look at them straight in the face, and this is precisely what he makes us do…. I recall images – of a skeletal corpse still being comforted by a child; of a round up of Jews in the ghetto leading to a summary execution by a bullet to their heads, carried out with a shockingly matter-of-fact indifference; of the starving pianist struggling to open a jar of pickles; of his fingers silently playing above the keyboard. And I remember how moved I was when he is finally reunited with his friends at the radio station and, with the quietest (and perhaps saddest) exchange of smiles, they all just get on with the business of doing their jobs and trying to live again.

"The Pianist" won a basketful of prizes all over the world, including the Palme D'Or at Cannes. And rightly so – it really is an excellent piece of film-making and one which I admire and moves me to this day.

* * *

While we are here, I am going to stay a little longer in Warsaw during the time of its sufferings in the war to recall the work of another great Polish director – Andrzej Wajda.

I confess to having a soft spot for Poland and all things Polish. This is entirely due to the fact my very first real girlfriend in my 'teens was an effervescent Pole, full of life and forever in trouble with the nuns at her Catholic school. Her family were exiles during the war, including her grandfather, a sculptor of quite some repute, and one of the warmest and nicest men an awkward, gauche adolescent such as myself could ever hope to meet. I adored him almost as much as I adored his granddaughter. At that time, the famous Lodz film school was in its heyday – with teachers such as Wajda, Munk and Kawalerowicz making it a Mecca for any would-be film student. My girlfriend's grandfather knew the people there and suggested that he could help me find a place at the school. I was incredibly excited at the prospect, but my father put his foot firmly down – it was to be Cambridge, not Lodz, end of conversation. He might have well been right, but I didn't quite forgive him at the time, and it sometimes niggles me to this day at what might have been….I still haven't got to Poland – and, like the character in Pinter's "The Caretaker" who is always vowing to get down to Sidcup and collect his papers but never does, I wonder if I ever will…

74. "ASHES AND DIAMONDS"

(1958. Director; Andrzej Wajda)

This is the last in Wajda's great war trllogy, preceded by "Generation" and "Kanal". I would dearly like to cheat and include them all – especially "Kanal" with its stupendous sequences in the sewers with the Resistance fighters during the ill-fated Warsaw Uprising. "Ashes and Diamonds", however, can stand on its own, a triumphant conclusion to this important trilogy of films – and a triumph, too, of Polish cinema.

The film may well be described as social realism, but at times it's images (as they were, too, in the sewer scenes of "Kanal")have a poetic, expressionist feel to them as if inhabited by the stuff of dreams, remaining in the mind over the years to haunt you…Its over half a century since I saw "Ashes and Diamonds", so I am not even going to pretend I remember it in any detail – but I am damned if I'm going to scuttle off to Google to refresh my memory until I have at least dredged up for myself those fragments I have still retained – and piece them together like archaeological clues. Of course, the hero of the piece is unforgettable for two reasons – the name of the actor playing him, Zbigniew Cybulski (heavens, how those Poles can cook up a name!) and for the dark glasses he wears. Cybulski was a kind of James Dean and Marlon Brando rolled into one – the dark glasses he wears the ultimate in cool, but actually worn (I think) because he had spent so long in the sewers fighting with the Resistance during the Warsaw Uprising that his eyes had become light sensitive. He was a terrific actor and , like Dean, died at an early age in a car accident. I remember him, too, dancing with a girl he is in love with, alone together in the deserted ballroom of a hotel, a place of faded splendour, festooned for a party. I remember her name, too, because it was the same as my Polish girlfriend – Krystyna. And there was a poem they see together (inscribed on a wall?) which talked of how the flames of our endeavours lead us to ashes out of which maybe a diamond can be born. At the end of the film, Cybulski's own endeavours lead him only to ashes – he is shot and killed, dying on a desolate wasteland of garbage.

The film takes place in a small town outside Warsaw during the very last moments of the war and the actual day when hostilities ceased. This must have been a time of very mixed and ambiguous feelings for the Poles. On one hand, their country had been liberated from the Germans who had left most of it in ruins; but, on the other, their liberators hardly promised them the autonomous freedom they sought. For many of the Resistance fighters – or Home Army – the enemy now, therefore, were their new communist rulers. Cybulski and a friend have been ordered to go in and bump off a new Commissar for the town – a job which they bungle, ending up killing two innocent bystanders. They are given a second chance to do the job during the celebrations installing some minor functionary at the town's best hotel, with its dusty echoes of Poland's more glorious past. It is there that Cybulski meets and falls for Krystyna – who believes there has been conflict and destruction enough and that he should put his past behind him and start anew. In truth, like a tortured James Dean, Cybulksi has indeed had enough of violence – and he doesn't want to go through with the assassination anymore. An order is an order, however, and he doesn't want to show himself as a coward either. As fireworks announce the official end of hostilities, the Commissar is killed, but during his attempt to escape Cybulski, too, is shot and dies on a rubbish tip...

Wajda shows us a Poland whose national identity has been left fragmented and confused, and is painfully trying to find it again, unsure what to stand for or which way to turn. The film is not without moments of dark, absurd humour and Wajda is careful not to take sides or pronounce judgements. Bleak and sad, but honest and true. I can vividly recall the fantastic black and white photography, glittering and evocative and as wistful as the situations the film explores. As with other films in this list, I may have forgotten it at one level – but it is not lost, but rather residing in another area of the brain and manifesting itself as an impact, a sensation which lives on. It is a film I would dearly love to see again, along with the other two in the trilogy – they reached deep inside me.

* * *

Derek Malcolm, film critic of The Guardian, tells of asking Wajda if he didn't sometimes wish to come to the West and work in freedom from the communist censors. Wajda replied you could always find a way to get round and escape the censors – but there was no escape from the censorship of money! In many ways, how right he was!

East European film-makers became something of past masters in finding ways to get around the Censors and going beyond toeing the official Party lines. It was a challenge which encouraged them to develop a distinctive subtlety and often a brand of subversive humour all of their own, which merely confirms what we all already know – that your average servant of the State machine is not gifted with much imagination and even less sense of humour. The next film remains, for me, one of the very best for showing both – and stands out as one of the most lovable…

75. "CLOSELY OBSERVED TRAINS"

(1966. Director: Jirí Menzel)

Made 2 years before the 'Prague Spring' and that brief (and doomed) period of hope for the Czech people under the liberalizing government of Alexander Dubçek, this most charming of films takes gentle pleasure in taking the piss out of their Soviet masters by the simple (and I would have thought immediately transparent) device of setting the film in the 2nd World War and substituting them with the German occupiers.

It is also a Rite of Passage film: for a virginal young man taking up his first job as a very junior railway platform assistant at a small country station. He loves the uniform, but loves even more the fact there are barely any responsibilities and plenty of time to idle away in daydreams – mostly concerned with his obsessive wish to lose his virginity. His station master is a pompous bureaucrat, prone to lecturing from the rule book, and harbouring a jealous resentment against his Number 2, a Lothario whose success with women drives him to distraction. In this idyllic, lazy setting – occasionally interrupted by one of the Nazi's cronies delivering propaganda pep-talks which everyone ignores – the young man develops a crush on a pretty young girl who is a train guard. It is she who eventually takes the lead and initiates him into the mysteries of sex. Disaster – in his total inexperience he ejaculates so prematurely that he hasn't even had the time to penetrate her precious body. So great is his shame and despair that, apart from becoming impotent, he is driven towards a bungled and half-hearted attempt at suicide. The station Lothario advises him to seek out a more mature and experienced woman who can sort his problem out.

During a night shift, our Lothario makes a pass at the station's telegraphist and ends up covering her handsome buttocks in as many of the numerous rubber stamps bureaucracy so reveres as he can lay his hands on. It is hilarious – but it is also a scandal which the station master can use to block his junior's promotion. It is also unfortunate inasmuch that a glamorous Resistance leader decides to show up and delegate him to plant a time-bomb on a German ammunition train due to pass by in the very near future – but at precisely the time when he will be up before a committee led by the Nazi crony to investigate the "buttock" scandal and the misuse of government property involved. On the plus side, however, this winsome and athletic agent does have enough time to show the young man how things should be done and relieve him of his despair in so doing.

It also effects a quiet sea change and, now that he has proved himself as man, he shakes off his habitual lazy torpor and goes into action. While his *roué* friend is up before a farcical committee for a grilling, he takes the bomb, climbs onto the bridge over the tracks and drops it into the passing train. But, alas, he is spotted by one the troops guarding the precious consignment and shot dead…. Minutes later, as the train disappears around the corner, there are a series of massive explosions bringing not only an end to the Germans' ammunition wagons but also to the absurd committee meeting. The force of the blast blows the young man's cap, his pride and joy, back onto the platform…and it is left to the pretty young guard to pick up and mourn all that remains of her lost sweetheart…Bitter sweet.

Jirí Menzel's humour is gentle and quiet – affectionate in its human observations, astute in its laconic underhand way of sending up the "system". I have seen the film 3 times and, on each viewing, it stands up to the test of time – and stands out for the economy and simplicity of its craftsmanship…I wonder, therefore, whatever happened to Jirí Menzel and where did his talent go….?

* * *

In the same year that Jiří Menzel was making his beautiful and unforgettable film, I directed my second and altogether forgettable (and forgotten) one. Made through the small production company I had set up with the same Mark Fisher I have referred to before, it was a documentary about the human and emotional impact of redundancy, filmed in a small Scottish town built around a car factory, which had been suddenly closed down throwing pretty well everyone out of work. Most of it was shot on actual Christmas Day and centred on a young family who, in this bleakest of bleak mid-winters, were neither able to give their young children any tidings of comfort and joy, nor anything more than a painfully meagre dollop of the festive spirit most of us enjoy and associate with the season. It was pretty grim stuff: indeed they could not see even a glimmer of hope for their own future. Although our hearts were in the right place, our skills and experience, however, were still trailing far behind. If our previous effort, "Margins" (mentioned after Number 10 on the list) was unintelligible because neither director or writer really knew what the hell that highly abstruse piece was all about, this one was unintelligible too, but for altogether different reasons. We were unlucky, to say the least, to be shooting on a 16mm self-blimping (self-silencing) Éclair camera which developed an insuperable problem (not what you want on a Christmas Day up in Scotland with no access to maintenance back-up down in London) with the result that, throughout the film, the family's dialogue sounds rather like it is being invisibly accompanied by someone hard at work on a sewing machine. This, combining with the challenges of deciphering the strong Scots accents, did not exactly help matters... The film wasn't bad...it just wasn't very good and disappeared into the dust without an airing, but, comfortably, not before that eminent film critic, Penelope Gilliat, had written some generous and kind words about it in her weekly Sunday film reviews in The Observer ... We were young and knew far less than we thought we did – "si la jeunesse savait, si la vieillesse pouvait"...

The year before, my Uncle John also made a film which would turn out to be the last he ever directed, as he became ever more burdened by managing the financial fortunes of a British Lion struggling to survive. A five minute walk away from its HQ in Broadwick Street was "Le Jardin des Gourmets" in Greek Street, favoured by "those bloody twins" as their local restaurant of choice. Over lunch with them there one day, my father turned and asked me (with a mischievous glint in his eye) what I thought of my Uncle John's last work. I'm afraid I found myself saying to this director of the excellent "Brighton Rock" and "I'm Alright Jack" that I inclined towards the opinion that his latest offering was not entirely unlike it's title – "Rotten to the Core". This cheeky and rather rude reply amused my father and, to be fair to Uncle John, after his initial "What a bloody sauce!", he reluctantly chuckled too. They weren't beyond laughing at themselves – and Uncle John was under no illusions about this harmless enough caper film: it was tired...and so perhaps was he. Nevertheless, had I known then half as well as I know now the difficulties facing every film-maker, I would have been – and should have been – very much less arrogant. Bloody sauce indeed!

By the end of the following year, during which I had charged off up to Scotland to set the world to rights by taking up the cause of the half million or so unemployed and redundant workers at that time, my father had gone 'up North' also to film Bill Naughton's play "The Family Way". Since the beginning of the '60's, 'the North', the industrial working-class, hitherto largely ignored, had become something of a vogue in literature, stage, and film alike. It was a world which lay way beyond the gardens outside the French windows of the genteel middle-class, and it spoke with a very different accent. To be sure, there was still a fair amount of cod "there's trouble at Mill, lad" and "where's there's brass there's muck" caricature, but, by and large, the issues and concerns being voiced were more authentic and real. Perhaps my father wanted, a little belatedly, to show that he could be up there and as 'modern' as the rest of them (and as he and John had certainly been back in the 1940's). Whatever his reasons, "The Family Way" managed to excite attention and then some notoriety for two different reasons.

Firstly, this was the film in which Disney's world famous and incredibly successful child star, Hayley Mills, was going to grow up – Pollyanna *leaving her childhood behind her to become a woman(and show a glimpse of it) on screen. Secondly, in the process of doing so, and despite their differences in age (Hayley was 19 and Roy 55) star and director, much to the delight and glee of the tabloids, but dismay of others – not least, I suspect, the star's mother – seem to have discovered they were rather seriously in love. Scandal. Cue the predictable and prurient 'Oooh's' and 'Aaah's' the British so enjoy indulging in, as if they had nothing better to do with their lives...*

As for the film itself? Hayley had already shown in Bryan Forbes' "Whistle Down the Wind" that she could "do North" as well as anyone else, as could her father John Mills, appearing alongside as her father-in-law. Hwyel Bennet, as Hayley's newly-wed husband who finds he can't perform in the bedroom, Marjorie Rhodes as his Mum and Wilfrid Pickles as the sympathetic uncle offering the homespun advice which eventually helps the young couple to finally consummate their marriage, all do a perfectly good job of it also. Just to show they were up to the mark of the times, The Boultings had secured Beatle Paul MaCartney to write the music score, the veteran cinematographer, Harry Waxman's work was perfectly respectable – indeed, it was all very solid. But, much as I really wanted to like and admire the film, to see my own father creating a really exciting piece of cinema, I had to admit to myself in private that perhaps it was all a little too bland for my tastes....that, at the age of 21, I found it just a wee bit 'old-fashioned' and that I was being forced to realize, as perhaps every son of every father must do one day, (and as Hwyel Bennet does with his own on-screen father John Mills in the film) that it was figuratively and literally time to leave 'home' ...Perhaps my expectations had been too high – and, as for many other sons, the disappointment inevitable.

The edge, the danger and excitement in film, the radical I was hungry for seemed lacking in English-speaking films, be they American or British, but I only had to turn my eyes towards Europe – or 'the Continent' as it was and is still referred to – to find the kind of cinema I could really admire. I had seen the following film only a couple of years before – and it went straight into my heart....

76. "SALVATORE GUILIANO"

(1962. Director: Francesco Rosi)

This is another film I saw 3 times when it showed at the Paris Pullman off the Fulham Road, another great little 'art house' cinema which bit the dust. It is one of my favourites and I would love to see it again. Francesco Rosi comes directly out of the neo-realist tradition, following in the footsteps of their social concerns, but possibly with less of his predecessors' sentiment and more of their politics. He is also altogether more a formalist – setting aside the more conventional 'documentary' style to bolster it with a more structured approach to 'realism'. It had an important influence on me for that reason alone, as well as for the brilliance of its film-making.

Salvatore Guiliano was a Sicilian guerilla fighter in the 1950's – fighting, like a latter-day Robin Hood, against corruption ... amongst the politicians, the police, the Mafia, the communist cabals. Initially, it won him the support and protection of the impoverished Sicilian peasantry – but over time, less and less so, and he and his band were shunned and hunted down as common criminals – in the end he was killed. But by whom? Who betrayed him? What was the truth behind his death?

Throughout most of the film, Salvatore is only seen as a corpse on a slab – Rosi moves back and forth through time, often without the audience realizing it at first, in search of the truth. In the process, he exposes the stinking fish of corruption lurking in every corner. But the truth as to who killed Salvatore Guiliano? One of his own disenchanted followers? The Mafia? Police spies? The answer is never given because it was never known, but you could say it was all of them.

There are some terrific set-pieces – a police raid on a remote mountain village, with the terrified womenfolk running in panic down the stone steps mounting the village; an attack Salvatore orders on a communist rally and the violent police shoot-out that follows. The harsh landscape, the white stone, the burning light, the sombre shadow of interiors are all scintillatingly photographed in black and white by Gianni di Venanzo, one of the great masters of the craft. There is also an exceptional and memorable score by Piero Piccioni, written for the plaintive twang of the Jew's Harp and strings. (He went on to compose the music for Rosi's next film, scoring this time for massed 'cellos. Di Venanzo also photographed this film, "Hands over the City", about property development corruption in Naples, starring none other than Rod Steiger. It won the Golden Bear at Venice). Structurally a piece of cinematic bravura, tense with action, "Salvatore Guiliano" has an underlying melancholy...you could say, almost despair. Rosi was clearly – and actively – committed to bringing the compromised values of his country to public attention. There may be more than a hint of pessimism in his approach to the subject-matter, but apart from making a magnificent film, he could take some satisfaction in knowing that it did also lead to enquiries being opened and a few rotten heads beginning to roll ...

77. "LAND AND FREEDOM"

(1995. Director: Ken Loach)

And talking of the political....

Someone once described Ken Loach to me as a 'romantic idealist'. Its not difficult to see why – the main corpus of his work has always been politically committed and adheres, often passionately, to his convictions and belief in the socialist ideals. Hardly surprising, therefore, that some prefer to label him as a good old-fashioned, communist 'leftie' or others take refuge in their outrage at some of the causes he espouses. Nor is there any doubt about it, his films can be very provocative – sincerity and the pursuit of truth often are.

It is easy enough to understand, therefore, how he would be drawn to this story of a young Liverpudlian worker (Ian Hart) in 1936 who drops everything and goes off to join in the fight against Facism, alongside other foreigners fighting with the Republicans in the Spanish Civil War; and how he ends up in the POUM militia, with their Marxist ideals of collective ownership, their atheism and loathing of the Church's corrupt hold on the people, their belief in men and women fighting as equals alongside one another, not only on the Aragon front, but also in the workplace and community of a better and fairer society. Their's was a heady radical vision of a brave new world to replace so many centuries of injustice and inequality in Spain....and perhaps too radical ever to survive.

The story is told in flash-back after the death of Ian Hart as an old man. Going through his affairs, his grand-daughter comes across a sheaf of letters he has written which piece together his story... The militia Ian Hart joins on the front is ill-equipped, inadequately trained, and not receiving the back-up it requires. But, bonded by their solidarity, they fight on bravely, free villages and bring their message to the newly emancipated villagers. Amongst those also serving in this brigade is a young woman (Rosana Pastor) with whom Hart forms an attachment. Wounded (by one of their own ancient rifles back-firing on him), he is sent back to recover in Barcelona where he meets up again with the girl and they start an affair. But it is also the time when the new Republican Army is being established, and as the 'official' army, Ian Hart feels he should join them. POUM was ordered to disband – their refusal to do so led to inevitable bloodshed and the unhappy spectacle of people, supposedly on the same side, shooting at one another. Comrade against comrade. Disenchanted by this, he decides to return to his old brigade in Aragon and fight on with them for the ideals he believes in. The Republican Army arrive at their camp, as they rest after a battle, lining up and ordering them to lay down and surrender their arms – in the extremely tense stand-off between the two sides, a shot rings out and the young woman is killed....Ian Hart takes her body on an ox-cart back to her village to bury her...Years later, his own grand-daughter buries him in Liverpool. Amongst his memorabilia she has found a red handkerchief in which he has wrapped the earth of Spain. She pours it into his grave – and raises a clenched fist into the air...

Loach has an extraordinary ability to generate 'performances', immersed in great intensity and realism, from professionals and non-professionals alike. To achieve this emotional depth and spontaneity he employs, apart from some unique alchemical talent all of his own, some equally extraordinary techniques. I was able to watch these at close hand when he kindly allowed me to spend a few weeks in the Maestrazgo region, up in the mountains above Valencia, where he was filming. Apart from filming in strict chronological order(which, incidentally, Dreyer also did on "The Passion of Joan of Arc"), his cast never know what they will be doing the following day – they are fed their scripts each evening, page by page, learning their story only as it unfolds. More than that, they only know what they, personally, will do, say – as the other parts in the script are blacked out and the actor has no idea of how his fellow actors around him will be responding.

To create a distance between the camera and all the mechanical paraphernalia so that the cast can feel more free and real in their environment, Loach always works on long lenses, endeavours to keep any lights necessary shielded from their view, and generally tries to make him and his crew as absent as possible. He never tracks the Camera, often uses multiple cameras, and runs a lot of film through the gate to get what he wants – but get it he does. Together, these techniques allow for a lot of freedom to improvise and build upon the scenes – and his mix of professionals with non-professionals can ignite some remarkable results – certainly, the atmosphere on the set of "Land and Freedom" was electrifying: the cast playing the militia were bonded by an intense comradeship which, at times, felt like some weird 1960's 'love-in'. I have a particularly fond memory of seeing them all, cast and crew, surprising Ken on his birthday, by downing both the weapons of war and the tools of film-making to whip out bright fluorescent water pistols with which they proceeded to drench their director, before pursuing his redoubtable Producer, Rebecca O'Brien, across the sun-scorched earth where they were filming. In straw hat and long skirt, for a moment the fleeing Rebecca conjured images of nothing less than a latter-day Joyce Grenfell in the St Trinian's films, a hapless and good-natured victim of children in a Ronald Searle cartoon. It was a charming and funny moment – Loach makes serious films, but that doesn't stop there being a bit of fun from time to time as well…

There are scenes of great power in "Land and Freedom" – the debate in the landowner's 'big house' amongst the people of a village, freshly liberated by the POUM militia, on whether to establish a collective or not is magnificent for its authenticity (and contains a magical little cameo from an actual veteran of the war) and is quite outstanding cinema – as is much of the film. Loach has sinew and guts, but above all he is completely free from sham and artefact. This is a damn good film.

I have frequently referred in this list to the British lighting cameraman, Roger Deakins – but another Brit, Barry Ackroyd, who has filmed much of Loach's work, is right up there also and ranks, for me, amongst the very best. Nor should I forget the formidable challenges Loach's films present to the Sound Recordist to capture direct location sound – he was lucky (as we all are) to have placed this responsibility in the hands of Ray Beckett who is, quite simply, a genius, a gentleman and a poet of sound. Amongst his cast which came from all over the place (God knows how he found them!) there was also the fiery spark of Iciar Bollain (whom I had last seen playing a young girl in Victor Erice's achingly beautiful "El Sur") as well as a non-professional actor, and clearly very gifted Scotsman called Paul Laverty, who has gone on to become Loach's regular screenplay writer. I also understand that he and Iciar became "an article"... and that the "article" continues to flourish to this day. I don't know why but it warms my heart – perhaps, like the admirable Mr Loach, there's a trace of the 'romantic idealist' in me too…

* * *

The Spanish Civil War was as brutal and cruel as any civil war can be – and the Republican cause was so riven by political factions and in-fighting it was tearing itself apart. Nor were they helped by Anthony Eden's Anglo-French sponsored Non-Intervention Pact with Germany and Italy, because Hitler and Mussolini simply ignored it and went in with their tanks and planes to help the Fascist cause as incarnated in the portly shape of Generalissimo Francisco Franco, armed and replete with his legendary bladder control. Britain's and France's refusal to get involved also gave Stalin the chance to slip in and support the communists (before the war they only accounted for less than a 10% following in the country) and exert control over the Republicans (quite apart from filching the entire Spanish gold reserves in exchange for his 'help', it also suited Uncle Joe's book to see them fail). Remind you of anything?

The shadow of this terrible war has hung over Spain ever since. My own Uncle John joined up and went out to serve in the International Ambulance Brigade. He returned disillusioned,(but with an enduring love of Spain) as did Orwell, which he describes in his book "Homage to Catalonia"…But many others, as in Loach's film, hung onto the dreams embodied in that struggle. Ken also told me he thought it was also one of those rare moments when the course of history really could have been changed. I am wary of "what if" scenarios, but I think I probably agree with him – although gloomily looking around me at the world today, I am not sure it would have necessarily changed for the better....But as long as we have the likes of Ken Loach around, there is always a chance that, one day, it will. Avanti Popolo!

* * *

Until quite recently, Ken Loach was far more appreciated on the other side of the Channel than he ever was in the country of his birth. I think that's partly to do with an innate hesitation in the British sensibility to consider and accept film as both an 'art' form and also a reluctance to engage head-on with 'political' issues on film – (unless, of course, they are films made by 'foreigners')... The next director in my list has also been more admired outside the UK than in it – but that has changed recently too. Both he and Loach now enjoy a respect and appreciation by their fellow countrymen which hitherto was not spontaneously forthcoming. When it comes to film, as a language, I can't help thinking that the Brits always have to follow someone else's lead...and I wonder if that is why I have included so few of them in my list...

78. "MR TURNER"

(2014. Director: Mike Leigh)

Mike Leigh seems to me to get better and better as a true film-maker with each successive movie. From his first film, "Bleak Moments" (1971) until today, what was a bloody good wine to start with has become exceptional. Taut, dense, stripped of any excess fat, with "Mr Turner" sometimes I thought I was watching a series of well-wrought *haiku*'s. It lifted my spirits and I rejoiced to know such films could still get made and even enjoy popular, as well as critical, support in Britain. A rare bird indeed!

Leigh's methods of developing his films and shaping his final 'story' through extended workshops with his cast is well-known. It is a fairly radical approach – and, in this sense, he shares something in common with Ken Loach in that both employ highly individual techniques to craft their work. But that's as far as any similarities between today's two foremost talents of British cinema go. They may be on the same planet, but they're living in very different countries…

Timothy Spall plays the great painter during the last 25 years of his life, and plays him quite superbly: blending a coarse carnality and gruff, verging on rude, demeanour with the depth of sensitivity and spirituality rumbling beneath the surface. He does so without ever descending into sentiment or rhapsody – this is a Turner who might very well be on the edge of the Asperger's Syndrome scale. Greatly affected by his father's death, Turner lives alone with his housekeeper, a woman who loves him, but whom he ignores except when it suits him to use her to gratify his sexual urges. He goes on to form another attachment, however, with the landlady of a seaside boarding house. Later they will move into a Chelsea house, living together incognito until Turner's death…All the while, he visits the great country houses...exhibits as a member of the Royal Academy where he is something of a misfit ... gives Ruskin (one of his earliest and greatest champions) a dismissive snub...sees his paintings disparaged by the Royal Family...turns down a magnate's offer to buy his entire work so that he can leave it all to the nation... And walks, walks and feels the light, Nature, the elements which he turns into those great paintings of the last years which we know and love today...On his death, two women are left to mourn him – and in his studio, the roof leaking in the rain, his housekeeper, loyal in her unrequited love to the end, must now grieve alone...

It may be a reprehensible shortcoming on my part, but, to be honest, I couldn't really give a monkey's about the historical accuracy (or inaccuracy) of this portrait – because I am much more interested in how Mike Leigh has crafted it, more concerned about it as *film*. Without being too fanciful, "Mr Turner" might equally well have been titled "Mr Leigh", as his signature is so very evident throughout the film. No, not in an egotistical way, but invisibly like the puppeteer controlling the strings of his puppet: we know he's there although we never see him – it's a presence – steering and guiding us with a sure and dexterous hand. From the opening shot (which many found baffling and I found glorious) in which two Dutch women come strolling slowly towards us in a peaceful countryside setting, passing by Camera to reveal Turner in the distance gazing up at the sky to the closing shot of the unloved housekeeper in her lonely grief, Leigh knows exactly what he is doing – there is a conviction in every shot which lends them an inevitability as if they could be framed no other way. He stands back at a remove, doesn't complicate his scenes, plays them out without fuss or 'drama'. Turner, seized by sudden desire, throwing himself like some brute animal at his unresisting housekeeper is watched dispassionately with a steely, unblinking eye. Turner listening to a lady of the nobility playing Purcell on the piano to him in a country house is finely sustained to allow us to feel Turner being moved by the loveliness of the music with feelings he can never show. So sure is Leigh of what he is doing that, in one scene, he plays it with Turner's back to the Camera and allows his hands to do the real talking for him behind the slightly stilted formal words coming out of his mouth. All in all, it's a joy to watch – and I think it's a film which will endure through time and be remembered as Mike Leigh at his best...

79. "DISTANT VOICES, STILL LIVES"

(1988. Director: Terence Davies)

Terence Davies has even been described as "the greatest living English director" – even Jean-Luc Godard, who has never been slow in dismissing English Cinema in general out of hand, was moved to praise this early Davies film – and with uncharacteristic enthusiasm (not that I'm suggesting that Godard's opinions are necessarily sanctified by the breath of God, but, even so, it gives you an idea of the high esteem in which Davies' films are held – worldwide). For me, as with Humphrey Jennings, he is a true poet of Cinema – and an English one at that, whose work reaches levels which I can only call sublime. No wonder, however, that at the age of 70 the corpus of his work remains small (I think 5 features in all), because, to achieve what he has achieved, also has required of him an unflinching resolve not to compromise and remain absolutely true to his own, personal vision. This purity, if you will, has won him admiration and praise *after* the event, but has made financing his films *beforehand* even more difficult than it usually is. His struggle to get his films made must have been painful as well as frustrating – but, like Erice, or Rivette, or even Kurosawa and Welles, he has stuck to his guns throughout, rewarding us with works which will be around to be admired a long, long time after we are all forgotten dust and ashes...Quite unique.

Terence Davies was one of 10 children growing up in a Catholic family, during the 1940's and '50's in Liverpool, and "Distant Voices, Still Lives" is clearly autobiographical. It is divided into 2 parts and, in fact, shooting them both had to be separated by two years – I assume for reasons of finance, rather than artistic choice. The first part, the "distant voices", explores the early years of this family, dominated by a brutish, abusive, physically violent father(the excellent Pete Postlewaite) and it is dark, fearful, tormented by anguish and sadness. The second part, the "still lives", shows the same family emerging into the 1950's – and it is more optimistic, at moments even more joyful although the shadow of the past still hangs tangibly in the air like a shroud over them all....The past – more precisely how we remember the past, what substantiates memory and, vice versa, what memories give substance to – seems to lie at the core of this beautifully composed and evocative film. In some ways it feels like a portrait of Memory itself, for which the film-maker is just its vehicle, shaping,through it, a composition of a life, a time, the moments which make us what we are.

Associations, elisions run like the different weaves and threads in a tapestry to build an overall picture with a rich emotional depth, stunningly framed visually with a highly personal yet classical or formal style. I was reminded at times of Jennings' "Listen to Britain" and, at other moments, of Alain Resnais' "Providence", but at the end of the day this is an intensely personal work which belongs alone to its author. Davies also uses music – the popular music of a time before The Beatles – and refers to the great MGM musicals throughout the film, seamlessly allowing them to emerge and disappear into and out of the scenes. Combining all these elements with a sure touch, Davies presents us with a picture, delicate in its sufferings, gentle in its regrets, warm in its sense of life. Yes, you might agree, a masterpiece.

* * *

Davies' films, needless to say, are hardly likely to be big box-office winners – its been a painful struggle for him to get them made, but I think, once they have been, they deserve better support from the exhibitors than possibly they have been given. In 2015, for instance, his last film "Sunset Song" came out – again universally admired – but released before Christmas only to be gazumped by the arrival of the latest "Star Wars" which swamped all the cinemas and shunted "Sunset Song" off into a siding. The mechanics of the market... Cruel!

But returning to the 1960's which, after all, was the decade which most shaped and influenced me...While the French were busy having their "nouvelle vague", the British were following suit and having a bit of the same for themselves. The curtain had already long gone up at George Devine's Royal Court Theatre on John Osborne's "Look Back in Anger" and suddenly we were into the era of "the kitchen sink drama" – without a polite accent or doily under the china in sight. Genteel went out of the window and in came the working-class men and women, gritty, grimy, rebellious – and, above all, sexy. Tony Richardson, Lindsay Anderson, John Schlesinger, Joan Littlewood, not forgetting the excellent Jack Clayton, all had their hands up to their elbows in the suds of the kitchen sink – including, to my mind, a naturalized British citizen who was far and away the best film-maker of them all: Karel Reisz.

80. "SATURDAY NIGHT, SUNDAY MORNING"

(1960. Director: Karel Reisz)

Apart from Eisenstein's writings on film theory, my other great mainstay as a 15 year old teenager searching to understand what film was really all about, was Reisz' invaluable book "The Technique of Film Editing". Gratifying though it was that he had chosen to cite a sequence from my father and uncle's film of "Brighton Rock" as an example of how to build montage editing, it was more important to me as an indispensable manual on the basic building blocks of film-making which, with its yellow dust-cover and black lettering, remained a work I consulted frequently. Reisz was, at that time, the bee's knees for me – so much so that I wrote to invite him to come and talk at our school Film Society. He declined – but with such a polite and thoughtful hand-written postcard (a Gainsborough) that he merely shot up even more in my estimation. I kept the card for many years until, along with pretty everything else in my life, it was stolen and vanished forever except in my memory...So when his film of Alan Sillitoe's "Saturday Night, Sunday Morning" came out, you could say he was preaching to the converted and I was ready to praise it before the first frame even flickered onto the screen...

Favourably predisposed or not, Reisz' film was pretty bloody good anyway, irrespective of my bias. There must have been exceptions, but until then my own memory of the portrayal of the British working-class on film was of the cod Cockney "Cor Blimey, guv'nor" variety, a pastiche which had little relation to the real man on the street. Certainly, I cannot recall hearing an authentic Northern or Midlands accent before this film – but then I was living the sheltered and privileged life of an English public schoolboy: I hadn't the foggiest clue of what was going on in the real world at large, and my ignorance was shameful. I was a virgin in every sense. So Reisz' film was an eye-opener in more ways than one. And, of course, in the process it introduced me and everyone else to the remarkable Albert Finney...

Finney plays a young factory worker in Nottingham – fed up with the grinding monotony of his job and equally exasperated by his own parents' mindless acceptance of the social status quo. He is part of rebellious youth wanting more out of life than this dull, unquestioning existence – and they're going out there to get it. Cocky, self-assured Finney is also living life dangerously – apart from his 'steady' girlfriend (the lovely and probably underrated Shirley Anne Field), he is having an affair with an older and heavily married woman (the splendid Rachel Roberts). Things get pretty sticky, however, when she discovers she is pregnant by him. As a married woman, there is no question of her keeping it, but nor is there any chance of her having an abortion – still illegal and a criminal offence at the time. Finney seeks the help of his Aunt (the formidable Hylda Baker) who knows the 'back street' way of helping women out such a predicament. It is dangerous, painful, sordid – and, in this case, doesn't work... Her husband finds out – and also discovers the culprit. He and his mates corner Finney in a fairground – and beat the living shit out of him...Rachel Roberts returns to her life, trapped as a housewife and, at the end of the film, Finney and his 'steady' girlfriend talk about finding a nice little house and making a home.. There is every prospect that the rebel, too, will 'settle down' ... The Swinging '60's still hadn't yet swung...

Taking a film out of the studios and into real-life locations was a new departure, made more possible, of course, by advances in camera and sound technology. But this social realism really was a breath of fresh air which cleared away a lot of dusty old cobwebs. Reisz' film is classical – almost conventional – in structure and style, but he injects it with a fresh authentic vitality. Crisply photographed by Freddie Francis (one of the two great 'Freddy's' of British cinematography – the other being Freddie Young), the film takes us into an environment hitherto only really seen through the fine school of British documentary. Reisz learnt a trick or two from their example and married their techniques to drama – and what a good marriage it made! "Saturday Night, Sunday Morning" made a deep impression on me and made me realize that if I wanted to see what life was really all about I had better get out there and see it....(but I would have to wait a little bit longer before that became possible...)

* * *

Since it does involve Cinema, a short detour into my own Rite of Passage might be excused. It was to take place a year later in Spain – specifically in Granada, where I fell in with a bunch of working-class lads who soon set about showing me the ways of the world. They were streetwise and knew the ropes, but were also in the grip of a poverty such as I had never encountered before in real life, so their spontaneous generosity and friendship was all the more touching. At that time, Spain was very backward, economic hardship was everywhere and Franco's stranglehold over the country very much evident. People were careful of what they said and to whom – while the dreaded Guardia Civil in their green uniforms and patent leather tricorn helmets were loathed and feared in equal measure. The other great institution making its presence felt on every corner was, of course, The Church. Up the road from the bar where we used to hang out was a massive cinema (and I think it really was called the Alhambra) where they were showing de Mille's "Ten Commandments" (badly dubbed into Spanish) and we all went along. There must have been well over a thousand people inside, it was so huge – and when God spoke to Moses (aka 'Chuck' Heston) from the burning fiery bush, I was gob-smacked to see hundreds of women (and some men) so caught up in the story that they were dropping to their knees in the cinema and crossing themselves: they believed what they were seeing was real! God was speaking – in wide-screen Technicolour. I had seen something of a similar sort a few weeks previously in an open-air cinema, which very thoughtfully had provided a bar at the back so you could get yourself a drink and a 'tapa' without losing a second of the film. It was some quite ludicrous black and white bandit film (and I suspect the reels were being projected in the wrong order to boot)but the audience were very vocal in shouting insults and obscenities at the 'baddies' and applauding the 'goodie' whenever he appeared. It was riotous and tremendously entertaining – and I thought how wonderfully amusing it would be to see the same audience participation taking place in, for instance, the Odeon, Leicester Square. But the spectacle of so many devout women genuflecting before a fairly dubious Special Effect AND a similarly dubious 'Chuck' Heston brought it forcefully home to me just what a powerful tool film can be and how manipulative.

But the suspension of disbelief, once it has cast its spell has to be maintained – and, dear me , how easily it can be punctured. Which leads me to a second story I will allow myself to indulge in...

I went to see the American William Friedkin's "The Exorcist" at a late night screening at the Warner Theatre, Leicester Square on an extremely hot summer's night. The heat plus the terrible tension of seeing the little girl (she was called Linda Blair, was she not?)possessed by Satanic forces, spewing green bile, revolving her head through 360 Degrees whilst mouthing obscenities combined to make an audience jam-packed to the roof come out in a plentiful muck sweat. The film was truly terrifying. Come the scene, however, when she levitates, ranting obscenities, while Max von Sydow and his fellow priest kneel at her bedside and incant "Come down in the name of God! Come down in the name of God!" to no avail, something quite extraordinary happened. From the first row of the stalls, a deep, sonorous West Indian voice boomed out in an easy drawl "Now you just come down, baby, you hear me?! You just come down nice and easy, niiiice and eeeeasy" – a request to which the tormented child on the screen meekly acceded. The audience broke up into laughter – their disbelief no longer suspended anymore than the child was. And that was that – all credibility went out of the window and didn't come back. Throughout the rest of the film what were meant to be scenes to scare you witless were met with anything from a ripple of giggles to outright howls of laughter. I am sure the point is clear – it is quite one thing to create an illusion, but altogether another to sustain it. It is, therefore, despite a natural human inclination and susceptibility which precisely wants to suspend its disbelief, quite remarkable how many films have succeeded in doing so – and indicates the complexities of the skills required to achieve this…

Enough of that – back to almost my last of the very few British films which feature in this list… Look, there are some admirable and wonderfully made British pictures I can think of – the work of Michael and Emeric Pressburger, of David Lean, Robert Hamer, the Ealing Comedy stable, Launder and Gilliat and even, dare I say it, some of the early works of "those bloody twins", my father and uncle. And what about John Boorman, Nic Roeg, Peter Greenaway, Derek Jarman, Stephen Frears, Danny Boyle, Michael Winterbottom or, even closer to today, Tom Hooper, Steve McQueen or Lynne Ramsay? Well, as I keep repeating, this is a personal list of films which have, in one way or another, come into my life in certain ways and at certain times and shaped my sense of what film is. So I make little apology for leaving out so many considerable creative talents from the country of my birth. Put it this way, however: they are not excluded… just not included…well, not for now.

This last film is a classic – and there are many reasons why it deserves to be so. I include it in this list for another reason as well – I could see it's closing shot again…and again….and again…

81. "THE THIRD MAN"

(1949. Director: Carol Reed)

Graham Greene wrote the screenplay, later turning it into a novella, of this highly atmospheric film set in the crumbling ruins of post-war Vienna then under Allied control. Holly, a 2nd-rate writer of pulp Western novels, (Joseph Cotten), comes to Vienna to find his childhood friend, Harry Lime (Orson Welles), only to learn he has been killed in a hit-and-run car accident, but just in time, though, to attend his burial. In the cemetery, he is approached by a Major in the British Army(Trevor Howard, dry as a biscuit) who informs him Lime was a thief and a murderer and advises him to leave town. Holly finds it hard to accept this news about his friend and, ignoring the Major's advice, stays on in the hope of clearing Harry's name. The more he looks into Lime's death, however, the more convinced he is it was no accident. His enquiries introduce him to a succession of curiously evasive Viennese characters with ambiguous and conflicting stories about the death – and eventually to Lime's girlfriend, Anna (here she is again – the lovely Alida Valli). When Holly starts demanding a police investigation, it pushes the Major into revealing that Lime, in fact, was running a racket stealing the highly valued and scarce commodity of penicillin from the military, diluting it and selling it off on the black market…where, now riddled with impurities, it was causing many deaths. The Major again advises Holly to leave Vienna.

The police investigation Holly has instigated also backfires on Anna, despite his intentions to help her. It leads to a search of Anna's apartment where they discover her passport is forged. Anna is detained … and now faces being deported to the Soviet sector. And then, after leaving her home, briefly illuminated by a light being turned on in a window, Holly sees Harry Lime, insouciant smile on his face, very much alive and standing in the shadows of a doorway.

The light goes off, Lime disappears, but chasing after him, Holly can find no trace: he has simply vanished. When told of this, the Major deduces he has escaped through the sewage system running beneath the city – Lime's supposed body is exhumed and discovered not to be him. The hunt is on…

Lime has, however, made contact with Holly and arranged a secret rendez-vous. Circling above the ruined city in Vienna's famous Ferris Wheel, Holly struggles to understand how Lime could have sunk so low, ruthlessly disregarding the value of human life for his own profit. Pointing down at the ant-sized figures of the people on the ground below them, Lime poses the morally bankrupt question to Holly – can the lives of these anonymous creatures really be of any significance at all in the great tides of history? Do any of them really matter?

Disillusioned and sickened by it all, Holly finally decides to take the Major's advice and leave Vienna . But before he goes, the Major shows him a ward in a children's hospital where the results of Lime's profiteering can be seen in the rows of children slowly dying from meningitis. Holly changes his mind and agrees to help the Major bring Harry Lime to justice – on condition that Anna is given safe conduct out of Vienna. The trap is set to ensnare Harry but it is Anna, loyal to her man regardless of everything, who warns him he is about to be betrayed. In the famous climactic sequence, Harry tries to make his escape through the sewers once more, but this time he cannot get away. Wounded by the Major, it is left to Holly to administer the *coup de grace*.

At the cemetery gates, with the last leaves fluttering to the ground, Holly waits in the hope of explaining himself to Anna. She approaches from the distance, walking on and on towards a fixed unmoving Camera, on and on, without even a glance at Holly, on through the gates and away…

Is it *noir..*? Well, I suppose it is…Robert Krasker won the Oscar for Best Cinematography, providing a magnificent look, evoking a

Vienna of dark contrasts, long shadows fleeing across glistening cobbles, tilted Camera angles and an almost expressionist sense of a city in a time of decay and ruin. The decision to use Anton Karas and his music for the zither was inspired and has gone into history, with the Harry Lime theme becoming almost as classic as the film itself. Being a Graham Greene story, it is, of course, shot through with tortured moral ambiguities ... loyalty, betrayal, love, duty...where do you put them all? How do you decide which side of the fence you are standing on? But Carol Reed is not laying these questions on with a trowel – he allows them to surface in the wake of the suspense-thriller narrative he is unfolding – and he does it very well... "Odd Man Out"? "Fallen Idol"...Yes, Carol Reed was better than good when he was good – he was very, very good! But unlike the child in the children's cautionary tale, when he was bad he was still pretty good too...Interesting director...

As for that famous last shot? The Camera fixed, Holly waiting, Anna walking? How long does it last? A minute? Two minutes? Forever? I don't know, but, as I said before I could watch it again...and again.... and again...

82. "CITIZEN KANE"

(1941. Director: Orson Welles)

With the link to both Orson Welles and Joseph Cotten from "The Third Man", this seems as good a moment as any to include what many people in the past have voted 'the greatest film ever made'. Well, such superlatives have no more real meaning to them than, say, voting the Mona Lisa as the greatest painting ever painted. Nevertheless, "Citizen Kane" certainly is an outstanding piece of film-making and Welles a tremendous creative talent. In real life, he was very fond of performing magic tricks and in this, his first feature film, he has a whole box full of them.

Super-magnate Kane lies alone on his deathbed in the castle of his massive estate, Xanadu. The last word he whispers is 'Rosebud'... What did he mean? The film is told in a series of flashbacks as a reporter sets out to find an answer to this riddle – interviewing past friends, associates, a broken down alcoholic ex-wife, his butler...A portrait is built up of Kane, from a happy childhood playing in the snow on his sleigh to a young, idealistic man who slowly, as he builds a newspaper empire, seeks political office, relinquishes his integrity and early ideals in the ruthless pursuit of yet more power and wealth...ending up alone, a defeated tyrant and a bully in his vast empty tomb of a home, abandoned by all...And the enigma of 'Rosebud'..? The reporter concludes no-one will ever really know – but as the thousands of contents of Xanadu are labelled and stacked to be stored or destroyed, one of the objects consigned to the incinerator is Kane's childhood snow-sleigh...and painted on its side, its name – Rosebud.

The similarities between Kane and the life of real newspaper magnate, Randolph William Hearst, are all well too known: and it is true that Hearst prohibited any mention of the film in any of his wide chain of papers and tried to have the film banned and its negative destroyed. This may account, in part, for the film's dismal failure at the box-office and its disappearance from view until its 'rediscovery' in the 1950's. But, I think personally, this is only partly the reason – certainly von Stroheim, in his witty review of the film, felt the unfamiliar 'flashback' structure was a mistake and, whilst praising it as a masterpiece of film history, chastised 'Citizen Welles' for putting 'Citizen Kane's' death at the beginning of the film – and not at the end, where deaths belong.

And, indeed, what is important about the movie is not so much the story itself but the manner of its telling. Think about it – how often (unless Fred Astaire feels the urge to tap dance his way up onto one) do you see *ceilings* in films of that period? Pretty well, never! "Citizen Kane" has enough ceilings on view to serve for them all. Frequently favouring Low Angle Shots (thus emphasizing Kane's stature), the ceilings had to be placed artificially low on the sets – barely a few feet above the head of the actor(s) – to accommodate the shot. Combining this with the equally innovative use of complete depth of field – in itself requiring considerable skills in the lighting and choice of lens which legendary cinematographer, Gregg Toland, masters with stylish flair – the film takes on an air of a kind of hyper-realism, over and above the conventional 'naturalism' of those times. This is further enhanced by his occasional use of over-lapping dialogue – another novel technique in those days.

There is a huge cast in the movie – hundreds of small roles pop up (anyone care to spot Nat King Cole in one of them?) – but for the mainstay, Welles called upon the members of his Mercury Players (famous for sending the good American folk into a gibbering panic with their radio hoax of The War of the Worlds). So there's Joseph Cotten, Agnes Moorhead, Everett Sloane and Dorothy Comingore as Kane's bullied, oppressed and almost tragic wife. Herman Mankiewicz, sent away with a minder and told to keep off the bottle which had almost wrecked his career, wrote the screenplay and Welles brought in one Bernard Hermann to write the music –

it was his first movie score, (I think), but he went on, of course, to become Hitchcock's collaborator on all his films until they fell out on "Torn Curtain" and, sadly, never spoke to one another again. And the film was edited by a certain Robert Wise, better known years later for directing "The Sound of Music" in which the hills resounded to exactly that – almost *ad nauseam*...Back in 1941, however, the Hollywood Hills were resounding to another tune altogether...

In life, as on screen, Welles was always slightly larger than both – flamboyant, charming, highly gifted and something of a showman, standing centre stage. A touch of *hubris* perhaps? "Citizen Kane" certainly confirmed him as 'the boy genius', but it wasn't only the Greeks who were worried about *hubris* – and it was precisely this tendency that did not readily endear him to the Studios... I wonder whether, even at that time, he saw the writing on the wall...and realise they were just itching for the moment they could kick his ass right out of town..?

* * *

Many directors have had a crack at filming Shakespeare – Olivier, of course, Polanski, Peter Brook, Franco Zeffirelli come to mind, and more recently, Kenneth Branagh and Mike Radford...Hollywood also had a go back in 1935 with the great Max Reinhardt's rather bizarre and tinselly "A Midsummer's Night's Dream" with, of all people, James Cagney as Bottom. But for my money – apart from Kurosawa's personal takes on both "Macbeth" and "King Lear" – there is one Shakespeare film which has stuck in my mind more than most – and, as it happens, is another work by Welles.

83. "CHIMES AT MIDNIGHT"

(1966. Director: Orson Welles)

Anyone who is inspired enough to cast Margaret Rutherford, all wobbling chins and jowls, as the ageing bawd Mistress Quickly and then go on to trump that by throwing in Jeanne Moreau as the tart, Doll Tearsheet, for good measure, certainly gets my vote for pulling not one, but two such unexpected rabbits out his magic hat. That's just for starters – up pop John Gielgud as King Henry IV, Alan Webb as Justice Shallow, Norman Rodway as Harry Hotspur and Ralph Richardson added to the mix as the Narrator. There's even Fernando Rey there as the rebel Worcester. Although, to be honest, I'm not sure about Keith Baxter as Hal…

With Welles himself playing Falstaff in this, his version of "Henry IV: parts 1 and 2", the film centres on his relationship with young Hal, the future King Henry V, still a tearaway youth keeping low company and up to no good in the taverns and brothels to the growing despair of his father. But, finally, this is Falstaff's story – and Welles plays him magnificently. He is a Falstaff creaking in his bones, a boasting coward who hides himself in a bush during battle, full of warm, paternal fondness for Hal and deluded that this affection is reciprocated and will lead him to honour. Rheumy-eyed and mischievous in equal measure, Welles plays him as an essentially good man with a head full of foolish ideas, yet commanding the genuine love of his friends. And it works – he is very touching. Finally rejected by Hal, reconciled to his father on his deathbed, and vowing to turn over a leaf and be a good and noble king, the pathos of Falstaff is genuinely moving – a man dying of a broken heart for a son who never was his son. Gielgud's King Henry IV is also marvelous, an ascetic, brooding man troubled by not only his wayward son, but also the responsibilities of the kingship he fears he has wrongly usurped.

The battle at Shrewsbury in which Henry confronts and defeats the rebel Hotspur is masterly – a brute, sordid business of men rolling around in mud and dying (and, incidentally, is a fine example of what you can achieve on a limited budget with only a handful of Extras). I don't know why, but it also had faint echoes for me of Eisenstein's Battle on Ice in "Alexander Nevsky' – both stylised, ritualized events. Indeed, much of Welles' film has a formalism to it which may be a nod of the head in the direction of the Russian master.

Despite its English setting, all of the film was shot in Spain – including some scenes in the little medieval town of Pedraza outside Madrid, (where I had a most unforgettable lunch of roast lamb with my ex-wife and a friend ….doubtless Welles, who was quite a gourmet, ate there too while he was filming). He had endless problems putting the finance together, shooting it over 2 years, while he cobbled together the cash. Edmond Richard, later Buñuel's cinematographer in his final 'Paris years', filmed "Chimes at Midnight" in a grainy, moody black and white, at times utterly compelling to watch.

I loved it, but the critics weren't quite so enthusiastic. Since then, however, opinion has changed and now are there many who consider it to be one of Welles' very best works. Its hard not to make a comparison between Falstaff and Welles himself…certainly they have an affinity and Welles' sympathy for the big, boasting braggart with a hedonist's love of life is apparent throughout. There are quite a few ways in which Welles could identify with his hero… Hollywood's turning its back on him, just as Hal does on Falstaff, not being the least… Falstaff and Welles were both giants in their own ways, and, as we all know, we have a habit of slaying them…or at least cutting them down to size… But, like a thief in the night, the giant still slips in through the back door and leaves his calling card to remind us the more you cut them down the more they seem to grow…

* * *

I wonder if it is those long, dark winters of the Northern countries which engenders the deep, brooding angst the work of their peoples so often carries.. Its there in the Russian sensibility, but also across the entire belt of the Scandinavian countries. Certainly, at the time I was living in Sweden, it seemed to me that, during those endless winter months, people could – and sometimes did – behave as if they were on the perpetual brink of being seized by some demonic madness, an intensity simmering away just beneath the surface. For the most part, however, they always managed to rein it in – possibly waiting to uncork it during the endless Midsummer's Day/Night when the 'madness' was sanctioned… I cannot easily forget the spectacle of a few dozen men and women, their white bodies stark naked, running through the shadowy pine forests of Dalarna, shrieking and laughing in some kind of frenzied pagan ecstasy. And remembering that now brings to mind, of course, another of the great film directors of all time, that extraordinary Swedish creative genius, Ingmar Bergman…

84. "WILD STRAWBERRIES"

(1957. Director: Ingmar Bergman)

Death playing chess with the Knight by the seashore, innocent women being burnt as witches, the plague, Death dancing a line of victims across the brow of a hill...."The Seventh Seal" was the first Bergman film I saw, and unforgettable it was. Then so many of his films, with his great creative drive, are truly memorable – but I have chosen the earlier "Wild Strawberries" because it is one of his loveliest films and one of his most redemptive works. And, for me, unquestionably one of his greatest.

Victor Sjöström (himself one of the greats also), plays the aged Professor, an eminent scientist, on his way from Stockholm to receive an Honorary Degree from a university in another city. Life has gone sour for him and now he is an embittered old man, disillusioned with himself and everyone else and there's clearly little love lost between him and his daughter-in-law, who is driving him there. She is played by Ingrid Thulin, one of Bergman's regulars – as were Bibi Andersson, Gunnar Björnstrand and Max von Sydow who also appear in the film. On the way, they stop and pick up a couple of hitchhikers (and you don't see many of them around these days, do you) who trigger a series of dreams/daydreams in which he looks back on his life and slowly starts to re-assess and indeed reassemble it before the impending death he is aware approaching takes him away forever. His lost love, his failed marriage, his relationship to his mother – we are in familiar Bergman territory, soul-searching, introspective and scarred by guilt. But this is also a lyrical and poetic film, with a lightness of touch about it as well – as delicate as the little wild strawberries he recalls sharing with the girl he loved and lost. By the end of the film, (and the end of his journey into his past) after receiving his Honorary degree and the accolade that goes with it, neither of which have any real meaning for him anymore, he has, in a sense, been reborn – his humanity restored, his capacity to love re-instated and peace replacing his anguish and guilt. Now he can approach his own end made whole.

Bergman is very clever in the way he places the present tense into the past – Victor Sjöström quite literally looks in on and at his earlier life – sees himself now as he was then in a woodland glade picking the wild strawberries. Bergman takes us in and out of these dreams so deftly, subtly eliding the two realities and showing that mastery of his craft which he would refine and distil right throughout his long and very distinguished life. Like so many of these films on the list, I was an adolescent teenager when I saw it first – apart from developing a crush on the lovely Bibi Andersson, who seemed to epitomize the sensual bubbling Swedish beauty, and being moved and full of admiration for Victor Sjöström's performance(I think it was his last film rôle ever), the most important realization was knowing I was in the presence of a master of film. I was in awe of him then and have been a devoted fan of Bergman ever since.

85. "FANNY AND ALEXANDER"

(1982. Director: Ingmar Bergman)

I have chosen this film (virtually his last) because it brings together the two central poles that run through so much of Bergman's work: the warm, sensual, life-affirming and joyous pitted against the cold, repressive, puritan and sterile. Besides that, it is also a wonderful, wonderful film and a late masterpiece. Originally conceived to play in several parts on TV, (and there is a compete version running at a whopping 300 minutes plus), it was re-cut and first released in the cinemas as a 3 hour film.... 3 hours, 5 hours, 10 hours – what the hell, I would have been gripped by it whatever its length...

Fanny and Alexander are brother and sister. They are growing up around the 1900's in an affectionate, warm environment with their theatre-loving parents. This home is full of friends, laughter, celebrations, games and a relish for the creative, the imaginative, and life-positive fun. A happy home! When their father dies, their widowed mother re-marries with a Lutheran Bishop. The regime of his home is the complete opposite: cold, strict, severe and repressive – utterly unlike their previous life. An unhappy home! The punishments meted out on the children, particularly on Alexander, are cruel, and their lives are being deliberately stunted and emotionally cauterized. It is a heartless prison from which they wish only to flee. Eventually, it is too much for their mother to take as well – now pregnant by him, she asks for, but is refused a divorce by the Bishop. She can take the risk of abandoning him, but, under the law of the time, the children would remain in his custody. Eventually, however, a friend manages to smuggle the children away and they take refuge in his home. The Bishop insists on their return, but his wife defies him. Full of that puritan self-righteousness he vows he will hound them down and bend them all to his will (aka God's will) or ruin their lives. Desperate situations require desperate remedies, as Hamlet reminded us – his wife drugs his drink and flees herself. An accident leads to a fire and the worthy Lutheran man of God dies within it….Good riddance!

The film has a happy ending – or does it? There is a christening of Fanny and Alexander's new sister, life and colour and warmth return, celebration enjoyed. But the spirit of the step-father whose death he has wished for so many times hovers before Alexander to remind him he will never ever be entirely free of him. Bergman talking of Bergman and his own unhappy childhood as the son of a Lutheran pastor? The scar of childhood trauma which can never be fully healed and expelled?

This skimpy outline doesn't even begin to do justice to the film – which, finally, is laced with enchantment, magic, daydreams blurring the line between fantasy and reality. It is a childhood vision seen through the eyes of a mature and compassionate man. It cannot express either the extraordinary 'ensemble' acting throughout the film which bonds the cast together with an easy familiarity. Nor can it do justice to the sumptuous photography of Bergman's long time associate, Sven Nykvist (he got an Oscar for the film, and I should bloody well hope so too) – which is all light, reds, oranges, yellows, glowing colours for the happy home of the first marriage and then cold, blues, greys, blacks for the unhappy misery of the second marriage to the Lutheran bishop. This works hand in glove with the excellent art direction and set dressing(also awarded an Oscar) – again, fecund and rich and generous on one side and austere, parsimonious, mean on the other. And at the helm, in what he intended to be his valedictory film, Bergman moves his Camera and the people in front of it with all the masterful assurance gained through the experience of years – and with all the magic of a Prospero casting a spell.

A few self-regarding critics condescendingly labeled the film as being too populist and accessible (oh, come down off your precious pedestals!), but most saw it for the enchanting masterpiece that it is – a grand work by a grand master, made in his mature years and as heavenly as "a green thought in a green shade".

* * *

However, without in any way detracting from his greatness, no-one would claim that Bergman is known for being a bundle of laughs. And, to be perfectly honest, I wouldn't wish to subsist on a daily diet of Bergman alone. My tastes are catholic and, like most people, from time to time I need to escape into froth and fantasy. I am not much of a fan of the American musical or any musical, either on film or stage(with the exceptions of Leonard Bernstein and Stephen Sondheim), but three examples of this genre come to mind, each of them having made an impression on me for very different reasons. The first of them comes, surprisingly perhaps, not from America but from France, although it would be only fair to say that, in no small degree, it looks back across the Atlantic pond to pay homage…

86. "LES DESMOISELLES DE ROCHEFORT"

(1967. Director: Jacques Demy)

It is not readily apparent where Jacques Demy fits into *La Nouvelle Vague,* because he inhabits a very different world from the one we customarily associate with their work. Yet he is their exact contemporary and, whilst no Rivette or Godard or Truffaut, his films remain as singular and radical in their own way, if not in content, then most certainly in style.

Following on from the huge success of his musical "Les Parapluies de Cherbourg", Demy decided to go the whole hog with this one – and do it all over again, but this time exploding into song and dance all over the screen in 70mm with the full Dolby treatment to go with it. When I saw it, I was completely charmed and surrendered myself without any protest to its fantastical fairy-tale silliness. Or, should I say sweetness ..? Sweetness of heart…?

Catherine Deneuve and her real-life sister, the adorable and highly talented, Françoise Dorleac (how I sorrowed when she died so young in yet another car accident) play twin sisters living in the seaside town of Rochefort. One teaches ballet and the other gives music lessons. They yearn to find true love and be whisked away to the bright lights of Paris – while their mother, (the versatile Danielle Darrieux) who runs a bar in the centre of town, in turn yearns to find a lost love she had jilted unfairly years before. So does Michel Piccoli, playing a melancholy man recently arrived from Paris to open a modest music store, also lamenting his own lost love. And the members of the fair coming into town are on the look-out for love as well … Love, love, love – there's enough of it in the air to give you a surprise attack of hay fever – all weeping eyes and dripping noses! And, *bien sûr,* they are all going to find it, aren't they – because this is a fairy-tale.

Coincidence, paths unexpectedly crossing, dreams coming true – all these are elements that interest Demy in his films. One of the twins will find it with one of the fairground workers (George Chakiris, with Demy tipping his hat to American musicals), and the other with a sailor (Jacques Perrin) who aspires to be a painter. As for their mother, Danielle Darrieux, she will learn eventually that Michel Piccoli is none other than the love she lost so many years before and be reunited. And, for good measure, Demy now throws none other than Gene Kelly into the mix, as a well-known performer and friend of Michel Piccoli. And between them all, they sing and dance themselves all over town and into happiness. Its irresistible.

The distinctive technique Demy employs – and, to begin with it feels incredibly bizarre, like listening to the chanted Responses in church – is that *everything* is sung. So a line of dialogue (and I'm not quoting) as banal as, for instance, "Please pass me the ketchup" or "My feet are killing me" are delivered in a plain chant to initially weird, then curiously compelling effect. The tone behind the most mundane of exchanges becomes loaded with possibilities and longings the words themselves are shielding. It's a little bit bonkers, but bold and surreptitiously hypnotic. Demy draws you into the spell, so much so that the next time you find yourself in, say, a supermarket when, yet again, the wretched blind electronic voice bleats its "Please place your items in the bagging area" or " Have you swiped your Nectar Card?", you are tempted to chant a *sotto voce* "Sod off!" in response. Or, in other words, just in case my point remains unclear, it makes you, the viewer, focus on the moment – on the 'now' – as if seeing the most mundane of daily events for the first time ... a sensation of slow-motion observed through the lens of a magnifying glass .

Michel Legrand's score (he wrote "Les Parapluies..." as well) is also studded with some pretty good songs and, naturally, from time to time everyone breaks into a dance routine here and there in the streets and squares of Rochefort. Demy fills his 70mm screen with a range of soft pastels – the blues, pinks, yellows you see in the piping around the edge of wedding cakes and so forth. Indeed, the whole picture is not unlike some glorious confection on display in an upmarket patisserie... a froth of "sugar and spice and all things nice". Charming, enchanting and as make-believe as they come. Emerging from the cinema and the world outside seems dull and grey by comparison, and you rather want to go back inside and see it all over again...

* * *

...Which I did – with the young orphaned cousin of my girlfriend at the time. She was a troubled and lonely teenager and I thought seeing this film would cheer her up. Which it most certainly did, although it did also bring on a brief spate of tears after which she felt much better... Years later, I learnt that she had met and married a Frenchman and had left London to go and live in France, where she was happily living, if not for 'ever after', then at least with her sadnesses left behind her... Not unlike a story out of Demy's film – although I don't suppose she chanted in plainsong to her husband over breakfast when asking him to pass her the butter...But then, on the other hand, perhaps she did...

87. "SINGING IN THE RAIN"

(1952 Director: Stanley Donen/Gene Kelly)

Like pretty well everyone else in the world, Demy must have heard the title song of this film dozens of times and perhaps even remembered it when he invited Gene Kelly fifteen years later to come and sing and dance with the desmoiselles in Rochefort. Its an infectiously happy song – and how well it has travelled through time and space to become part of everyone's repertoire. The last time I heard it was a couple of years ago being sung by three bubbly African girls in, of all places, the remote bush of Swaziland where I was making a little film for the NGO Garden Africa. It was a charming moment...they even danced as they sang...

Teaming up Gene Kelly with Stanley Donen makes for a potent combination of talents – and, although the film is mostly remembered for its title song and Kelly's brilliant choreography of it, Donen was there also to make sure there was more meat on the bone than you're going to find in your average Hollywood musical. And I include it in my list for both reasons – the title song sequence, which I have seen more times than I care to remember (and I have still failed, despite numerous attempts, to count how many edits there are in it); and the structure Donen imposes on the story which has some clever and amusing comments to make on the problems faced by the advent of 'the talkies'.

Gene Kelly plays Don, a movie star and something of a matinee idol in the silent era, alongside his regular co-star, the lovely Lina Lamont (Jean Hagen, showing a wicked talent for comedy). They are about to make another silent period drama together just as the 'talkies' are being ushered in with "The Jazz Singer". Don's studio boss hastily decides they must re-shoot with sound. Along the way, much to the vindictive and spiteful fury of the lovely Lina, Don has come across a nice, unpretentious and straight-talking chorus girl called Cathy (all American, nice girl next door, Debbie Reynolds) and has been somewhat smitten. The other problem facing the lovely Lina (and the studio boss) is that, despite the best efforts of a voice teacher, she cannot escape the fact that her voice still sounds like something between a cat being slowly strangled and someone with a terminal case of adenoids. This, together with the technical headaches of early sound(mics hidden in flowers vases, actors turning their heads and going off-mic, losing synch, etc), pretty well guarantees that the film is an absolute turkey….Then, hey, Don and his friend(Donald O'Connor – no mean performer either) come up with an idea – why not re-shoot it yet again, but this time as a musical? And, since the lovely Lina is never going to win points as a warbling nightingale, why not get down-to-earth, sweet-as-Mother's-apple-pie Cathy to dub her voice? And why not, indeed, thinks the studio chief. There's absolutely no question, however, as far as the lovely Lina is concerned that Cathy should receive even one ounce of recognition for saving her bacon – and she brings in the lawyers to make sure credit is not given where credit is most emphatically due. Of course, it all comes right at the end – and the lovely Lina is given a humiliating lesson in how to be on the receiving end of a raspberry, whilst an admittedly rather tearful Cathy is publicly recognized as the real talent of the film….A Star is born…Somewhere in all this, Gene Kelly has also sung, danced, splashed, tapped his umbrella, swung round a lamppost right through the rain and into cinema legend… Oh, its good alright.

Donen is one of those directors who has been long admired and respected, but who sometimes gets overlooked. He has a strong sense of style, rhythm and pacing and, like many a good craftsman knows how to make it all look so easy. When the 'talkies' came in, there were many casualties – some quite tragic – amongst the fraternity of silent stars who couldn't make the transition. Donen makes good use of the many devices and facets involved in early sound-recording to show just what an uphill task it was, and although the lovely Lina thoroughly deserves what she gets, you can't help reflecting how cruel and merciless the medium (and its public) can be at times when you get it wrong...Little touches, here and there, suggest that Donen(and Kelly) were only too aware of that as well...

* * *

Kitsch, camp, sexist, jaw-droppingly vulgar – to be seen to be believed! Busby Berkeley has become a synonym for a certain style, has he not, and there has been no shortage of imitations and parodies – and while we are in the world of musicals, I am wondering if I should include him on this list...or should I?

All those lines of men, in tails and toppers, perfectly drilled, descending the steps in their shiny patent shoes (oh my God – surely not the Cossacks on the Odessa steps again?!); and those rows upon rows of smiling ladies, all white teeth and shiny lipstick, peeling back in their swimsuits or gowns, one after the other, in strict uniformity (oh no! – please not the massed rallies at Nuremberg?), like lotus flowers opening, petal by petal. The Ladies becoming kaleidoscopic patterns, permutating in precise order; the Gents removing their toppers, one by one like a rippling wave. And everyone smiling, oh, God, how they smile as they tap their canes, click, swirl to the beat of the music – how very, very American they all are! And its all so very gay before that word meant gay! I watch these routines, frozen like a rabbit in front of headlights. I'm not sure I even breathe until its all over – my mind is boggled good and proper! Its brilliant! Its horrible! Its amazing! I can't even blink and sometimes the puritan in me is appalled at how compelling Busby Berkeley is to watch, like an attraction to a loathsome habit I simply can't renounce – but his influence is undeniable. Of one thing I am sure, however, and that is I really would not have liked to have been inside his head....and maybe his six wives also felt there was something not quite right and didn't want to be there either...When all is said and done, there's an uneasy feeling its all just a wee bit unhealthy ...so I'm leaving him off the list – in favour of turning towards another director and another genre, both of which are favourites of us all...

88. "THE MALTESE FALCON"

(1941. Director: John Huston)

Humphrey Bogart, Sidney Greenstreet, Peter Lorre, Elisha Cook Jr and ice-cool *femme fatale*, Mary Astor? The whole gang all in the same bag? Plus Dashiell Hammett's story and John Huston, making his directorial debut? Simply got to have it!

In the film *noir* genre, it already ranks as a classic – and "The Maltese Falcon" perhaps sets a benchmark. This is a murky world in which the tough guys are just tough – tough-talking, tough acting, tough feeling – while the small guys try and act even tougher, ending up with their pretensions punctured and more than likely with either a bullet in their guts or, at the very least a punch on the nose. As for the dames, just watch out for them – svelte, alluring, sexy, but dangerous as hell to go with it! And, of all the tough guys with the really smart talk and ready riposte, who can equal private dick, Sam Spade? Or his hats – in a genre in which there are considerably more hats on view than hot dinners – quite apart from a generous dosage of curling smoke from all those cigarettes they are endlessly lighting up.

Bogart plays Sam Spade as if the role had been invented for him. He is hired by the dangerously attractive Mary Astor ostensibly to track down her missing sister. But Miss Astor is lying through the back of her charming teeth, indeed is pathologically incapable of telling the truth. Thereafter, as is characteristic of Dashiell Hammett's underworld of low-life criminals, harassed cops and endless deceptions at every level, the plot becomes complicated and as murky as the world which they all inhabit. But one thing is for sure – they are all after something, and their greed to lay their hands on it means they will stop at nothing to get it. The 'something' in question is, of course the much coveted and priceless artefact, the legendary statuette of the Maltese Falcon. And, lurking in the background, master-minding it all is 'The Fat Man' (Sidney Greenstreet, also making his screen debut) working in cahoots with our duplicitous Miss Astor and sidekick associate, (the fantastically mournful Peter Lorre, all these years later from Lang's "M") as well his remarkably pathetic 'heavy' in the shape of the diminutive Elisha Cook Jr (really excellent in his portrayal of cack-handed ineptitude dressed up as the would-be tough guy).

Between them, they are no match at all for Sam Spade, but they do manage to bump off two of his associates in pursuit of their goal. And, sorry, Sam does not like this – in fact, he doesn't like this at all, anymore for being taken for a sucker. The Fat Man, such a charmingly well-mannered gentleman, would like to cut Spade into the deal if he can arrange to lead them to the statuette they all so desire, but we know – as Sam knows – you don't go around killing people and believe you're going to get away with it: someone is going to have to pay. Even a *femme* as *fatale* as Mary Astor. Sorry, babe, Sam Spade seems to say, but this is how its got to be…In the closing shot, the iron gates of the lift close across her face…and Miss Astor goes down…in every sense…Neat! …And the Maltese Falcon itself? – the one Spade finally lays his hands on and gets delivered to them turns out to be, to his amused satisfaction, a fake.…which does momentary wonders for The Fat Man's otherwise usually impeccable composure and solicits a rather irritable display of discomfort in them all.(Oh, such greedy boys and girls!)…

The dialogue sparkles with smart one-liners, the performances are as polished as the hats and Huston's direction firm and sure in its handling of the *noir* mood, without ever falling into the trap of taking it all too seriously. Indeed, there is a sense of fun about it all – (Peter Lorre trying to pull a gun on Bogart still makes me laugh, as does the lugubrious Elisha Cook Jr's trying to act the tough guy). Huston doesn't ask us to suspend our disbelief – rather, he wants us to sit back and enjoy. Its an entertainment, and none the worse for that. And, as entertainments go, it ranks amongst the very best. (See if you can spot Huston's own father, the renowned Walter Huston, giving his son a helping hand in a cameo role…)

* * *

Talking of hats, there's nothing like the wide brim of a felt hat to help the Lighting Cameraman cast the perfect moody shadow on her face in the Big Close Up when She has to say the Big Good'bye to Him and turn away and get on that 'plane however much its breaking her heart.(But they'll always have Paris, won't they… ?) Of course, they will – if they are Ingrid Bergman and Humphrey Bogart standing together on the airport tarmac in a town called Casablanca…

89. "CASABLANCA"

(1942. Director: Michael Curtiz)

This was meant to be just another solid Hollywood movie, one of hundreds, and a job well done. That it became and remains one of everyone's all-time favourites must have been as baffling back then to Jack Warner of Warner Bros who made the movie, as it still is to me today. I love the film – who doesn't – but I am far from sure I know why…

"Play it again, Sam…"(which is *not* what Ingrid Bergman *actually* says in the film) has gone into the vernacular and "As Time Goes By" is known and sung by us all. But apart from Woody Allen in his "Play It Again, Sam" seen mouthing every line of the film a second *before* it comes up on the screen, I doubt anyone else can recall the film in that much detail (*maybe my friend, the Calcutta Police Inspector, on that memorable evening circa 1972? Although I am pretty sure it wasn't on the list of films he sampled for me and his family that night. Come to think of it, though, I should add that his delivery of Clark Gable's "Frankly, my dear, I couldn't give a damn, (isn't it?)" and Vivien Leigh's famous last line "Tomorrow IS another day, (isn't it?)"from "Gone with the Wind" both had a certain ring to them*). Yet, there it is – "Casablanca" has become 'iconic' (a word everyone seems to insist on using these days). And, like "The Sound of Music", I don't quite get it – (although give me "Casablanca" any day over those hills resounding again and again to Julie Andrews' nun *manquée*! I can't even see a dirndl now without panicking she might pop up out of a bush and start resounding all over again).

We all know the story, don't we – Rick (Bogart) runs a bar in Vichy-occupied Casablanca, which is a magnet for an assorted bunch of waifs and strays fleeing the Nazi occupation of their own countries and desperate to get hold of the papers which will give them safe passage to neutral Lisbon and then on to freedom. Rick is prone to wearing a white tuxedo and smoking cigarettes, both of which he does to good effect. He also has his faithful pianist, Sam, alongside him, still tickling the ivories for the benefit of his guests. Rick is a bit of a cynic and professes to be on nobody's side but his own, and there is clearly something brooding from his past which has hardened his feelings. However, that doesn't stop him offering a helping hand from time to time and getting his croupier (Marcel Dalio – remember him from Renoir's "La Règle du Jeu"?) to fix the roulette table so a young couple can win and pay for their papers to freedom.

With all these refugees swilling around, it is also only natural that the Vichy Police Chief (Claude Rains at his suave best) should keep an eye on what goes on in Rick's bar, and is not averse to turning a blind eye if his palm is crossed with silver, whilst remaining outwardly and vocally loyal to the official rule book. They have an understanding and he and Rick know each other's game inside out. Sidney Greenstreet with a fez on his head is always around, ready to make a deal with Rick and so is Peter Lorre, wandering around and being mournful and very Peter Lorre.

Into this one evening steps the past – in the lovely incarnation of Ingrid Bergman in a hat, and her husband, Viktor, (Paul Henreid) a well known resistance fighter, without one. Cue for Sam to look alarmed. Cue for Miss Bergman to ask him to play 'it' again ("Play it, Sam ...play "). And cue, too, for Rick to come storming across the bar to remind Sam he had told him never to play 'it' again. Time indeed has gone by – and there, before Rick, is the love he lost those years ago in Paris...Oh...ouch! Viktor and wife are also looking safe passage out to Lisbon so that he can continue the fight. Can – won't Rick, help them? Will he ever – he's not inclined to after the way Ingrid B. upped and left him in the lurch when the Germans occupied Paris. So why should he lift a finger now?

Into this already heady mix, now steps a very polished nazi Nazi (Conrad Veidt) and his men, intent on imposing the Führer's will on all and sundry. He's a bit of a bully, but of course, he can't touch Viktor while he is on Vichy soil without the indispensable help and connivance of Claude Rains. Well, he's not going to get that assistance anymore than Ingrid Bergman is going to get Rick to help her and freedom-fighter hero hubby. Well, not true in the latter case: Rick has softened up somewhat and Ingrid Bergman also feels their love being re-kindled and whipped up into a pretty darn hot flame. A dilemma – Viktor is a decent man and can Rick and Miss Bergman allow their passion to get in the way of 'doing the right thing'? Yes… I'm afraid they can ….Or, then again, can they?

All's well that ends well – despite his best efforts Conrad Veidt cannot stop Viktor and wife getting to the airport with their safe passage to freedom and instead gets shot dead by Claude Rains (or was it Bogie?) for trying to do so. Ingrid Bergman intends to stay behind and be with Rick once more, but duty calls to both of them – and, the brim of her hat framing her very prettily indeed, she listens to Rick's insistence she should join her hubby on the waiting plane. But they'll always have Paris, won't they…? As for Claude Rains and Bogart – well, you can't go around killing senior Nazi officers and hoping no-one of their ilk is going to raise an eyebrow. As the plane takes off carrying Paul Henreid and Ingrid Bergman to take the fight to the free world, Bogart and Rains stride off across the misty airport to join the Free French. As one of them remarks, "I think this is the start of a beautiful friendship…"

Michael Curtiz was no *auteur* director – I think he was what is called a good "jobbing director". But that would be to disparage his skills in crafting a film which, with ""Casablanca", he shows he can do remarkably well. Why it has become so 'iconic', however, still remains a mystery to me….but I think I would put it down more to those simmering Close-ups of Ingrid Berman and the brim of her hats than I would to anything else. Although, it has to be said, Sam playing "As Time Goes By" certainly knows how to tug at our hearts when combined with Miss Bergman's Close-Ups…

* * *

Michael Curtiz had a busy 1942 – he went on to direct Cagney as the showman George Cohan in "Yankee Doodle Dandy" in the same year – (and it is hard to forget Cagney, "just a regular American guy", tap-dancing down the stairs of the White House after a meeting with Roosevelt. Oh, that American Dream!) It was a pretty busy year for Paul Henreid too, who must have been practicing how to light two cigarettes at once so he could pass one across to Bette Davis at the end of "Now Voyager", thus inspiring her "Oh, Jerry, don't ask for the moon – we have the stars" ... which I was to hear re-performed for me so unforgettably in that Calcutta Police Station so many years later ... (isn't it?).

Reflecting for a moment on Conrad Veidt's performance as the German officer, with the slight sneer and Aryan superiority always close to the surface, makes me ponder again on what a powerful conditioning tool film can be. And prompts me to remember another little anecdote – which I tell at my own expense.

Germany is not a country I know at all well – and my impressions of it's people, I realize, were formed in my childhood by the endless war films we all saw. In the majority of them, Germans were portrayed endlessly shouting shrill guttural orders at one another, like "Schnell, schnell!", "Raus, raus!" or leering at another captured Tommy to tell him "Ve haf vays of making you talk!". They were the bad guys, of course, and they were played as bad, incapable, so it seemed, of stringing a sentence together in an ordinary tone of voice. They were all in a mould close to the apoplectic, as in those speeches by Mr A. Hitler when he loses his trolley and goes right off the scale. That was the Germany I knew.

Very recently, I went to Berlin for the first time to visit my daughter, doing a university internship there. We went out for a supper together and when the very nice and friendly waitress came to take our order, she might have been worried for my sanity in the way I gave it – certainly she looked a little bemused. After she left, my daughter lent across the table and told me very gently, "Daddy, its okay, you don't have to talk to them in that way – just speak to them normally"... Yes, so conditioned had I been in those early formative years by all those war movies, that unconsciously I had been addressing the waitress in a full-blown 'Ve haf vays of making you talk!" and 'Schnell, schnell!' voice...Oh, the shame of it! Oh, the power of film! (And what a really exciting city Berlin is, by the way, and what nice people!)

* * *

I am not going to dwell long on the next film, but how can I possibly NOT include the wonderful Audrey Hepburn somewhere in this list? "Funny Face", "Roman Holiday" and so many others mark her out for the absolutely captivating actress she was...This is not my favourite film of her's, but it is representative of that radiant loveliness, innocence even, and sensitive vulnerability she projects so well. And it does contain one scene which most certainly is a favourite...

90. "BREAKFAST AT TIFFANY'S"

(1961. Director: Blake Edwards)

I suspect Truman Capote's novella on which it is based had a darker edge to it than the Blake Edward's film, which veers towards the sentimental and sometimes tips into it. The story of kooky, enchanting Holly Golightly, (Hepburn) who has left her country past behind her to parade as the Manhattan socialite which, in reality, is not much more than a fantasy in her mind, is a promising one – and Hepburn nails the role fair and squarely on the head. She is a troubled, lonely and confused girl pretending to be what she isn't and suffering for it. And Tiffany's represents the glittering world she can only dream of – she is window-shopping her life away. George Peppard, (whom I find a little insipid) plays the struggling writer she meets and will fall in love with – and the splendid Patricia Neal plays the wealthy and genuine socialite who keeps him supplied with cheques in return for favours rendered in the bedroom. All well and good, and we know how its all going to work out in the end.

However, there is one scene which is a little gem for me – and that is owing to the immaculately judged performance of John McGiver playing a Tiffany salesman. McGiver is one of those excellent character actors who never puts a foot wrong, never upstages and is always memorable – P.K.Simmonds is another more recent example ("Juno", "Burn After Reading", "Up in the Air", etc). McGiver, with his pudgy face and small jug ears, plays the salesman, trying to find a sufficiently cheap Tiffany's item to suit Hepburn and Peppard's non-existent bank balance, with such serene and professional good manners, never condescending and always kindly, that he effortlessly steals the scene and makes it his own. And *that's* "The Breakfast at Tiffany's" I remember. The role these character actors play in bolstering up a film sometimes doesn't receive the attention it deserves – but the importance of their contribution to a film's overall success and their own incredible professionalism should never be undervalued. They are there in their legions (the Coen Bros are brilliant at casting them!) and I salute them as the flesh and blood of so many otherwise rather pedestrian films.

Audrey Hepburn is wonderful – because she *is* wonderful (and doesn't she know how to wear those famous dark glasses!). Henry Mancini's "Moon River" has gone into the canon of classics, if you like that sort of thing, and Hepburn manages to ration the amount of sugar when she sings it. The film is better than competent too – but, for me, when all is said and done, it belongs to pudgy-faced John McGiver and the slightly pained regret of his expression when he remembers a 'crackerjack' from a packet of cereals...Just a lovely, lovely moment to be cherished...

* * *

Audrey Hepburn's natural elegance, John Mcgiver's polished good manners put me in mind of another director whose sense of style and equally elegant manner I have long admired. His son, Marcel, is perhaps better remembered now than his father for his searing epic documentary "Le Chagrin et Le Pitié" which tore apart the myths the French invented for themselves after the war, but old man Max Ophuls was no slouch either and could teach us all a trick or two about film-making...And, for one American critic risking his reputation as well as his neck, the following film was simply "the best film ever made"...

91. "LOLA MONTES"

(1955. Director: Max Ophuls)

Here's another one which cost a lot of money to make and was a resounding flop at the box-office – only to re-emerge as an influential classic a decade later. It was Ophul's last film after a career starting back in the 1930's and it really is tremendous.

Historically, Lola Montes was a renowned courtesan whose many, many affairs and exploits scandalized Europe and the world. Ophuls tells her story in flashback from inside the confines of a New Orleans circus where she is the star attraction feeding the vicarious appetites of the general public. Late in her life but still beautiful, Martine Carol plays Lola as a tired but proud woman stoically resigned to her fate. A tragic woman keeping her dignity – someone we can really believe was special and whose plight we empathise with.

The circus – the ring – seems so apt for the telling of the story and Ophuls was clearly fascinated by the circular, cyclical nature of life. His earlier "La Ronde" and "Letter from an Unknown Woman" both have a similar circular structure and even his slightly baroque camera style repeatedly plays on graceful waltz-like turns: as elegant as a well-made suit and as discreet. Peter Ustinov plays the circus ringmaster who has befriended Lola and now exploits her in the ring. Through the crack of his ring-master's whip, the horses perform, the trapeze artists fly through the air and everything goes round and round. Ophuls uses this structural device to take us back first to Lola's affair with Liszt, her unhappy marriage, then her very public and scandalous one with a conductor and the ups and downs of her career as an 'actress' which finally lead to her fatal affair with Ludwig I of Bavaria (Anton Walbrook) which so shocked his subjects that it triggered the 1848 revolution which brought him down and sent

Lola into exiled disgrace. From the outset we know we are looking at a woman doomed to be rejected and to end up little better than an act in a freak show. She is a victim of moral hypocrisy, of course, but also of her own beauty and appetite to conquer men. But Ophuls makes it clear that she is 'more sinned against than sinning'.

Towards the end of this moving film, Lola, who has sunk so low in life, is lifted high on a trapeze bar to the very top of the big top where she sparkles like a queen before making a death defying plunge. If this irony isn't painful enough, Ophuls closes his film with shots of a long queue of punters paying their money for the privilege of entering Lola's kiosk so they can get to kiss her. The humiliation and the stoic way she bears it is truly awful...

Max Ophuls ranks high on my list of favourite directors and I think he merits being re-visited. Baroque as his style may be, it is nevertheless lean and economical at the same time. No fussy frills and no gratuitous thrills, there is a grandeur and nobility to the manner in which he crafts his often sad and tragic stories. Yes, he is up there with the best of them and I could watch his work time and time again.

* * *

So, indeed, is the next director, one of the great names of Cinema whose work has commanded such respect and exercised such influence...I know those who loathe him and those who love him – one thing, for sure, is no-one can ignore him or remain neutral about his work...

92. "PICKPOCKET"

(1959. Director: Robert Bresson)

Bresson is an ascetic – in his films, sometimes no more than a trembling of a cup in someone's hands can signify the deepest of internal dramas. When the poet George Herbert writes "Give me simplicitie that I may live", he is talking about distilling matters to their essence and this is how I feel about Bresson's work as well: they are not so-called 'minimalist', they are distillations from which impurities have been carefully extracted to present us with an uncompromised vision of his moral universe. It doesn't make for easy viewing, but it has a compelling strength by which it holds us. Its hard to choose a film for this list – "A Condemned Man Has Escaped" and "Diary of a Country Priest" are both supreme Bresson works, as is his later version of the Joan of Arc story, but I have chosen "Pickpocket" if for the only reason it was the first Bresson film I saw and its impact was immediate and enduring. It opened the door into his highly individual world and introduced me to a director whose work – like Pialat or Franju – stands outside any category beyond its own…

This is another film which I must trawl through my mind in order to recall it in any detail; another instance of elusive memory tucking itself away from immediate reach. The Pickpocket of the title is a small-time, petty thief for whom stealing is a compulsion, a kleptomaniac who cannot help himself. He steals at the race-tracks, steals from his friends, even steals from his mother. A gang of professionals teach him the mechanics of the pick-pocketing trade and Bresson shows us, dispassionately but excitingly so, them putting their skills into practice on trains, subways etc (it really is fascinating stuff!). The police have an eye on him, but no tangible proof. And there's a girl who also has an eye on him concerned, more than anything else, for the well-being of his soul. And, I suppose, that is what the film is about – the authority of that mysterious thing called Love to pull us back from the brink of falling into the darkness of the void and haul us up into life again...redemption. The Pickpocket's mother dies, he wanders Europe stealing, the girl has a child by another man, but remains single and the police finally nab him and he is sent to jail. The girl, however, visits him regularly there – and this man, whose life has been drained of all sentient meaning the more he steals from the lives of others, can finally feel love and, imprisoned as he is, nevertheless a kind of freedom as well. Bresson liked to work with non-professional actors – and draws from them equally 'non-performance' performances: everything is internalized and compressed, but this can produce a terrible intensity – in the eyes, in a gesture, in impassive silence even. Like a monk in his cell, he works with the bare necessities and no more. His work always deal with moral dilemmas – and you could say he is a 'religious' director – but he is never a preacher, rather someone profoundly concerned with the spiritual side of life. As the actual pick-pocketing sequences show, he was also a very adept craftsman and I admire him enormously.

* * *

I recall sitting one evening in the infamous Byron Restaurant in Inverness Street, Camden Town with a French film director, making a film about the whirling dervishes, and a very good friend of mine who was his producer. Over several bottles of Retsina, The Frenchman and I both became quite vocal in expressing our admiration for Bresson – and my friend equally vocal in dismissing him as a pretentious bore, an art-farty, snail-eating, charlatan of the first order. The Byron (scene of many a dubious debauch) was about the size of a broom closet and any conversation at one table above 'piano molto cantabile' level, became the common property of any other guests present and could do wonders in livening up a plate of Peter the Greek's kleftiko. My friend later confessed he hadn't actually seen any Bresson movies – but he was to get his revenge on me some years later at an Uruguayan restaurant in the Granada Sierra when I tore into the works of the writer, Herman Hesse, in an equally abusive manner – only to find myself owning up I hadn't read a single word of him either. We remain the best of friends to this day... (Incidentally, not that it is in any way relevant, but The Byron came to an ambiguous end after Peter the Greek had gone home to Greece to shoot his young wife's lover, before returning to London to burn down his own establishment, some say so he could cop the Insurance money....We shall not see its like again...)

93. "L'AVVENTURA"

(1960. Director: Michelangelo Antonioni)

There's a shot towards the last part of "L'Avventura" in which Monica Vitti runs away from Camera down a very long corridor for a very long time. She enters a room as dawn is breaking and then stands for another very long time at an open window looking at the softly swaying palms below. At Cannes Film Festival, where they like to express their feelings vocally, this was greeted by a lot of booing and hissing. As a 16 year old boy in London, I just couldn't understand why – I thought it was a stunningly beautiful moment! More than that, Antonioni was a revelation to me – the dawn of a new kind of film-making every bit as exciting as the French *nouvelle vague*. When he followed it up with "La Notte", I was even more in his thrall and by the time he finished the trilogy with "L'Eclisse" I was ready, if needs be, to cut my flesh, draw blood and swear an oath of undying loyalty. But would I do so today..?

To be perfectly honest, I wasn't much taken by his "Blow-Up", nor his American venture, "Zabriskie Point", although rather more with "The Passenger", not that I could readily admit that to myself at the time. His fluid camerawork, the compositions of the frames and the prolonged moments in which nothing seems to happen have a sureness of touch and sense of purpose and meaning to them, which, to an impressionable adolescent with his own existential crises, were powerfully seductive. Nor is there any doubt that Antonioni was his own master of Form...but today, can I be so sure about the Content? . I saw "L'Avventura" 3 times, ditto "La Notte" and "L'Eclisse' twice – but that was a long time ago. Now I find myself hesitating at the idea of seeing any of them again for fear having my adolescent sense of wonder cruelly dashed on the rocks of disappointment. "L'Avventura" was such an important moment in my life at 24fps and I would hate to have to relinquish it to the bogeyman of hindsight...

A woman, involved in a relationship with an architect (Gabriele Ferzetti), invites a close friend, (Monica Vitti), to join them on a boating trip along the Italian coast. On one of the islands they stop at, the woman just suddenly disappears – why, how, where? For the remainder of the film, as they travel on, they try to find out what has happened to her ... In the process of doing so, Garbriele Ferzetti develops feelings for Monica Viitti which, out of loyalty to her friend, she resists at first but finally reciprocates – only to be deceived by him as well. At the end of the film, both weep – regret, dissatisfaction, a sense of failure, of lives unfulfilled ....disillusion pervades. And, in terms of story line, there's not much more to say about it.

Not that the 'story' in itself is what really matters – because this is more a study of an emotional landscape which has become barren and infertile, slowly drained of its vital life-blood. There is a fatigue in these people which is corrosive and soul-destroying... The disenchantment of the time? The malaise of a wealthy Italian middle-class which Fellini was also looking at in the very same year, but through very different eyes, in "La Dolce Vita"? *"Ennui"* is the word that comes to mind – there's a lot of it about as Monica Vitti wanders the streets of Palermo, so blatantly stared at by those dark Calabrian eyes standing there on the street corners; a restless, aimless wandering. The only moment of relief, I recall, is when she accidentally sets off a church bell which triggers a succession of carillons from across the other churches of the town – a moment of happiness, even joy...otherwise the mood is sombre, depressed and dusty. Monica Vitti plays her beautifully and Antonioni films it superbly .... but do I dare see it again?

I think I probably do – just to see Monica Vitti running *away* from Camera down that long, long hotel corridor again, in much the same way I can always see Alida Valli in "The Third Man" walking *towards* Camera down that equally long cemetery avenue...and passing Joseph Cotten by...

94. "THE THIN RED LINE"

(1998. Director: Terrence Malick)

Terrence Malick is another director whose undoubted brilliance nevertheless also makes me a little uneasy at times. He has been given a cult status and it seems half the world queued up to play in this, his first film in 20 years, but I am wary about the danger of legends believing in their own myth. I shouldn't have worried in this case – this was the last film I saw in 1999 before the new millennium arrived – and it wasn't a bad way to usher it in, cinematically speaking: because I think it is very good indeed…but then again, as with Antonioni, am I sure…?

The war in the Pacific. Gudalcanal. An American company re-taking the island. Sean Penn, John Travolta, Nick Nolte, George Clooney, Woody Harrelson, John Cusack, Adrien Brody, just to mention a few of those illustrious names who joined the queue to be part of a Terrence Malick film, as well as many other luminaries who ended up on the cutting-room floor. And one other – a comparative unknown, (Jim Caviezel), who plays the Army Private who, at the outset of the film, has gone AWOL to live an idyllic and peaceful life amongst the indigenous people. Re-captured, he is sent in with the others to clear out the Japanese. Without in any way being flagged up and hammered into our heads, he is a kind of Zen figure, touched by a little of the mystic or the poet John Clare – close to the rhythms, powers, ubiquitous beauty of Nature in the midst of the awful business of war. Not that Malick dwells on this – he is unfolding so many collateral stories at the same time, as well as leading us through the physical practicalities of what is involved in being at war. And this he does with great panache and verve – the battle scenes, such as they are, have a ruthless, sickening brevity and finality about them which make them truly disturbing. There is no bravado – the great machine of an army goes in, does its job, moves on. People get killed, blown apart, senselessly …Its awful. Yet Malick is never far away from pointing out the tiny details of this earth Paradise to remind us how we have lost it – as the Company advance up a grassy hill, bending and swaying in the breeze, an insect crawls up a leaf of grass, close to the face of a soldier….in the face of possible and imminent death, he nevertheless can find time to focus, not on the unseen enemy waiting to mow him down, but on this fragile manifestation of life. It is moments such as these that lend the poetry to Malick's film and lift his work to a special level. He did it in his wonderful first film, "Badlands", with the young Martin Sheen and Sissy Spacek, and there are moments in this film when he does it again – he soars right up into the ether where the air is pure and so is the film!

By the end of the film, the Company wades upstream through the jungle to flush out the enemy – and the Private is surrounded by the Japanese, shot and killed … a sacrifice which he meets with an almost ecstatic acceptance. The closing shot of a film is of a coconut husk on the seashore – out of which sprouts new life…

John Toll was the cinematographer and the picture is ravishing to look at – as I understand it, Malick doesn't like to work with artificial lights and this makes Toll's achievements even more impressive. The film was nominated for everything under the sun and was garlanded with enough prizes to light up a Christmas tree. Malick went on to make "The Tree of Life" …and I rather wish he hadn't – for all its many virtues, I had the nagging suspicion that Mr Malick had been begun looking in the mirror at himself and rather liking a little too much of what he saw there…But in "The Thin Red Line" – that fragile division between sanity and madness, life and death, the real and the unreal – no such trend is yet discernible. Its one of the very best war films ever.

* * *

For a few days in 1962, when I was 17 years old, the spectre of a war which would annihilate us all loomed as a very real possibility. The Cuban Missile Crisis was a very frightening moment – and I was soon off, along with thousands of others, cultivating blisters on my feet out by marching from Aldermaston to London to Ban the Bomb. The next film on my list was made 12 years before the crisis but, in the light of it, seems quite relevant. And looking around at the world today, with all the uncertainties of 'terrorist' threats, and 'dirty bombs', it is not without prescience.

I have assiduously avoided including any films made by "those bloody twins", my father and uncle, the Boulting Brothers, because their influence on my life was not really through their films, but simply by their presence. Better known for their later satirical comedies, their earlier work was altogether more serious – and this film one of their best. The studios spent ages not making up their minds whether they should finance it – so they took it to Alexander Korda one Friday evening and signed a deal with him the following Monday. Korda knew how to decide and was, in that respect, a formidably real film Producer – regardless of the massive debts he left behind him, he knew how to dare and take the risk ...

96. "SEVEN DAYS TO NOON"

(1950. Directors: John & Roy Boulting)

A nuclear device in a suitcase? Seem improbable? Not any more, its doesn't – but in 1950…? A scientist, (the unknown Barry Jones), working in a nuclear establishment is so unhinged by the appalling implications of nuclear warfare that he constructs such a bomb and writes to the Prime Minister to tell him he intends to explode it in seven days at noon in London, unless the government immediately ceases its stockpiling of nuclear weapons. And then he goes on the run.

In an increasingly disturbed state of mind as he tries to avoid detection and the hour to explode his bomb gets closer and closer, the film follows the hunt to find him in time to avert catastrophe. Taking lodgings, first he arouses the suspicions of his landlady (the admirable Joan Hickson) by his pacing up and down all night. And then seeking alternative shelter he takes up with a blowsy, brassy lady of questionable virtue (Olive Sloane, well known in her day) who also quickly gets a whiff of something sick about this man she invites back to her home after a drink together in a pub. In the meanwhile, Scotland Yard are hoping that, if they can contact him, his devoted daughter might be able to persuade him out of going ahead with his mad scheme. However, plans are under way to evacuate London, troops take to the streets to intensify the search, and the scientist ends up in a blitzed bombed-out church, agonizing over his decision as the seconds tick by. At the last moment, he is discovered there and his daughter makes a desperate last attempt to get him to hand over the bomb. Panicking, the scientist runs from the church and is shot by an equally panicky soldier (Victor Maddern – remember him?). The bomb is defused in the nick of time. London is saved.

Paul Dehn and James Bernard won the Oscar for the Best Screenplay and it is indeed a taut and suspenseful 'thriller'. The major production problem the Boultings had to face was how to show a London which had been completely evacuated. With the help of the police, and on a limited budget without any of the special effects available today, they did a pretty convincing job in showing both the process of evacuation itself and then an empty, deserted London as noon approaches on the seventh day. Gilbert Taylor, who worked many times with the Boultings, and went on to photograph Kubrick's "Dr Strangelove", did a better than solid job lighting the film and John Addison whom I think was one of the very best British film composers wrote an intelligent score.

The Boultings were good at their craft, good with their actors, and Roy, my father, was especially good at editing. My uncle John told me he thought his twin was the better director of the two of them – more of an artist and poet, he thought – but, although I would never have dared express this opinion aloud while they were alive, I sometimes thought it was John who made the better films and the more enduring ones as well....Is that being disloyal to the memory of my father? Just a little perhaps...not that they would have given a toss for anyone's opinions except their own.... Identical twins, you know...funny creatures...

The Cuban Missile Crisis, the Nuclear Threat, the Cold War ...and eventually that Wall coming crashing down piece by piece...Its hard now to remember just how tense those days of the great Iron Curtain divide could be at times...but virtually impossible for us to imagine what daily life was really like if you happened to born on the other side of the wall. The following film on my list, made 17 years after the Berlin Wall came down and Germany was re-unified, apart from being such a convincing and authentic portrait of life in the GDR under the thumb of The Party and the Stasi, is a terrific piece of film-making in its own right – the first feature of a director too young to have ever known East Germany for himself...

97. "THE LIVES OF OTHERS"

(2006. Director: Florian Henckel von Donnersmarck)

It is extraordinary to think that in the days of the GDR, and the dreaded all-pervasive Stasi, every typewriter had to be registered so that any subversive material typed on them could be traced back immediately to its author. Snooping, surveillance, bugging, informing …it was a way of life and the Stasi were masters at creating an atmosphere of fear and suspicion in which no-one could be certain whom they could trust or what thoughts they dare utter aloud.

In this paranoid climate, a dedicated Stasi Officer is set to work conducting the surveillance of a prominent and internationally recognized playwright, himself a Communist sympathiser. The Officer and his team bug the playwright's apartment and he starts a routine of systematic eavesdropping in the hope of digging up some treasonable dirt on him. But the Officer also discovers that the real motive for bugging him is that the Minister for Culture harbours amorous feelings for the playwright's girlfriend, a successful but insecure actress. It shakes his previously rock solid faith in the State, the Party, the System and plants the first seeds of his disillusionment. This disenchantment is paralleled by the playwright's own growing belief that there is something "rotten in the state of Denmark".

With his power to make or break her career, the Minister also plays on the actress' insecurities to make her give way to his advances. This, too, disturbs the idealistic values of the Officer … and as time goes by he finds himself increasingly sympathetic towards his quarry and less and less inclined to do the State's dirty work. At his birthday party, the playwright is given a present of a piece of music by a fellow writer who has been blacklisted and cannot work. When this same writer then goes out and promptly hangs himself out of despair, the playwright decides to write an article denouncing the State for this death and the many others driven to suicide and smuggle it out to the West for publication. To write it he uses a secret and unregistered miniature typewriter which he hides beneath his floorboards...The authorities are enraged when it comes out in Der Spiegel some days later but, as they cannot trace the typewriter, they cannot pin it on the playwright despite all their well-founded suspicions. The Minister, too, is furious because the actress has rejected him to follow her true feelings and be with the playwright – the Officer is ordered to interrogate her and get her to reveal where the typewriter is hidden and, in her fear, she cracks and tells all. However, when the Stasi go to search the apartment, there is no trace of the typewriter at all...Where has it gone? Who has taken it? Nevertheless, in despair at betraying the man she really loves, the actress runs out into the street and throws herself under a lorry...

With no evidence to go on, the investigation into the playwright is called off, but the Stasi Officer also finds himself demoted in disgrace and consigned to a back room to steam open envelopes for the rest of his working days. And then the Berlin Wall comes down...

It is only much later, now with access to the Stasi files on him that the playwright finally understands that all that time he was under surveillance he was also being protected – by the very man sent to spy on him and bring him down. It is he who has removed the incriminating typewriter; he who has not passed on any damaging information he has monitored. In gratitude the playright dedicates his new book to that same Officer, using only his code name and number. Now a lowly employee distributing leaflets, the Officer passes a bookshop one day and sees copies of this new book – and sees the dedication. Very moved, he buys a copy and when the shop assistant asks him whether he wants it gift-wrapped, he replies: "No – this is for me"....

Limpid in its stylistic purity, intelligently scripted, the film doesn't put a foot wrong. The scenes showing how the Stasi go about their business in bugging the lives of others are terrifically staged and the journey of the Officer from being loyal servant of the State to one who questions, then rejects what it stands for is portrayed with a sincere and quiet conviction in an excellent and memorable performance by an actor (Ulrich Mühe) who, I believe, died shortly after the film was released. Sad, but at least he lived long enough to see the film and share in the great success it enjoyed world-wide. More than a good film – it is an exceptionally good one in which he gave an exceptional performance.

* * *

There are some directors whose thumbprint is almost tangible and visible in the films they make. This is true about many of the film-makers in this list, but there are also a few whose singular style and unusual approach to their material sets them apart and their personal voices seem to shout out at us from the screen.. To conclude, therefore, I have chosen four of them...

98. "THE ENIGMA OF KASPER HAUSER"

(1974. Director: Werner Herzog)

There are stories of Herzog and his lead actor, the mad-eyed Klaus Kinski pulling pistols on each other during the shooting of "Aguirre, the Wrath of God" in the steaming Amazon jungle. Easy enough to believe when you think of the closing shots of that film, with the deranged Kinski in his rusting conquistador armour, floating alone down the Orinoco on his raft, still searching for El Dorado with only monkeys scrambling around him for company. There is more than a touch of the fanatic and obsessive about Herzog in both his films and he, their creator.

Deluded Aguirre, establishing his 'empire' in the jungle...Fitzcarraldo, hauling a ruddy great ship over a mountain so that he could bring Opera to the Amazon...A man living with grizzly bears ... Herzog has a taste for the oddballs – and a distinct, unique talent to put them on film. "The Enigma of Kasper Hauser" is no exception, but remains for me one of his finest films for also having an almost mystical, certainly spiritual tinge to it...

Kasper Hauser was discovered in the early 19th century – a grown man who had been kept all his life confined in a cellar with only a wooden toy horse for company. Every day a mysterious figure in a top hat comes to feed him. For reasons as inexplicable as the confinement itself is his sudden release by the same mysterious man, taking and leaving him out into a totally alien world in Nuremberg. Unable to speak words, barely able to walk, he is like a half-formed creature – more than an oddity, a freak and seen as such by the good burgers of Nuremberg who put him on show in a circus. Rescued from this degrading spectacle by a kindly doctor, Kasper Hauser shows himself to be a fast learner – forming some unorthodox and highly individual views on everything from religion to politics to philosophy. And he develops a deep love and passion for music. Under the tutelage and protection of the good doctor, he soon attracts the attention of professors, pastors and the curious of the nobility. In a word, he becomes famous, not simply because of his history but because it has led to him shaping a highly unique understanding and vision of the world to which he has now been exposed. He makes the familiar unfamiliar – re-invents the way we see it. Then, just as mysteriously, the same strange figure in the top hat reappears and attacks Kasper Hauser, leaving him unconscious. He recovers, only to be attacked again and this time stabbed in the chest. As he lies dying, with that same detached imperviousness to the concept of death one might see in an animal, he has visions of the Sahara, of nomadic tribes, of other peoples and worlds. A kind of ecstasy. And then he simply dies.

When I walked out of the Paris Pullman cinema and into the Fulham Road after seeing Herzog's film, the world I saw looked completely different too: everything looked strange, as perhaps it did to Kasper Hauser. Herzog has that effect at times – his cinematic language is direct and unshowy, he can linger on a static shot (Kasper sitting cross-legged and hunched up into himself with his back to Camera, gazing across the hills, for instance) with telling results. The camerawork is simple, the acting subdued, the dramatics restrained. Throughout the film, there is a diminutive Town Chronicler recording the events of Kasper's life and I believe these actual archives formed the basis for Herzog's script. He also turned to Mozart and the Baroque composers to provide the music for the film. Kasper Hauser does not come across as an *'idiot savant'*, but more as a kind of universe all to himself…not unlike, I suspect, the extraordinarily gifted and unique Werner Herzog who has re-created him in this beautiful, simple and moving film….

99. "WILD AT HEART"

(1990. Director: David Lynch)

David Lynch is another director who lives in a world all of his own – and let's face it, a pretty weird one at that. Think of "Eraserhead", of "Blue Velvet"..? And think of this film too… But he is also a consummate and highly original creator, with an incredible feel for the language of film. This he demonstrates in "Wild at Heart" across the spectrum of his compelling, if utterly bizarre imagination. I think this is Lynch at his very best – and probably at his most hallucinogenic as well.

As an example, how about a character who is the mentally deficient cousin of the heroine and likes to put cockroaches down his pants and has a really weird obsession with Christmas? Where, in God's name, did Lynch dream that up? This gives an idea of the tone of the film – it is peopled with oddities such as this and everyone hovers on just this side of psychosis, sometimes tipping completely over the edge and into it. No-one is 'normal' in the accepted sense of that word.

In truth, I struggle to recall more than the bare bones of the plot line but it revolves around the love between a bungling, wild-haired criminal (Nicholas Cage) and his slightly saner and loyal girlfriend, (Laura Dern). Cage likes to wear a snakeskin jacket, croon Elvis Presley and can't stop either getting into a fight or being sent back to jail. Laura Dern waits it out and waits also for him to commit himself to her for good. She also has a mother (Diane Ladd) who is seriously short of her marbles and seems hell-bent on removing Cage from her daughter's life (and his own as well). When Cage decides to break his latest parole and escape to California with Dern, Mother, as well as sending a private investigator to track them down, also hires in a hit man to polish Cage off. Everything goes wrong, of course, and

Cage turns south to Texas to seek out another criminal – this time Isabella Rossellini (in life, Lynch's long time Ex). She in turn puts him to work with her latest squeeze (William Dafoe) sending them off to rob a bank. Yet again, a complete balls-up during which Cage shoots two clerks and Dafoe manages to blow his own head off. Back to prison for Cage, and more waiting for Dern who, along the way, has got herself pregnant by him. When he is eventually released from prison, Cage finally sees the full errors of his ways via a visitation of no less than the Good Witch from "The Wizard of Oz" to remind him of the power of love. Reformed, redeemed, Cage runs across the roofs of a line of cars to find Dern and declare his undying love with a rendering of Presley's 'Love me Tender, love me True"…Yes, all very strange… And utterly mesmerizing!

Lynch won the Palme D'Or at Cannes with this film, nor is it hard to see why – its an utterly original *tour de force*. Leave aside the grotesqueries and exaggerated mannerisms of his strange characters (superbly judged as they are) and just watch how he puts his camera to work, his use of colour and composition. Like Herzog, Lynch stamps himself across every frame and, although the world he leads us into is as weird as anything you are ever likely to see with a morality all of its own, he has a truly masterly control over it. A road movie? A love story? A semi-surreal crime thriller? All of those in part …but I rather fancy, at heart, beyond all the aberrant images, Lynch, too, sometimes yearns to be able to turn to someone and simply sing them "Love me Tender, Love me True"… There is a terrible innocence lurking in his dark, dark world.

* * *

And so we arrive at 100…Perhaps I should also call it "Amour a 24fps"…

100. "AMOUR"

(2012. Director: Michael Haneke)

Remember Emannuelle Riva from way back in Resnais' "Hiroshima, Mon Amour"? Or Jean-Louis Trintignant in Lelouch's "Une Homme et Une Femme"? Here they are, octogenarians both, in Haneke's heart-breakingly beautiful film about the travails and sufferings of old age. Haneke's voice has also been so distinct and uniquely creative in his films that he must rate as one of the most powerful directors of this age.

An old woman lies on her bed, surrounded by cut flowers. She is dead – and has been so for quite some time before she is discovered by neighbours alerted by the smell of decomposition...

We go back in time: Anne and George (Riva and Trintignant) are retired music teachers, rubbing along comfortably in the old age of marriage. Over breakfast one morning, Anne becomes catatonic – she is having a stroke. At first George thinks she is playing a joke on him, but when she comes round, unable to recall anything of this event but equally unable to lift her cup from its saucer, he realizes what has happened.

The surgery she undergoes to repair the damage to her artery goes badly wrong, leaving her paralysed down one side and confined to a wheelchair. She makes her husband promise not to send her away to a care home and George dutifully takes on the responsibility of caring for her. Inevitably it strains the patience, and there are times when he gives way to irritation and tetchiness. There comes the moment when she tells him she doesn't wish to continue living... A former pupil comes round to help care for her and there's a sense of hope that she will really improve – but a second stroke leaves her demented and incapable of coherent speech.

Their daughter (Isabelle Huppert) who lives in London wants George to put her mother into care, but he refuses to break his promise to his wife. He brings in a nurse – then another, whom he has to fire because he discovers her mistreating Anne. The toll it is taking on him and her pitifully and humiliatingly dependent state become too much to bear and one day, after telling her a childhood story, George takes a pillow and smothers her…It is he who buys and cuts the flowers, who dresses her and lays her out on the bed…It is he who also frees a pigeon which has become trapped inside the room…In an achingly poignant scene, he imagines he sees Anne washing the dishes then asking for her coat and leaving their home…Dutifully, he follows after her…

In the letter he leaves behind, George explains that 'he has set the pigeon free'. At the end, their daughter wanders through the rooms of the now empty apartment…

"Amour" is aptly titled. This is a deeply tender and gentle film which looks unflinchingly at the painful challenges faced when trying to cope with the sufferings of someone you love. Inevitably, it is also about the frailty of old age and death itself. Michael Haneke has a mastery of technique, which is disciplined and cool-headed, never allowing himself to be either maudlin or sentimental. His markedly detached style, however, never undermines the very real presence of his compassion. The film swept the board at Cannes with the Palme D'Or and pretty well all the other major prizes, as well as scooping up a basketful in the rest of the world. Cobbling together the budget can't have been easy – there's a good baker's dozen of Producers credited on the film. That, these days, is how you get it done…

* * *

There you are – there's the list, the 100 of memories, reflections, meandering this way and that through time, looping back and forth and in some curious way telling me as much about my own life as it describes the films which have been so much part of it….But I can't leave it there, neat and pat with a tidy number because that would be like closing a door..At least it should be left ajar, so I include one more...special and strange...

101. "THE COLOUR OF POMEGRANATES"

(1969. Director: Sergei Paradjanov)

The crimson juice of a pomegranate seeps slowly across a piece of cloth and quite naturally forms itself into a map of the boundaries of what used to be Armenia… On the steeply pointed roof of an ancient Orthodox church, dozens of finely leather-bound volumes lie drying in the sun, their pages flapping this way and that… A grave-faced young woman takes on the role of half a dozen characters sometimes incarnating as a man… Churches, books, bells…the landscape of an elusive dream…Snatches of images and voices caught on the air and carried away by the wind…a semi-mystical vision…

I have saved this film for Number 101 (and curious I should end as I started with another Russian director whose work can be almost as abstruse) quite simply because I have never seen anything quite like it: it really is as unique and revolutionary now as Eisenstein was back in the 1920's and 1930's – both re-invent the language of cinema and take it to a new level. So I place it here at 101, because it strikes me as being so completely 'modern' and 'liberated' from all the cinematic conventions we have come to accept and a vivid glimpse of what can lie beyond their boundaries.

The film portrays the life of a celebrated 18th century Armenian poet – but in a series of painterly miniatures, densely compressed and almost as abstract as a particularly recondite piece of poetry. But also as brilliant and dazzling as a flawless diamond – no, a pearl of peerless purity! The superlatives come easily – the precise memory, less so…Childhood into manhood, the discovery of women, of his Muse…his poems and eventual retreat into a monastery and his death – all visualized by Paradjanov in highly personal and internal re-expressions of the man's poems themselves, imagined with an intensity enough to give you a nose-bleed and see your own blood seeping into a handkerchief and creating your own cosmographic vision of the inner universe.

A little bit of research tells me the poet was the *Sayat Nova*, or King of Song, an an Armenian national hero, and the tribulations suffered by that oppressed nation in its fight to preserve its own identity lies close to the surface of this film. Some further research reveals that Paradjanov's film did not go down well with the Soviet authorities who withdrew it from circulation shortly after its release. It was some years before it got to be shown internationally where it was quickly acclaimed as a 'masterpiece'. There is something of a paradox about such a radical and 'avant-garde' film ever getting to be made in such a tightly supervised and censored society in the first place – but perhaps this bears out Wajda's observation that you can always find a way around the censors – but not around the censorship of money...Certainly it is hard to imagine such a film ever having a chance in hell of getting off the ground in the good old capitalist West!

'Artistic Freedom', for what that term is worth, comes with a price tag and, because of the huge sums of money involved, perhaps film-makers have to pay it more than in all the other arts. Paradjanov is not the only one who had to pay the price by any means – but at least he got it made! And the history of film as a language, as an art, is all the richer for it. Yes, truly wonderful...

* * *

And a little Epilogue before the curtain really does come down and the cinema lights go up...

P.S. 101 + 1. "TOM & JERRY" CARTOONS

Flattened by a mallet to his head, electrocuted at high voltage, desiccated, shot into space, drowned in paint, smacked around the face by closing doors, ironed, frazzled on hot stoves, pinioned in the jaws of the bulldog, exploded into smithereens – there are very few forms of humiliating ignominy to which Tom, the cat, is not subjected in his forever doomed quest to catch that pesky Jerry, the mouse, and finally have him for dinner. Yet whatever they throw at him, however painful, lethal and downright impossible, Tom reconstitutes in seconds, resurrects from certain death a thousand times, like a Terminator, and gets back to the business at hand – nail that wretched mouse! He never gives up! How can one not include them on any list? (And how can one resist anything which is produced by anyone called Fred Quimby!? Quimby! What a glorious name!) I loved Tom and Jerry as a child and still love them now...

But, as every Loony Toon cheerfully announces at the end – "That's all Folks"...My list is done and the rest is silence ...

POSTSCRIPT

...Well not quite as absolute as Hamlet's silence....there's always a Puck or Robin Goodfellow appearing with his broom before we go to tell us "If we shadows have offended – Think but this, and all is mended – That you have but slumbered here – While these visions did appear"... Akinesis... Time re-timed at 24fps...a month, a year, a century re-invented and passing before our eyes in 90 minutes, two hours, fifteen minutes...Film – such a strange visitor into our lives ... Listen to the clatter of the film as it passes through the projector's gate, taking us to where it will...

But Luchino Visconti, Marcel Carné, Jean-Luc Godard, Claude Chabrol, or the great Rossellini? Where are they...? Shouldn't they be here? Or Dovzhenko, Vertov and Pudovkin? Chaplin, Keaton or the immortal W.C. Fields? And what about the likes of Douglas Sirk, Nicholas Ray, William Wyler, Francis Ford Coppola, Quentin Tarantino ? Or Mr Spielberg? And Wim Wenders, no sign of him nor of Fassbinder (remember him?) or 'I-really-am-the-flavour-of-the-month', Lars von Triers (sorry, but no thank you)... Impolite oversights? Any list could be as endless as the rebukes and protestations for all these omissions are likely to be. But each one of us must make our own list – that's part of the joy of it all, isn't it – "You say Tomayto, I say Tomahto"...: the diversity of taste in each individual and the cornucopia of choice available.

Although I make no apology for what I have left out, there is one obvious omission, however, which does leave me feeling a little sad: apart from Leni Riefenstahl, there are no women directors included. I don't think I should be pilloried for this (although doubtless someone will throw a tomato or two at me because there are those for whom tomato-throwing is an indispensable part of their lives) because the truth is that, in the period of film-making that most impacted upon me, women directors were, to say the least, pretty thin on the ground. And I surely can't be held responsible for that. There were a few though, weren't there – Agnès Varda, Lina Wertmuller, Agnieszka Holland…even Mai Zetterling, but perhaps I should have included Jane Campion, not for "The Piano", however, but for her wonderful "An Angel at my Table", and deserve, for that at least, a rotten tomato being launched in my direction for failing to do so…

That's all changing now, little by little, and more and more highly talented women are putting their original thumbprint onto the history of Film. Of course, everything else is changing too – celluloid, emulsion, film laboratories are almost a thing of the past as the digital age replace them and there is a whole generation of film-makers now who will have never seen streams of film hanging in their trim bins, heard the crunch of a splicer joining A to B and making C, or experienced the distinctive thrill of sitting alone in the middle of the night amidst a forest of fluttering ribbons of celluloid waiting and whispering to be brought to life.

How we look at films is changing, too: downloaded onto our lap-tops, or onto the miniscule screen of a smart-phone, we can call up a movie with a single click. So, too, with this new technology, the very shape and structure of what constitutes being a film is evolving into a new language. And that is how it should be. Whatever the new tools, however, the creative process itself will remain essentially unchanged. There will still be all the same old struggles, disappointments and frustrations every film-maker has faced in the past – how to best express an idea, how to overcome the limits of time, of money, of people unable to grasp what the hell you're doing or trying to say. But I have no doubt whatsoever in my mind that there will also always be those magical moments when, faced by what might seem an intractable problem on the set, there will be someone in the crew who will suddenly, out of the blue, like the Script Girl in Truffaut's "La Nuit Americaine", pop up with an inspired solution and crown it all by adding "And can we do it with snow…?"

…Love at 24fps…here we go again…

THE END

APPENDIX – The List

1. "ANDREI RUBLEV" (1966. Director: Andrei Tarkovsky)
2. "TO LIVE" (1994. Director: Zhang Yimou)
3. "LISTEN TO BRITAIN" (1942. Director: Humphrey Jennings)
4. "OTTO E MEZZO" ("8 and a Half" 1963. Director: Federico Fellini)
5. "AMARCORD" (1973. Director; Federico Fellini)
6. "LA GRANDE BELLEZZA" (2013. Director: Paolo Sorrentino)
7. "I ALBERO DEGLI ZOCCOLI" (1978. Director: Ermanno Olmi)
8. "THE BICYCLE THIEVES" (1948. Director: Vittorio de Sica)
9. "THE GOSPEL ACCORDING TO ST MATTHEW" (1964. Director: Piero Paolo Pasolini)
10. "TEOREMA" ("Theorem".1968. Director: Piero Paolo Pasolini)
11. "LES QUATRE CENTS COUPS" (1959. Director: François Truffaut)
12. "LA NUIT AMERICAINE" (1963. Director: François Truffaut)
13. "LA REGLE DU JEU" (1939. Director: Jean Renoir)
14. "LA GRANDE ILLUSION" (1937. Director: Jean Renoir)
15. "ZÉRO DE CONDUITE" (1933.Director: Jean Vigo)
16. "VAN GOGH" (1991. Director: Maurice Pialat)
17. "CELINE ET JULIE VONT EN BATEAUX" (1974. Director: Jacques Rivette)

18. "LE GENOU DE CLAIRE (1970. Director: Eric Rohmer)
19. "HIROSHIMA, MON AMOUR"
    (1959. Director: Alain Resnais)
20. "GREED" (1924: Director: Erich von Stroheim)
21. "SUNSET BOULEVARD" (1950 - Director: Billy Wilder)
22. "TO BE OR NOT TO BE" (1942 - Director: Ernst Lubitsch)
23. "SULLIVAN'S TRAVELS" (1941 Director: Preston Sturges)
24. "HIGH NOON" (1952. Director: Fred Zinneman)
25. "REAR WINDOW" (1954. Director: Alfred Hitchcock)
26. "VERTIGO" (1958. Director: Alfred Hitchcock)
27. "ON THE WATERFRONT" (1954. Director: Elia Kazan)
28. "RAGING BULL" (1980. Director: Martin Scorsese)
29. "KUNDUN" (1997. Director: Martin Scorsese)
30. "DERSU UZALA" (1975. Director: Akira Kurosawa)
31. "THE SEVEN SAMURAI" (1954. Director: Akira Kurosawa)
32. "KAGEMUSHA" (1980. Director: Akira Kurosawa)
33. "TOKYO STORY" (1953. Director: Yasujiro Ozu)
34. "FIRES ON THE PLAIN" (1959. Director: Kon Ichikawa)
35. "PATHS OF GLORY" (1957. Director: Stanley Kubrick)
36. "WESTERN FRONT 1918" (1930: Director; G.W.Pabst)
37. "KAMERADSCHAFT" (1931. Director; G.W.Pabst)
38. "THE CABINET OF DR CALIGARI"
    (1920. Director: Robert Wiene)
39. "METROPOLIS" (1927. Director; Fritz Lang)

40. "M" (1931. Director: Fritz Lang)
41. "TRIUMPH OF THE WILL" (1935. Director: Leni Riefenstahl)
42. "THE APARTMENT" (1960. Director: Billy Wilder)
43. "A NIGHT AT THE OPERA" (1935. Director: Sam Wood)
44. "LES VACANCES DE MONSIEUR HULOT" (1953. Director: Jacques Tati)
45. "PLAYTIME" (1967. Director: Jacques Tati)
46. "THE LAVENDER HILL MOB" (1951. Director: Charles Crichton)
47. "THE LADYKILLERS" (1955. Director: Alexander MacKendrick)
48. "OH, BROTHER, WHERE ART THOU?" (2000 . Director/Writer: The Coen Bros)
49. "MEN WHO STARE AT GOATS" (2009. Director: Grant Heslov)
50. "DR STRANGELOVE" (1964. Director: Stanley Kubrick)
51. "2001: A SPACE ODYSSEY" (1968.Director: Stanley Kubrick)
52. "SOLARIS" (1972. Director: Andrei Tarkovsky)
53. "GRAVITY" (2013. Director: Alfonso Cuarón)
54. "SNOW WHITE & THE SEVEN DWARFS" (1937. Director(s): Walt Disney + crew)
55. "THE RED BALLOON" (1956. Director: Albert Lamorisse)
56. "SHANE" (1953. Director: George Stevens)
57. "THE SEARCHERS" (1956. Director: John Ford)
58. "UNFORGIVEN" (1992. Director: Clint Eastwood)

59. "LAWRENCE OF ARABIA" (1962. Director: David Lean)

60. "INTOLERANCE" (1916. Director: D.W.Griffith)

61. "BATTLESHIP POTEMKIN"
(1925. Director: Sergei Mikhailovich Eisenstein)

62. "ALEXANDER NEVSKY"
(1938. Director: Sergei Mikhailovich Eisenstein)

63. "THE PASSION OF JOAN OF ARC"
(1928. Director: Carl Dreyer)

64. "VIRIDIANA" (1961. Director: Luis Buñuel)

65. "THE DISCREET CHARM OF THE BOURGEOISIE"
(1972. Director: Luis Buñuel)

66. "EL ESPIRITU DE LA COLMENA"
(1973. Director: Victor Erice)

67. "LES YEUX SANS VISAGE" (1960. Director: Georges Franju)

68. "EL PIEL QUE HABITO" (2011. Director: Pedro Almodóvar)

69. "THE WORLD OF APU" (1959. Director: Satyajit Ray)

70. "BROADWAY DANNY ROSE" (1984. Director: Woody Allen)

71. "MANHATTAN" (1979. Director: Woody Allen)

72. "A SERIOUS MAN"
(2009. Writer/Director : The Coen Brothers)

73. "THE PIANIST" (2002. Director: Roman Polanski)

74. "ASHES AND DIAMONDS" (1958. Director; Andrzej Wajda)

75. "CLOSELY OBSERVED TRAINS" (1966. Director: Jirí Menzel)

76. "SALVATORE GUILIANO" (1962. Director: Francesco Rosi)

77. "LAND AND FREEDOM" (1995. Director: Ken Loach)

78. "MR TURNER" (2014. Director: Mike Leigh)

79. **"DISTANT VOICES, STILL LIVES"**
    (1988. Director: Terence Davies)

80. **"SATURDAY NIGHT, SUNDAY MORNING"**
    (1960. Director: Karel Reisz)

81. **"THE THIRD MAN"** (1949. Director: Carol Reed)

82. **"CITIZEN KANE"** (1941. Director: Orson Welles)

83. **"CHIMES AT MIDNIGHT"** (1966. Director: Orson Welles)

84. **"WILD STRAWBERRIES"** (1957. Director: Ingmar Bergman)

85. **"FANNY AND ALEXANDER"**
    (1982. Director: Ingmar Bergman)

86. **"LES DESMOISELLES DE ROCHEFORT"**
    (1967. Director: Jacques Demy)

87. **"SINGING IN THE RAIN"**
    (1952 Director: Stanley Donen/Gene Kelly)

88. **"THE MALTESE FALCON"** (1941. Director: John Huston)

89. **"CASABLANCA"** (1942. Director: Michael Curtiz)

90. **"BREAKFAST AT TIFFANY'S"**
    (1961. Director: Blake Edwards)

91. **"LOLA MONTES"** (1955. Director: Max Ophuls)

92. **"PICKPOCKET"** (1959. Director: Robert Bresson)

93. **"L'AVVENTURA"** (1960. Director: Michelangelo Antonioni)

94. **"THE THIN RED LINE"** (1998. Director: Terrence Malick)

96. **"SEVEN DAYS TO NOON"**
    (1950. Directors: John & Roy Boulting)

97. **"THE LIVES OF OTHERS"**
    (2006. Director: Florian Henckel von Donnersmarck)

98. **"THE ENIGMA OF KASPER HAUSER"**
    (1974. Director: Werner Herzog)

99. **"WILD AT HEART"** (1990. Director: David Lynch)

100. **"AMOUR"** (2012. Director: Michael Haneke)

    and

101. **"THE COLOUR OF POMEGRANATES"**
    (1969. Director: Sergei Paradjanov)

    plus by way of an epilogue

P.S. 101 + 1. **"TOM & JERRY" CARTOONS**

THE END CREDITS

The End Credits on most films nowadays seem to go on for almost as long as the film itself. By the time the last title has rolled up the screen – crediting everyone right on down to the Transport Captain's Best Boy's second cousin twice removed plus his grandmother, her canary, the goldfish, not forgetting Florrie down the road who made us all such a nice cup of tea – the audience has usually left the theatre and these acknowledgments are playing to an empty house...Because, to be honest, no-one is really interested in knowing who was the 3rd Assistant Wardrobe Mistress, are they, except perhaps the 3rd Wardrobe Mistress herself (or her grandmother)... Nevertheless, they deserve their credits, because the making of a film and the realization of the director's vision of it depends almost entirely on the collective input of everyone involved, each with his or her specific talents and skills. And sometimes that really does include a 'Florrie down the road who made us all such a nice cup of tea'...It is they who dress the stone, plumb the line and build the cathedral...

The same applies to a book – whilst writing can be a solitary business, it is neither completely hermetic nor immune to outside forces, subtly and often unwittingly exerting their influence. And to them credit is due too. I am also indebted in different ways to Duncan Beal, Clare Brayshaw and all the team at YPS who have guided this book safely through the pangs of birth thereby ensuring it now sits today in the hands of you, the reader. Just as meaningful is the debt I owe to true and good friends who, simply by virtue of friendship itself, have supported and encouraged me, a constant buttress against the uncertainties and doubts which assail us all. To name one would mean naming them all – it's a bit like the Christmas card list, isn't it (or the end credits on a film) – once you start, it goes on forever. So let me be forgiven for naming no names – they already know who they are and hopefully also how much I appreciate and value them all. However, I want to make one exception – this entire book was written from start to finish in the delightfully simple and modest surroundings of the Makati Apartelle, Manila, which has become like a home from home for me. The owner, Mama Tess Flores, her three sons and her lovely team of Divina, Marialyn, Rhonie, Leo plus the three girls who come to clean each day – chirruping sparrows, singing, smiling (and endlessly texting) 'angels' and '*buangs*' – have become like my Filipino family. Without them, their generosity of heart, their laughter and warmth, I doubt there would be a book at all. Their ceaseless goodwill has pricked and shamed my jaded Western soul, reminding me, in this country of so much real, grinding hardship, just how very lucky we are in the West and telling me to stop complaining and get on with it. And finally, I should remember, not "Florrie from down the road who made us all such a nice cup of tea", but a certain Celestine who dropped in from time to time to cook up one hell of a *caldereta* and then went on to do some remarkably interesting things with the humble Udon noodle as well – put it this way, she did not let me starve for anything!

To all and everyone, my sincere gratitude and thanks.

THE PATRONS

The publication of this book was made possible through the kind generosity of:

Gillian FitzHugh

Mark Fisher

Faustina Gilbey

Gina Glover

Julian Lousada

Tony Travis

Penny Turner